The stark theological polarities of damnation and salvation have haunted representations of guilt in Western culture for thousands of years. Friedrich Ohly's classic study of the damned and the elect offers a comparative cultural history of figures such as Oedipus, Judas and Faust, from Antiquity, through the Middle Ages into modern times. Looking at the works of writers as various as Sophocles, Dante, Marlowe, Bunyan, Goethe and Thomas Mann (and illustrating his ideas with reference to representation in the visual arts), Ohly's wide-ranging arguments weave deftly across different cultures and periods to illuminate one of the most salient themes in Western literature.

THE DAMNED AND THE ELECT

THE DAMNED AND THE ELECT

Guilt in Western Culture

FRIEDRICH OHLY

Professor Emeritus of German Philology, University of Münster

Translated from the German by

LINDA ARCHIBALD

CAMBRIDGE
UNIVERSITY PRESS

Publishers' note

The publishers are very grateful to Dr Rosemary Morris for her assistance in preparing this translation for press.

Published by the Press Syndicate of the University of Cambridge
The Pitt Building, Trumpington Street, Cambridge CB2 1RP
40 West 20th Street, New York, NY 10011–4211, USA
10 Stamford Road, Oakleigh, Victoria 3166, Australia

Originally published in German as *Der Verfluchte und der Erwählte: vom Leben mit der Schuld* by Westdeutscher Verlag GmbH 1976 and © 1976 by Westdeutscher Verlag GmbH Opladen. Gesamtherstellung: Westdeutscher Verlag GmbH ISBN 3–531–07207–2

First published in English by Cambridge University Press 1992 as *The Damned and the Elect: Guilt in Western Culture*

English translation © Cambridge University Press 1992

First published 1992

Printed in Great Britain at the University Press, Cambridge

A catalogue record for this book is available from the British Library

Library of Congress cataloguing in publication data
Ohly, Friedrich, 1914–
[Der Verfluchte und der Erwählte. English]
The damned and the elect: guilt in Western culture / Friedrich Ohly: translated from the German by Linda Archibald.
p   cm.
Translation of: Der Verfluchte und der Erwählte.
Includes bibliographical references and index.
ISBN 0–521–38250–5
1. Guilt in literature.   1. Title.
PN56.G803713   1992   809'.93353 – dc20   91–37210   CIP

ISBN 0 521 38250 5 hardback

Contents

Illustrations

Foreword

The pendulum motion between crime and punishment would appear to be incised in human consciousness. It may even be imprinted on the behavioural reflexes of animals which are in contact with man. One's dog is aware of the retribution which may follow on his wrong-doing. Such is the compelling logic of the sequence from transgression to chastisement or reparation that it intimates those obscure but probably generic dualities or binary structures which are thought to inform the human brain and psyche. Whatever its archetypal source, the dialectic of crime and punishment has been seminal in myth and in literature from *Genesis* and the *Oresteia* to Shakespeare and Dostoevski. It is the peculiar find of Kafka's *Trial* to suggest that the pulse of terror which emanates from punishment is of such ineluctable and persuasive force as to make innocence culpable. To those – and they comprise not only religious believers but also Marx and Freud – who postulate some initial fault in the history of man, some 'original sin' and fall from grace, human experience, with its incommensurable absurdities, injustice and suffering, is itself an enacted punishment. There is history because a primal crime, an originating biological, social or ethical wrong set in motion the pendulum.

Guilt and chastisement, the wrath of God and that of the Furies, literally generate the matter of biblical and classical narrative. Even Jesus, the master of pardon, enigmatically but irrevocably withers the fig-tree. False prophets, idolatrous monarchs, adulterers, are hideously found out. Dogs lap their blood. Often it is the wildness of the pendulum's arc, the unbalance between the minor or unwitting crime and the

xi

maniacal punishment – consider the seventy-thousand slain when David, tempted by an evil demon, imposes a census on Israel or consider the vengeance of the offended deity in Euripides' *Bacchae* – which appalls and solicits reflection. What malfeasance committed by imperfect (fallen) man or woman can conceivably merit everlasting damnation? What insult or neglect in respect of the divine can be equated with the razing of cities, with the metamorphosis of man into homeless beast? It is as if crime was made exponential by guilt, magnifying itself towards the excess of darkness, as in *Macbeth*, as in *The Brothers Karamazov*. The hunter is made quarry to himself.

In the Western legacy, this dread mechanism is rendered quintessential in the figure and tale of Judas Iscariot. What child has been named Judas since (whereas even Adolf will, before too long, return to our baptismal and birth-registers)?

This dense, suggestive monograph looks at the emergence of the figure of Judas in secular literature after the mid-twelfth century. Though unavoidably repetitive, many of these poetic and dramatic texts are truly harrowing. *The True Mystery of Passion*, finely rendered from a French mystery cycle by James Kirkup, is of particular power. As is the *Magnum Legendarium Austriacum* of *c.* 1190. But Friedrich Ohly's focus is one of moral psychology. It is not Judas' betrayal of his Lord nor the abject suicide that follows which mainly engage the argument. These have indeed been abundantly considered elsewhere. Here the issue is that of Judas' rejection of remorse. As these medieval and early renaissance texts make poignantly clear, there are versions of the tale in which intercession for the arch-criminal is fully available. The Virgin Mary is ready to pray for him, to urge his repentance. There are poetic texts which strongly imply Christ's willingness to forgive his betrayer. This is not the principal or canonic version, but an eloquent alternative to the determinism of immediate and eternal damnation once Satan had entered into Judas. What Dr Ohly investigates is the psychology of self-damnation, the psychology of despair which makes Judas incapable of seeking or accepting the very possibility of salvation through penitence. In maddening despair Judas passes a last judgement upon himself. (Charles Péguy, who lies outside Ohly's interests, combined the two traditions in a hair-raising conceit: it is when Jesus, on the cross, realises that he cannot save Judas, either because of God the Father's will or because of Judas' own desperation, that the carnal agony of the Passion begins.)

In counterpoint to Judas, Dr Ohly analyses the legend of the Holy Sinner Gregory as it fascinates the literary–religious imagination from the early Middle Ages to Thomas Mann. In this instance utmost transgression – parricide followed by incest in evident echo to the Oedipus motif – leads to impassioned confession and repentance. Terribly chastised (the Holy Sinner is immured or banished to a barren rock in midst the raging sea for decades), the evil-doer is restored to the communion of Christendom and, in the case of the legend of Gregory, elevated to the papacy. Seeking wretched death, as in Flaubert's narrative of St Julien, he comes home to radiant sanctity. No sin, no crime is, *pace* the Augustinian reading of divine law and Dante's picture of unremitted Hell, too grave for repentance. None is extraterritorial to hope. Where remorse is spiritually authentic, where punishment is borne as a salvational visitation from God, pardon and blessing can follow.

This study concludes with brief summaries of the deep-seated affinities between the Judas–Holy Sinner dialectic on the one hand and the great presences of Dr Faustus and of Oedipus in Western awareness. It rightly directs us to the tremendous theme of Faust's denial of God's power to forgive as it is sketched by Marlowe and expounded by Thomas Mann. There can be no pride, no doomed rationality more daemonic.

It is ironic that Dr Friedrich Ohly's work itself lies under a certain shadow. Nowhere does he bring himself to touch on the obvious central crux that, of the disciples, only Judas is, by his very name, defined as a Jew. It is in the name of Judas' alleged betrayal and of the deicide which it provokes, that Jews were hounded to pitiless death from those very times onward in which Judas looms in Christian literature and iconography. It is countless Jewish men, women and children who suffered ostracism and martyrdom in the black light of Judas' fate as it has been proclaimed and imaged by Christianity. Half a century after Auschwitz, it seems as if German scholarship is still lamed when it draws near the unspeakable; a condition which gives to this essay on 'life and guilt' a constraining pathos.

George Steiner

CHAPTER I

Judas and Gregorius

'How can I live with my guilt?'[1] The question first put to Adam, put more starkly at his expulsion from Paradise; the question which belongs among the most enduring problems of this world; a legacy for all times, though not every age has taken it with the same seriousness. 'How can I live with my guilt?': the question no one can avoid, though not everyone takes it equally to heart. It troubled the medieval mind more deeply than it does ours today. Through the centuries leading up to Dante, travellers in spirit followed their visions of the Beyond through heaven and hell: overwhelmed, so much so that what they saw could change their whole lives, they beheld those whose life had ended – not 'the dead', for none truly ceased to be – as souls sent to live for ever either among the damned or among the elect, in torment or in bliss. How a man lives with his guilt in this life decides his fate through all eternity. Dante teaches us to see that; and he was not the first. With a visionary assurance which seems to us starkly incredible, and yet impossible to dismiss as mere presumption because of its strange objectivity, Dante describes for us the very real and individual consequences which the next world holds in store for those who have served their time in this one. Like God at the Last Judgement, he sentences them to heaven, to purgatory or to hell. No theologian would dare to pronounce sentence on figures from our own recent past as Dante did on his contemporaries.

A hundred years before Dante, around the year 1200, an age of severe *contemptus mundi* had come to an end, and a new biblical maxim – 'be pleasing unto God and the world' – had ushered in an entirely new kind of secular poetry, which featured, among other things, the Arthurian romance. At the beginning of this period we find the courtly romances of poets such as Chrétien de Troyes, Hartmann von Aue and Wolfram von Eschenbach, which all have something in common that to modern eyes may seem surprising: in so far as women provide the motivating force – and in all these works the heroes are inspired by women – the works do not end with a marriage, but are *about* marriage. Unusually – from a literary point of view – they are not concerned with love outside marriage, adulterous love such as we find in Tristan, Lancelot and so many later novels, but with self-testing within marriage. Either the conjugal ideal has to be reconciled, to the satisfaction of both God and the world, with some equally legitimate imperative after one or the other has been infringed, or else some guilt connected with the entry into marriage has to be borne until life brings about its solution. Early in these works, the hero enters into marriage; but he also enters into a state of guilt, connected with the marriage or close to it in time: the main action then shows how he and his beloved live with this guilt. In no case does this guilt arise from the hero's deliberate fault: it is always unintentional, often incurred in pursuit of the best inclinations or intentions, and arising from a clash of obligations. Normally such guilt would attract little attention, and there would be no question of holding anyone else to account for it – were it not that the unwitting perpetrator has to awaken to the disturbing realisation that innocent parties are suffering unexpected consequences on his account. He is compelled to 'cast aside his guiltlessness',[2] to realise the growing power of guilt over him, to accept it and to live with it. Whence arises a paradox: it is 'the fact that the hero affirms his guilt that is important, not the objective existence of guilt itself'.[3]

   In Dante's visions of guilt in the next world also, literary characters by the dozen, from Helen to Tristan, find their place side by side with those whom literature led astray, as the tale of Lancelot did for Paolo and Francesca (*Inferno*, canto V). But we do not find among them those who, like the Arthurian knights Erec, Iwein and Parzival, or Hartmann von Aue's Gregorius, learned to live, as knights, with their guilt. The Gregorius legend, in Hartmann's version, takes the connection between guilt and marriage to its limits. Gregorius is the product of brother–sister incest. Fate decrees that the culmination of his knightly career shall be the liberation of an heiress and subsequent marriage with her; it is later revealed that she is his mother. The mother has to live with the guilt of a twofold incest; the unhappy son of the first liaison has to live in a marriage with his mother, a marriage into which both had entered in ignorance of their relationship. They separate and pursue their penitential ways apart. Gregorius languishes for seventeen years chained to a rocky crag in the middle of a lake until certain miracles induce the Romans, prompted by God, to make him Pope. Eventually Gregorius announces that his mother is forgiven. The great sinner has become a saint, one of the Elect. But this is no saint of the church, no liturgical figure, it is a legendary figure called into life by poetic creation alone. The story breathes airs from both heaven and hell; it plumbs the abyss and scales the heights: such depths and such heights that the sounding of them extends the potential of mankind to an incredible degree. Hartmann even goes so far as to prepare himself and his hearers for a joint invocation of the sinful saint, and so creates a community of prayer where none existed before. Such can be the power of literature.

When Thomas Mann was researching the Gregorius legend for his novel *Der Erwählte* (*The Holy Sinner*), he also came across the legend of Judas. He said of these legends:

The story of Gregorius belongs to the sphere, or rather the long succession, of Oedipus myths, in which the motif of predestined and abominable incest with the mother (alongside the murder of the father) has its part to play; the legend of Judas Iscariot is an example. According to this legend Judas was abandoned as a baby because of an ominous dream; he later returned to his home, killed his father in the course of a robbery and married his mother. When the entanglement came to light he became a disciple of Jesus to be cleansed of his guilt – which, as everyone knows, did not exactly turn out for the best.[4]

After comparing related legends from the Middle Ages, Mann concluded:

The story seems to have passed from Oedipus, via Judas, Andreas and Paul of Caesarea, to Gregorius.

In the first part of this book I shall endeavour to turn this conjecture of Thomas Mann's into a certainty. Let us now, therefore, turn our attention to the Middle Ages.

The real subject of the Gregorius legend is not guilt, but the consequences which guilt brings upon the guilty party.[5] The authorial intention which emerges from all the Gregorius texts is to examine the hero's relationship with his guilt.[6] The oldest version of the Old French *Vie de Saint Gregoire*, which is the one closest to Hartmann von Aue's text (B₁), promises to relate the life of a 'good sinner' (line 2) who suffered greatly for his sins ('pur ses pechez suffri grant peine', line 4). The author hopes that a stark relation of the hero's guilt may serve as a lesson to other guilty parties (lines 5–12). It may thus serve as a deterrent, for a story about guilt can only serve as a lesson in so far as it teaches us how to live with guilt in the future. It is not a case of suffering imposed from outside in the form of sentence and punishment: there is no external judgement in the Gregorius legend. It is a question of the *individual's* response to the experience of living under a burden of guilt. 'For what does any man bring upon himself by his misdeeds, if not a prison for his own conscience, so that he is oppressed by his awareness of guilt, even if no other accuses him?'[7] In such a case the guilty man has two choices: trust in God's mercy, and despair. The Old French poem, the earliest Gregorius text, ventures into the distressful regions between that trust and that despair, following the path indicated by the prologue. Gregorius did not despair (lines 37–43) – despair (*desesperance*) having already been defined (just as Hartmann will later define it) as a refusal to believe in God's power over sin, and as the sin against the Holy Ghost (lines 25–32). In the prologue to the Old French poem, the rhyme *desesperance/penitence* emphasises the possibility of falling and obtaining mercy after guilt. The reader will see

K'il ne chai en des(es)perance,
Ainz s'amenda par penitence,
Si ke puis fud sainz apostoiles
Et si out nun li bon Gregoires.

(lines 43–6)

That he did not fall into despair, but made amends by penitence, so that afterwards he was holy Pope, and was called 'the good Gregorius'.

It is the two concepts of *desperatio* and *poenitentia* which form the theological basis of these works on the subject of the 'good sinner'. They are fundamental to the prologues of Gregorius texts in French, German, English and Latin. Hartmann endows *desperatio* with a sister, *praesumptio* – the over-confident expectation of grace.[8] Both the despair of obtaining grace and the presumptuous expectation of obtaining it are sins against the Holy Ghost, for which there is no forgiveness; for the Middle Ages they were incarnate in the figures of Judas and Origen. In about 1210 Arnold of Lübeck wrote at the end of the prologue to his *Gregorius peccator*, a Latin translation of the Middle High German *Gregorius*: 'nunc ad gesta perveniatur, ut ab omnibus peccantibus venie desperatio auferatur' ('now let us come to the action, so that the despair of forgiveness may be taken away from all sinners', p. 3). The real question is not how one gets into guilt but how one gets out of it. Through living, one comes to terms with one's own guilt; as in the Arthurian romance, that guilt is neither voluntary, nor known, nor conscious. The characters have to live through their guilt when good turns to evil because the devil has a hand in matters; they have to make their way through the murky darkness of events, and only the author and his audience can see what awaits them on their way from appearance to being. Only take one step against your better judgement – as happened at the Fall of man – and you become a ready victim to the seductions of the devil and to well-meaning deception. There is only one conscious sin in the Gregorius story, at the beginning when Gregorius' father, seduced by the devil, becomes seducer in his turn[9] and sleeps with his own sister. But the guilty act takes place, becomes known, and the consequences must follow. The strange fascination which the guilty act itself may have from a literary viewpoint is beyond the scope of theology and is not the focus of the work: its spiritual weight falls on the repentance. The work is not a warning against sin leading to guilt – of all examples Gregorius is the least suitable for that purpose. It warns against the fallacy of *desperatio*. Hartmann says of his poem: 'Des ist ze hœrenne not / und ze merkenne in allen / die da sint vervallen / under bercswæren schulden' ('This ought to be heard and remembered by all who have fallen under the mountain-heavy load of sin').[10] Those who, so laden, turn to God are received with mercy:

> wan sîner gnâden ist sô vil
> daz er des niene wil
> und ez gar verboten hât
> daz man durch deheine missetât
> an im iht zwîvelhaft bestê.
> ez enist dehein sünde mê,
> man enwerde ir mit der riuwe
> ledic unde niuwe
> schœne unde reine,
> niuwan der zwîvel eine:
> der ist ein mortgalle
> ze dem êwigen valle
> den nieman mac gesüezen
> noch wider got gebüezen.

For his mercy is so great that he will not tolerate it, and has forbidden us to despair of him because of any kind of wrongdoing. There is no sin left that cannot be repented of, to leave us free and renewed, pure and fair, except for one, despair: that is a deadly poison leading to eternal damnation, a gall that no one can sweeten, nor can any man repent of it before God.

Adam and Eve tried to hide their fall into sin and refused to answer when God called. In the Gregorius story, the parents conceal their sin and its fruit, Gregorius himself, from the world – they cast him adrift on the sea – but they do not attempt to hide it from God, in that they do penitence though no man has accused them. The father makes a pilgrimage to the Holy Sepulchre ('dâ büezet iuwer sunde' – 'there repent of your sin');[11] the mother does penitence in her own land ('ir sünde unde ir schande / mac si sô baz gebüezen', 'so is she best able to atone for her sin and shame').[12] They do avoid shame before the world, but not guilt; this they acknowledge, repent and atone for, and so God is satisfied. This satisfaction 'aller sünden machet vri' ('delivers us from all our sins').[13] They are restored to their former state of grace – even the child of sin is rescued from the sea – and everything would be peace, if the son himself did not bear that inheritance of guilt which is gradually to be made plain.

It is with the best of intentions that what has happened is concealed from the world: the child is cast adrift 'ze helne daz mein', 'to hide that sin'.[14] His homeland and parentage are kept a secret from him: 'im wart dâ niht benant / weder liute noch lant, / geburt noch sîn heimuot: / daz was ouh in ze helne guot' ('he was not taught about his people nor his country, his birth or his home; that concealment was good' – i.e. it was good to protect him from the knowledge).[15] Thus the facts are blanketed in concealment, and an outcome made possible in which people have seeing eyes and yet are blind, demanding revelation all unaware of what its consequences will be. On all sides good intentions lead to evil. No accusations are made, except by the guilty parties themselves. God's purposes, laments the poet, are beyond our understanding:

> wâfen, herre, wâfen
> über des hellehundes list,
> daz er uns sô geværic ist!
> war umbe verhenget im des got,
> daz er sô manegen grôzen spot
> vrumet über sîn hangetât
> die er nach im gebildet hât?

Defend us, lord, defend us from the cunning of the hound of hell, for he is so set against us! Why does God decree that he is allowed to make such a mockery of God's own handiwork, which he has made in his own image?

Cain and Abel, the first brothers, could not live peaceably together. Cain slew his brother and despaired of mercy: 'Major

est iniquitas mea, quam ut veniam meream' (Genesis 4:13,
Vulgate Bible: 'Mine iniquity is greater than that it may be
forgiven'). But God sets his mark on Cain, to protect him, and
so he survives. As for Gregorius, he is cast ashore on an island
and brought up by fisherfolk, then educated in a monastery.
One day he strikes his foster-brother during a game: a blow,
though not (as in Cain's case) a fatal one. The victim runs
crying to his mother. He whom God has blessed strikes him
whom God has not blessed – and Hermann finds it hard to
justify this. 'Nû geviel ez eines tages sus' ('now it so happened
one day');[16] 'nû gevuocte ein wunderlich geschiht (ez enkam
von sînem willen niht)' ('now happened a strange thing – it
was not his will').[17] Gregorius did not intend to strike his
brother. Through this unintentional sin he realises that he is an
outsider: 'ich enbin niht der ich wânde sîn' ('I am not who I
thought I was').[18] He begins to realise what his origin must be:

> ich bin vervallen verre
> âne alle mîne schulde.
> Wie sol ich gotes hulde
> gewinnen nâch der missetât
> diu hie vor mir geschriben stât?

I have fallen very far without all my guilt. How am I to win God's
forgiveness after the wrongdoing which is here written before me?[19]

And so begins the search for his own identity:

> ichn geruowe niemer mê
> und wil iemer varnde sîn
> mir entuo noch gotes gnâde schîn
> von wannen ich sî oder wer.

I will never rest, and will always be journeying on unless God's mercy
shines upon me and shows me where I am from or who I am.[20]

This second sea journey brings the sometime castaway back to
his origins, to his mother. But his ignorance of his parentage
leads him into sin, because he fails to realise that what is
happening to him is linked with his own past history, which
came adrift when he was cast adrift. His search for his origins

brings him into his mother's presence, and she also fails to recognise him:

> vür einen gast enphie si ir kint:
> ouch was sîn herze dar an blint
> und im unkunt genuoc
> daz in diu selbe vrouwe truoc.

She received her son as a guest, and his heart was also blind, and he was not aware that this same woman had borne him.[21]

They mistake past history for present adventure, and so the devil finds a way to unite mother and son. They ought to have been on their guard: 'once bitten, twice shy', and since the son has had to abandon his monastery, and the mother has already contracted an incestuous marriage, this new (apparent) sin really looks like carelessness: 'culpa culpam cumulat', it heaps blame upon blame.[22] The devil has his way, and the 'messenger of God',[23] his mother's deliverer,[24] becomes her ruin.[25] Gregorius bemoans his parents' sin without recognising the load of sin that is on his own back ('erkande niht der schulde / diu ûf sîn selbes rücke lac'[26]) – once he has accomplished his adventure, delivered his mother, and won her to be his wife.

When the inscribed tablets bring recognition, mother and son are cast into the abyss. Has God rejected their penance and let the devil have his own way once more?[27] Gregorius is now at odds with God,[28] and his mother loses faith in Him because of the fearful way in which He has fulfilled her son's quest for his origins. Gregorius sought and found – and what he found was sin, his own and that of the woman he sought. Hartmann analyses the situation and announces his conclusions:

> Ich weiz wol daz Jûdas
> niht riuwiger was
> dô er sich vor leide hie
> danne ouch diu zwei nû hie.[29]

I know well that Judas, when he hanged himself for sorrow, was no sorrier than these two are here and now.

The darkness of death falls round mother and son, and in it lurks despair. No biblical names have been mentioned in the

poem since line 27 (Adam and Abel); but now two more are
quoted: Judas, who despaired, and David, who mourned.[30]
The mother feels she is damned:

> ouwê ich vervluochtez wîp!
> ...
> ist mir diu sêle nû verlorn
> sô ist der heize gotes zorn
> vil gar ûf mich gevallen
> als den vervluochten allen.

Alas, accursed woman that I am! Now my soul is lost, for the hot
anger of God has fallen far heavier on me than on all the damned.[31]

She puts her last hope in her son, who has read many books ('ir
habet der buoche vil gelesen')[32] and is thus well versed in
theology. The latter helps her in his wisdom:

> ez ist wider dem gebote.
> niht verzwîvelt an gote:
> ir sult harte wol genesen.
> jâ hân ich einen trôst gelesen
> daz got die wâren riuwe hât
> ze buoze über alle missetât.
> iuwer sêle ist nie sô ungesunt,
> wirt iu daz ouge ze einer stunt
> von herzelîcher riuwe naz,
> ir sît genesen, geloubet daz.

It is against God's law. Do not despair of God: you will surely be
saved. I have read some comforting words: that God has mercy on
those who truly repent, however terrible their sins. Your soul is never
so sick: if at any hour your eye is moistened by a tear of heartfelt
repentance, you were saved: believe that.

Medieval authors always looked to their sources, the Bible or
other works, before they committed themselves. They steered
through the darkness of their own doubts by following the pole
star of tradition. Traditional characters and words were a
guide through life, a model and a warning. To refer to Judas
was to hoist a warning sign against the unforgivable sin of
despair. If the Gregorius legend were to end in despair, rather
than repentance, then it would become, theologically speak-

ing, an irredeemable tragedy. And so mother and son now go their separate ways, as father and mother did earlier in the story: the mother to her own land, the son into the unknown, a crag in the sea, where he does penitence for seventeen years before emerging, elect and exalted, to say:

> vil liebiu muoter, sehet mich an:
> ich bin iuwer sun und iuwer man.
> swie grôz und swie swære
> mîner sünden last wære
> des hât nû got vergezzen.

Much-loved mother, behold me: I am your son and your husband. However great and serious the burden of my sin may have been, God has now forgotten it.[33]

At the end Hartmann is able to say:

> daz si nû iemer mêre sint
> zwei ûz erweltiu gotes kint!

that they are now forever more two of the chosen [elect] children of God.[34]

Here Hartmann implicitly challenges the abbot who tried to keep Gregorius in the monastery with the words, 'sun, ich hete dich erwelt / ze einem gotes kinde' (son, I had chosen you to be a child of God).[35] Gregorius followed his own destiny, but – whatever the abbot said – God could still 'elect' him after he had done penance. Critics often ask why the chief sinners do not confess to a priest. The answer has little to do with the evolution of the confessional sacrament and more to do with literary aims. The sinners – father, mother and son – impose on themselves the severest possible penance, reaching the limits of what God allows. Against the weight of their dark experience of guilt they set the counter-weight of their freely chosen experience of atonement: an absolution spoken by a priest would destroy that balance. Only the fisherman, a weak character, makes his confession. The shorter route to grace via absolution is theologically irreproachable but narratologically weak: the story gives God the time to elect those whose penance is not imposed, but chosen freely.[36]

Any confessor would have had to impose a heavy penance. The seventeen years of penance correspond only roughly to the penance for incest with sister or mother laid down by the church: usually fifteen years, though some medieval penitentials mention, for laymen, twelve years (the next most frequent), and also five, seven, eight, ten or twenty-one years;[37] for those in holy orders the penalties could be even higher.[38] The only text to mention a seventeen-year penance for incest with the mother is the thirteenth-century *Poenitentiale Laurentianum.*[39] In literary texts the period of seventeen years is used because the numbers one to seventeen, added together, give the number of the fullness of grace, 153.[40] St Alexis leaves his bride on their wedding night, without laying a finger on her, and lives for seventeen years as a poor beggar in a strange land, so as to serve none but God.[41] Honorius wrote a sermon on the broad left-hand road to Hell and the straight and narrow way to Heaven: in it he distinguishes fifteen paths on the true way of Love. Seventeen arms come down from the heights of blessedness to pull upwards those who follow these paths: they are the seventeen aids of the Holy Spirit on the climb out of the depths on to the path of salvation. Honorius characterises each of them by means of scriptural references; the seventeenth aid brings one on to the Rock.[42] The number of fishes in the Apostles' miraculous draught after the Resurrection, 153,[43] is recalled by the fact that the key to Gregorius' release from his penance is found in a newly caught fish.[44] The fact that Gregorius does penance for his sin upon an island is not mere poetic invention: it is based on the punishment for incest in Roman law, exile to an island.[45] Penitentials also demand, as part of the penance, *peregrinatio*: originally this meant exile, but in the Middle Ages, a pilgrimage.[46] Gregorius' father's penance after his incest with his sister, a journey to the Holy Land, also has a legal character.

Of all the legends of 'sinful saints', the closest to *Gregorius*, in both content and date (between 1178 and 1190), is that of St Albanus, which serves as a warning against the same sinful extremes. Albanus is born of incest and marries his mother. After a time of penitence he kills his father and mother, who had fallen back into sin, repents, does penance, and attains to sainthood through martyrdom.[47] The prologue of the *Passio Albani* sees the legend as an exemplary warning against presumptuous self-confidence and despairing of grace.[48] One Middle High German version furnishes a key at the end for 'der die materi wil versten' (him who wishes to understand this matter). He who bemoans his sins by day and night should

> an dem schepher nicht verczagn,
> des parmung er gepruefn chan
> an dem vil liebn Alban.

not despair of the Creator, whose mercy he can put to the test through the beloved Alban.

For despite the magnitude of Alban's guilt, his penance enabled him to become a saint.[49] One of the German prose versions is entitled 'Das kein sûnder verczweyfelen soll' (that no sinner should despair), and opens with the words:

Nu wil ich schreyben von eim grossen haubtsunder, der vater vnd muter, weybe vnd schwester erschlagen vnd sich mit der sûnde der unkeûschheit mit muter vnd schwester – doch vnwyssenlich – beflecket hat vnd durch seyn pusswertig leben an sein leczten zeiten selig vnd heilig worden ist. Darauss verstanden soll werden, das kein sûnder in seinen sûnden, wie gross die sein, verczagen vnd verczweyfelen solle.

Now I shall write about a great and mortal sinner, who murdered his father and mother, wife and sister, and stained himself – albeit unwittingly – with the sin of unchastity with mother and sister, and who through his life of penitence became in his last days blessed and holy. This should give us to understand that no sinner in his sins, however great they may be, ought to give up and despair.[50]

The Gregorius authors, almost all of whom belong to the Middle Ages, have in common a principle which exponents of an excessively formalistic critical method find incomprehensible and mercilessly dismiss: that literature can be a guide through life. This emerges clearly from all the prologues and epilogues, including Hartmann's:

Bî disen guoten mæren
von disen sündæren,
wie sie nach grôzer schulde
erwurben gotes hulde,
dâ ensol niemer an
dehein sündiger man
genemen bœsez bilde

dâ sol der sündige man
ein sælic bilde nemen an,
swie vil er gesündet hât,
daz sîn doch wirt guot rât,
ob er die riuwe begât
und rehte buoze bestât.

(lines 3959–65, 3983–9)

No sinner should receive, from this good story about these sinners and how they after great and guilty acts obtained God's mercy, any evil example. ... From it the sinner should receive a blessed example: however greatly he sinned, he will find help if he prays for God's mercy and does due penance.

In the epilogue to his Latin translation of Hartmann's *Gregorius*, Arnold von Lübeck develops the metaphor of sin as a snare or noose. *Gregorius peccator* – Gregorius the sinner – becomes a type of the man who, though caught in the noose of the devil, does not despair of obtaining the gift of grace, so that his bonds are worn away. In this he contrasts with Judas, who through his death – by the noose – remains an admonitory type of the man who perishes through despair:

Hec ergo forma omnibus
sit data peccatoribus,
quicunque dyabolico
irretiti sunt laqueo,
ne desperent euadere
quando per donum gracie
cernunt contritum laqueum
et saluam turbam passerum.
Iam absit desperacio
cayn nec non confessio
iude, qui non penituit
dum laqueo interiit.

Therefore, this example should be given to all sinners: whatever people are entrapped in the devil's noose, they ought not to despair of escaping when they see the noose worn through by the gift of grace, and the host of little birds safe and sound. Away, then, with the despair of Cain and the confession of Judas, who did not repent, and perished in the noose.[51]

> Sit igitur hec leccio
> piis edificatio
> scelestis exercicium,
> ut redeant ad gemitum
> post fallacem insaniam
> vite sperantes veniam.
>
> (IV, 1242–7)

Therefore, let this reading be an edification to the righteous, and a model of wickedness that after the madness of error they should return to penitence, hoping that their lives will be spared.

Through repentance, a man who has fallen into the dark pit of the devil can climb up again into the light of life:

> Si fueris iam cauea
> absortus dyabolica
> veraciter et penites,
> illic vere inuenies
> foramen, per quod exeas
> vt sic ad vitam redeas.
>
> (IV, 1230–5)

Even if you are already plunged into the pit of the devil, if you truly repent, there indeed you shall find a hole through which you can escape, so that you can return to life. [See full text lines 1224–35.]

Arnold von Lübeck clearly identifies despair with the sin against the Holy Ghost. Gregorius tells his mother:

> mater celestis medicus,
> qui sanare nos vouerat,
> omne ab nobis auferat
> desperandi periculum,
> quod sanctum tangit spiritum.
> Omne scelus remittitur
> quod a nobis committitur
> in patrem sive filium,
> in sanctum vero spiritum

peccare non remittitur,
quod desperare dicitur.
Mater, pro certo noueris,
si penitens dolueris,
ex corde fusis lacrimis
dico, quod saluaberis.

(III, 438–52)

Mother, may the celestial doctor who vowed to heal us take from us all danger of despair, which involves the holy spirit. All crimes we commit against the father and the son can be forgiven, but the sin against the holy spirit is not forgiven – and that is called despair. Mother, be sure of this: if you grieve and are penitent, and weep tears from your heart, I tell you that you will be saved.

Desperatio and *poenitentia*, penitance and despair, stand side by side: Judas and Gregorius.

The twelfth century's shuddering contemplation of Judas produced a *vita* (life) of the character,[52] which, like the Apocrypha, purported to fill in the gaps in the biblical account: Judas' parentage, birth, and life up to his death upon the tree. It was influenced not only by the Moses and Oedipus stories but also by the *vita* of Pontius Pilate,[53] an older text than the *Judas* but found alongside it in manuscripts, including the earliest manuscript to contain the *Judas*. Both texts satisfied readers' eagerness to know how the life they lived had driven these two wicked men to bring about the passion of Christ and then to die by their own hand. The first complete Latin life of Judas dates from the twelfth century; later, a similar story travelled the world via the *Golden Legend*, where it forms part of the life of Matthias, who took Judas' place among the apostles. This in turn served as the basis of *Judas der Ertz-Schelm* ('Judas the Arch-Villain'), by Abraham de Santa Clara (*c.* 1700), and literary re-workings continued to appear well into the nineteenth century. We know about fifty manuscripts of the Latin *vita*, and almost as many (and varied) vernacular versions. They are not long: the Middle High German *Alte Passional* tells the story in just 550 lines.[54] The Latin *vitas* largely abstain from comment and let the facts speak for themselves:

Reuben and Cyborea, Judas' parents, fear the birth of their son, for the mother has had a dream foretelling that he will destroy the Jewish people. Therefore they set him adrift upon the sea, which casts him up on the island of Scarioth – hence his surname. The childless queen of the island takes him in, but then bears a son of her own. Judas strikes the latter one day, in play, and the queen then reveals that he is a foundling. Stricken with shame, Judas slays his nobly-born brother and flees to Jerusalem, where he meets another wicked man, Pilate, and rises high in his service. Pilate covets the apples in the garden next door to his palace. He sends Judas to steal them; the owner of the garden catches him in the act, and in the course of the quarrel Judas slays him with a stone. It is his father, Reuben. Pilate gives Judas Reuben's widow to wife: thus, having murdered his father, he marries his mother, a fact which mother and son subsequently discover. On his mother's advice, the repentant Judas, seeking forgiveness, becomes a disciple of Jesus. He is loved by Jesus more than the other disciples, but robs and betrays him; however, realizing that Christ is guiltless, Judas throws away the blood-money and hangs himself. (See plates 1–4).

Vitae like those of Judas (as a warning) or 'sinful saints' like Gregorius (as an exhortation to repentance) may well have been influenced by medieval 'laments for sin' in verse and prose, which make a point of piling up long lists of dreadful deeds to be repented of. This is the more likely in that the laments also frequently refer to exemplary figures like St Peter and the penitent thief, St Mary the Egyptian and St Mary Magdalene – to name but a few. The repentant speaker of the laments grounds his own appeal to God in the redemption of such figures, who were released from their abyss of guilt by reason of their faith. Every overtone and argument in the Gregorius texts is prefigured in the laments, especially where the latter use the dialogue form to confront the arguments of the despairing sinner with the consolations of theology. An excellent example is the *Synonyma* of Isidore of Seville, later also known as the *Lamentatio animae peccatricis*, the lamentation of the sinful soul.[55] It is a monologue in the form of a lament for sin, a demand for consolation, and an acceptance of the latter.[56] Then the sinner's journey into despair, and his escape through trust in God's grace, are measured out in a lengthy conversation between *Homo* and *Ratio*, which takes them through extremes of darkness and enlightenment, from the uttermost

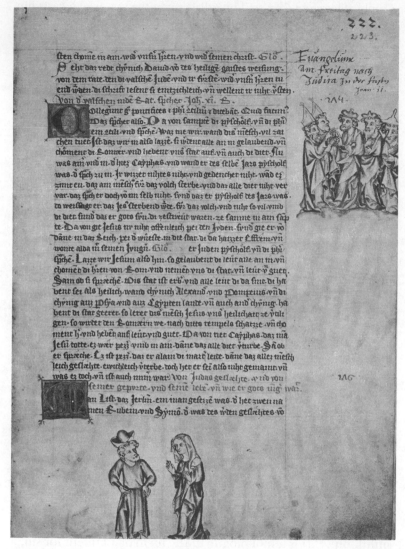

Plate 1 The opening of the Middle High German *Life of Judas* in the
Schaffhausen Lectionary (1330).

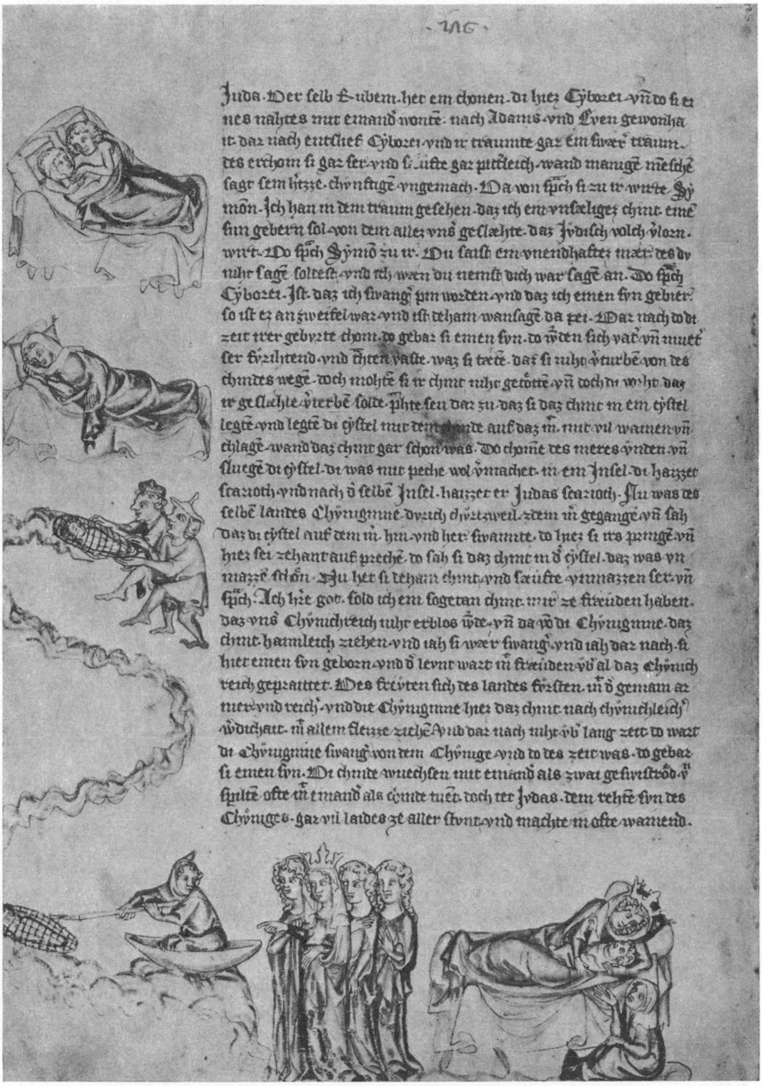

Plate 2 *Life of Judas*. Judas is cast adrift and rescued.

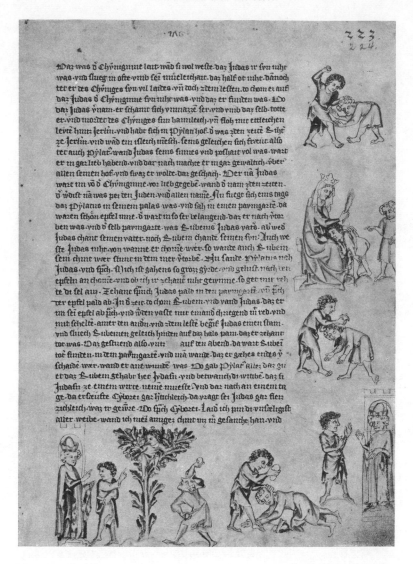

Plate 3 *Life of Judas*. Judas kills his foster-brother; Judas in Reuben's orchard.

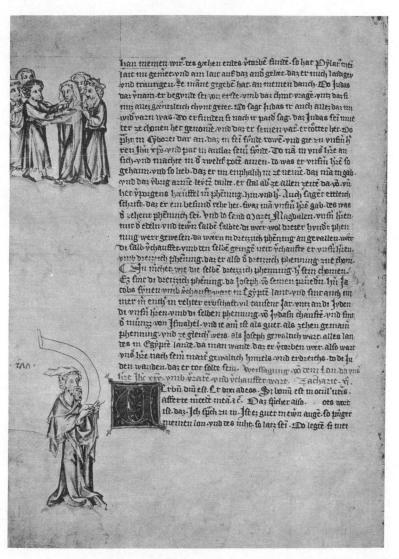

Plate 4 *Life of Judas*. Judas marries his mother.

abyss to the most dizzying heights. Thus the monologue of the
despairing sinner,[57] and the reply of his comforter[58] which
leads him towards self-knowledge, prepare the ground for a
genuine dialogue:[59] a very important progression, which illu-
minates the capacities of the human soul and guides mankind
towards the theological message – the search for a meaning in
life which will banish despair. The second book contains a
hundred pieces of good advice from the comforter to the sinner,
and concludes with the sinner's expression of gratitude. But the
culmination of the dialogue is the comforter's warning against
despair:

Believe, therefore, most strongly; do not hesitate, do not doubt, never
despair of God's mercy. Hope in confession, have faith. Do not
despair of the healing remedy; do not despair of salvation, if you turn
to better things. For he who despairs of forgiveness for his sin, damns
himself more by his despair than by the sin he has committed.

Despair increases the sin; despair is worse than any sin. Correct
yourself therefore, and have hope of mercy. Lay aside injustice and
hope for life; lay aside iniquity and hope for salvation. There is no sin
so great that it cannot be forgiven; though you be a sinner, an
evildoer, a scoundrel, burdened by endless misdeeds, the chance of
repentance will not be denied you. The divine mercy willingly comes
to the help of the penitent; through penitence forgiveness is granted;
by penitence all sins are wiped away.[60]

This is the sinner's answer:

Alas for me! I had lost hope, I had lost faith, I mistrusted in my heart,
my heart was broken, in desperation my heart wellnigh foundered.
Now I have returned to hope, now I have regained faith, now I have
hope of forgiveness; I hope in God's graciousness, I doubt not of
God's goodness. I shall dwell in hope, his graciousness has raised me
into hope, it has given me hope of life through penitence. Therefore if
God look upon me, if he come to my help, if he help me achieve what
I desire, I have decided and resolved to do it, my heart is set upon it,
it cannot be wrested from my heart.[61]

I shall not pursue the comparison between the *lamentatio* dialogue and the similar conversation between mother and son in
Hartmann (lines 2665–706), since we are speaking here in
terms of genres rather than of individual texts. Other *lamenta-*

tiones, actual prayers in monologue or lyrical form, also show a relationship to Hartmann's work. At an early stage (lines 97–170), Hartmann evokes the parable of the Good Samaritan: some explanation for this may be found through a comparison with the lament by Pope Leo IX (died 1054) which throws some light on the passage in *Gregorius*.[62] The content of its thirty-five verses is as follows:

1–4: invocation of Father (1), Son (2), Holy Spirit (3), the Trinity (4). 'Lapsum stude reformare, / prostratum erigere' (See that you restore the fallen and raise the prostrate.)

5–12: the sins of birth, childhood, boyhood, adolescence and youth – too much turned towards this world – are confessed and lamented.

13–18: the sinner is seen as the man who fell among thieves on the road from Jerusalem to Jericho.

19–23: the Priest (19), the Levite (20) and the Good Samaritan (21–3).

24–34: prayer to Christ (24), who had mercy on Peter (25), the Penitent Thief (26) and Mary Magdalene (27–30): may he, the Good Shepherd, take up the sinner (31), tend him (32), bring him home (33) and have him cared for (34).

35: invocation of the Trinity.

Closer similarities are apparent in the following passages:

Hartmann		*Leo*
der mordære gewalt.	14	Insperate laquaeatus
er was komen in ir gehalt		cecidi improvidus
(99–100)		In manus tandem latronum
		dire saevientium,
		Me quaerentem devorare
		leonina rabie.
dâ hâten sî in nider geslagen	15	Captum, caesum, vulneratum,
und im vrevellîche entragen		spoliatum, miserum
aller sîner sinne kleit		Reliquerunt semivivum,
und hâten in an geleit		ad terram depositum,
vil marterlîche wunden.		Duris flatibus spirantem
ez was zuo den stunden		peneque exanimem.
sîner sêle armuot vil grôz.		

sus liezen sî in tugende[63] blôz unde halp tôt ligen. (101–9)	17	Inde cadet in latrones, videlicet daemones, Vitiis misellum plagant, virtutibus spoliant, Immortalitatem demunt, rationem nequeunt.
dô enhâte im got niht verzigen sîner gewonlîcher erbarmekeit – (110–11)	18	Iam (jacet) velut captivus cui nullus proximus, Parens, notus vel amicus, doloris qui conscius, Nisi pius Deus meus, super omnes providus.
112–126 (The two children)		(Not parallel)
si tâten im vil guotes und ervurpten in des bluotes. si guzzen im in die wunden sîn	23	Plagis aptans legis vinum gratiaeque oleum.
beidiu öl unde wîn. diu salbe ist linde und tuot doch wê, daz öl diu gnâde, der wîn diu ê, die der sündære haben muoz: sô wirt im siechtuomes buoz. (127–34)	33	Oleum infundes sanctum vinum simul optimum, Tuum ponens interventum perducas ad stabulum, Pellens mortem, donans vitam fac, ut tecum veniam.
alsus huop in bî sîner hant diu gotes gnâde als sî in vant ûf ir miltez ahselbein	30	Bonus pastor oves tuis reportas in umeris.
und truoc in durch beruochen hein. (135–8)	31	Sic, sic, pastor, nunc iacenti languido ac debili Elevandum manum praebe, velis me erigere, Ut erectus possim stare coram te, dulcissime.
dâ wurden im verbunden sîne verchwunden daz er âne mâsen genas – (139–41)	32	Plagas meas (cicatrices) novas atque veteres Studeas sic tu curare, quaeso, bone medice, Sim per te ut hinc securus, sanatus languoribus.

1. H: the power of the robbers: he had fallen into their hands. L: improvidently, unexpectedly, I fell into the snare, into the hands of savage thieves, seeking like hungry lions to devour me.

2. H: there they struck him down and wickedly tore all his garments from him, and inflicted many terrible wounds upon him. So at that time the poverty of his soul was very great. They left him half-dead, clothed only in his virtues. L: they took the unhappy man, struck him, wounded him, despoiled him and left him helpless on the ground, gasping for breath and almost dead. . . . Then he fell among thieves – that is, demons – they struck the poor man with vices, despoiled him of his virtues, took from him his immortality, robbed him of his reason.

3. H: if God had not taken from him his usual mercy. L: now he (lies) like a captive with nobody close to him, parent, acquaintance or friend, who might be aware of his suffering, except my gracious God, who sees all things.

4. H: they did great good to him and cleansed him of the blood. Into his wounds they poured both oil and wine. The salve is gentle and yet hurts. The oil is grace, the wine is the commandments the sinner must have: so at the last he is healed of his sickness. L: applying to his wounds the wine of the law, and the oil of grace. . . . You will pour in the holy wine, best of wine; you will bring your help and lead us to the shelter; driving away death, giving life, bring me unto you.

5. H: Thus when God's grace found him, he raised him up in his hands, on his kind shoulders, and bore him home so as to take care of him. L: you, good shepherd, bear back your sheep on your shoulders. . . . Thus, thus, shepherd, raise your hand and show it to me as I lie weak and languishing: please, sweetest lord, raise me up so that I can stand erect beside you.

6. H: then his wounds were bound up, so that he was healed of his wounds. L: please, good doctor, do your best to heal my wounds (scars), new and old: from now on let me be safe through you, healed of my weaknesses.

The same theme reappears later in hymns (for example, in Herradis von Landsberg) and in other similar poems.[64]

Up to now, writers on *Gregorius*, while being aware of the *Judas*, have given it only a passing mention as a related text of the Oedipus type,[65] while *Judas* critics have done the reverse:[66]

neither group has progressed from study of the actual material to consideration of the story and its historical importance and real meaning.

Let us look again at the story of Judas. As a child he is cast away, unloved, because of an ominous dream; as a stranger in a strange land, he observes and envies the nobility of the prince believed to be his brother; his mother denounces him as a foundling and curses him; he flees and becomes an accomplice of Pontius Pilate; tempted by Pilate, he steals apples from his father's garden (= Paradise),[67] bludgeoning his father in the process; he is forced to marry his mother against her will, and through her becomes aware of her sin and his own. The story shows what it is like for a human being to live under a curse – a curse which seems to be removed when Jesus chooses Judas and loves him above the other apostles, until the devil rides him once again[68] and drives him, thief and traitor, through despair into suicide.

If the life of Judas had ended with his acceptance as a disciple it could have served as an example of *gratia superabundans*, the granting of superabundant grace to the repentant sinner – in spite of his murder of brother and father and his incest with his mother. Many similar lives of 'sinful saints' are exemplary in this way. But the pre-biblical life of Judas could not be read in isolation from the biblical story of his death. Thus the *vita* in its entirety became an example of despair and consequent damnation, all the more readily *because* the first part could have served as a counter-example to show that even the worst of sinners can be forgiven. The experience of such forgiveness only made Judas all the more guilty in his death. In lives of Judas the repentance which leads him to Jesus comes before the despair that drives him to hang himself; but because the character of Judas is irrevocably fixed by his role in the Gospels, the whole *vita*, from the very beginning, has to be read as a warning. Even the oldest Latin *vita*, dating from the twelfth century, ends thus, with his suicide as in the Bible. Jesus took the repentant arch-sinner as his disciple: the fact that he could then fall once again made his final position utterly unredeemable.

It is this which constitutes the emotional impact of the Judas *vita*. After the murder of the king's son and of his father, and again after the incestuous marriage, he found grace; but after the betrayal of Jesus he could find it no more. After his return to sin he could no longer recall his escape from horror by turning to Jesus, or his choosing as a disciple: in the darkness of despair no further thought of grace could come to him. The experience of Gregorius and his mother is quite different: they do return to sin, but even then, after the first frenzy, they are aware of the promised way of escape. Judas, like the parents of Gregorius, lies under the spell of circumstances imposed upon him, which he has not chosen but which becomes a part of him. Like them, he breaks out of the spell into the fresh air of grace. His path and theirs begin to diverge only at the point where the sin each thinks he or she has left behind unexpectedly catches up with them again, this time in an intensified form. Lava cools, and grass grows over it; but if the destructive stream breaks forth again, it is hard indeed to rebuild one's life over the still-smouldering grave of Hope. Judas falls, and falls for ever. Gregorius and his mother save themselves on the very brink of the abyss through trust in the promise of grace; through penance – which means half a lifetime of torment – they are eventually chosen as being fit to receive grace again.

When Jacobus de Voragine inserted the life of Judas into the *Golden Legend* (as an excursus in the *Life of Matthias*), he left some doubt as to whether the apocryphal part was suited to be read in churches: 'hucusque in praedicta hystoria apocrypha legitur, quae utrum recitanda sit, lectoris arbitrio relinquatur, licet sit potius relinquenda quam asserenda'. (What is read thus far in the aforementioned history is apocryphal; whether it should be read out, I leave to the judgement of the reader, though it is better to leave it out than to include it.)[69] No such doubts had troubled the author of the *Life of Judas* from Saint-Victor, writing in the twelfth century, a hundred years before de Voragine. This text ends with the usual concluding formula for public reading in a monastery: 'Tu autem domine miserere nostri. Qui perseveraverit usque in finem in bonum, hic salvus erit.' (But thou, O Lord, have mercy upon us.

Whoever perseveres in goodness until the end will be saved.)[70]
Similarly sanguine is the German *Alte Passionale* of *c.* 1300,
which introduces the life of Judas into the Matthias story on
the authority of 'a book', and says that he 'vz allen eren weich
zu ewenclichem vluche' (out of all honour turned to everlasting damnation, 312, 74–5). And the last doubt vanishes
when a mid-fifteenth-century collection of saints' lives introduces the lives of both 'the wicked Judas' and 'Gregorius on the
rock' into its 'Winter' section as a contrasting pair of good and
bad examples: the first time that this pairing is made in
hagiography.[71] The story of Gregorius, a saint, ends with an
appeal to him as intercessor: 'Now we pray to dear Lord Saint
Gregorius that he should intercede with God to grant us, after
this life, life eternal.' The life of Judas ends: 'Thus you have
heard how Judas came to a bad end. God give us all a good end
and, after this life, life eternal.' Obviously the *Judas* had now
found its way into the church's readings. Through collections
like the *Golden Legend*, the *Alte Passional* and the *Lives of the Saints*
it became known over a very wide area.

(A hitherto unnoticed allusion to the life of Judas, in a
sermon from Belgium, indicates that a completely different
version existed in the thirteenth century, though it was not
widely known. In this version Jesus, out of love for Judas, heals
his father of leprosy and his mother of lameness, despite the
incestuous relationship. In the pseudo-Augustinian *Sermones ad
fratres in eremo*[72] there is a sermon on the Last Supper which
quotes John 13:27: 'What thou must do, do quickly.' Christ
then goes on, as it were, to interpret his own words: 'As if Christ
were saying, "Since I cannot dissuade you by the fear of shame
or of eternal death, nor by love, I give you the power to do in
fact what you have already willed to do."' The preacher then
goes on, in his own voice, to ask Judas a series of reproachful
questions designed to bring painfully to his mind all the good
which Christ has done to him, and to hale him before the
tribunal represented by the congregation. The first accusation
again refers to the miracle which Jesus wrought for Judas'
parents and which Judas has forgotten: 'O Judas, what are you
doing? Think before you act; for after the deed you may not

have the grace of repentance.' Then follows the allusion to the apocryphal *vita*: 'Why do you want to betray him who forgave you so many sins? Has he not often delivered you from death? Did he not, for love of you, heal your father from leprosy, and your mother, with whom you had lain, from the palsy?')

The textual history of the two Lives makes it probable that the *Judas* is the earlier, and this is confirmed by the recognition that the *Gregorius* follows it in logical sequence: Gregorius is a recognisable antitype of Judas, the man who despaired.[73] The Judas story may have sprung from that of Oedipus, which was rediscovered in the West some time before 1150: Origen's juxtaposition of the two characters may have been the key.[74] Similarly, in the second half of the twelfth century the Gregorius story may have been a deliberate literary creation, the antitype or counter-story to that of Judas. Against Judas, who despaired, it sets the portrait of a sinner who passes through the same trials, but repents: the elect as against the damned. From the viewpoint of antithetical typology, Gregorius on his crag rises above Judas: creative opposition transforms an older tradition. Judas dies without ever being aware of his place in the divine plan of salvation, just before the saving death of the Redeemer. He is perhaps the last man to die under the Old Law, before the dawning of the Age of Grace. Gregorius, by contrast, lives after the first Pentecost, when salvation was made known to the world; thus, as a trained theologian to whom 'dîvînitas / garwe durchliuhtet was' (theology was made wholly transparent, lines 1187–8), he is well placed to express the antitype of the type represented by Judas.[75] If the warning against despair (*desesperance, zwîfel*) is so insistent in all the Gregorius texts, it is because they are rooted in the memory of Judas whom indeed Hartmann, and later Arnold of Lübeck, name as a warning to all sinners hereafter.

What exactly was Judas guilty of? As with the Gregorius story, it is sometimes difficult to see the answer. The *vitae* often take the edge off his responsibility by blaming it all on the workings of fate. Deliberate fault, predestination, catastrophe, fate or Oedipal tragedy: where, in all this, do our (often cursory) literary texts ground the unfathomable theology of

Judas' guilt? They give few indications; but the question is still worth asking. Let us just glance at one of the later *vitae*, the most detailed prose rendering, dating from the thirteenth century.[76] This author alters the prophetic dream, and pays more attention to the psychological aspects of the story, for example the parents' hesitation between patriotism and parental love just before they cast Judas adrift. He sees the element of predestination more as fate.[77] When Judas realises that he has committed incest with his mother, he cries, 'Unhappy man that I am! What accursed fortune is dogging me?' and is about to fall on his sword in a fit of madness when his mother intervenes. On her advice he goes with her to lay his story before Jesus; Jesus takes him so as to rescue him from despair, and promises him eternal life if he repents and avoids a relapse into sin:

tamen ne desperatione salutis cogeretur amplius periclitari, 'Potes,' inquit, 'adhuc salvus fieri si digne penitueris, sed et hec et cetera peccata deinceps vitaveris ... sequere me meque imitando in veritate vitam aeternam habere poteris.' (p. 508)

However, lest by despair of forgiveness he might be forced into further danger, [Jesus] said, 'You can still be saved if you duly repent, but also if you hereafter avoid this and other sins ... follow me, and by imitating me you may indeed have eternal life.'

It is possible that this version has been influenced by the Gregorius legend.[78] It is the first in which the barrel containing the infant Judas is found at sea, by a fisherman (not cast up on the beach, by the queen), and in which the infant is accompanied by evidence of his origins. Judas is brought up by the fisherman's wife and shows such ability that he is sent to Greece to study. This allows for a change of scene. Judas is a favourite for the Olympic games, but his envious rivals have him barred because of his base birth. He rushes to his mother, extracts the secret of his origins from her at sword-point, and the 'desire to know himself' thus awakened leads him home to Jerusalem.

Gregorius is but one of a great chorus of 'holy sinners' out of the Bible, history and literature whose legends reached their full flowering in the twelfth century, when their example assured even the poorest that grace was available to all. There was a rich variety of sins against God – unbelief, backsliding, lust, avarice, murder and incest – and a goodly number of sinners, including Mary Magdalene, Charlemagne and Gregorius, to commit them. But they all found God's grace, and even became saints, because they avoided committing the only unforgivable sin, the sin against the Holy Ghost: despair. Judas committed murder and theft, patricide and incest; he repented and became an elect of God. But not only did he relapse – into embezzlement and betrayal – he also despaired, and all that could still have been forgiven became thereby unforgivable. He was damned. Judas and Gregorius fit together, as type and antitype. The saintly sinner and the damned sinner, bound together though originally poles apart, were both elect of God and near to Him. The more ancient of the two, Judas, fell far away from God because he did not trust in the grace that follows on repentance. (Why did he not? Why was he not allowed to? It is a question we might ask God as much as Judas himself. By putting himself beyond redemption he made redemption possible.) Things are easier for his more recent counterpart: Gregorius can read the scriptures of divine revelation. Indeed he is well acquainted with them, and his mother's hope in this familiarity is not misplaced.[79] The scriptures bring counsel:

> ez ist wider dem gebote.
> niht verzwîvelt an gote.
> ir sult harte wol genesen.
> jâ hân ich einen trôst gelesen
> daz got die wâren riuwe hât
> ze buoze über alle missetât.
> iuwer sêle ist nie sô ungesunt
> wirt iu daz ouge ze einer stunt
> von herzelîcher riuwe naz,
> ir sît genesen, geloubet daz.

(lines 2697–706)

For translation, see page 10.

Gregorius knows something to which Judas, though a chosen disciple of Jesus, is blind because he fails to recognise his place in the plan of salvation, fails to recognise Christ. Yet to the medieval mind, Judas could have been another Gregorius:

> het sich Judas nit in der stunde
> vor grossem leide erhangen,
> *got het ine gerne entphangen.*

If Judas in his great grief had not hanged himself on the spot, *God would gladly have received him.*[80]

If Judas had not despaired he might have been a saint. So François Mauriac, writing in 1936, assures us:

Very little would have been needed for the tears of Judas to be allied in the memory of mankind with those of Peter. He might have become a saint, the patron of us all who constantly betray Christ ... Judas was on the border of perfect contrition ... God might still have had the traitor needed for the redemption ... and a saint besides ... While there exists a ray of hope in the most guilty soul, it is separated from infinite love only by a sigh. And it is the mystery of mysteries that the son of perdition did not heave this sigh.

Judas and Gregorius stand in a creative relationship to each other as exempla, and were expressly designed as such by all authors up to Abraham de Santa Clara. These authors intended people to look to their work for guidance in life, just as Gregorius himself looks for salvation in written tradition. Hartmann appeals directly to the experience of real life:

> des ist ze hœrenne nôt
> und ze merkenne in allen
> die dâ *sint* vervallen
> under bercswæren schulden:
> ob er ze gotes hulden
> dannoch wider gâhet,
> *daz in got gerne emphâhet.*

(lines 150–6)

This ought to be heard and remembered by all those who have fallen under the mountain-heavy load of sin: if he thereafter returns to God's mercy, then God will gladly receive him.

Medieval literature is intended to shake people out of their indifference. If we fail to realise this, our study of it becomes

absurd, a pointless game. We must realise that there could be
no form without content, no literature unconcerned with the
destiny and potential of mankind. Aesthetic value was insepar-
able from spiritual and human values; originality had to be
grounded in tradition.

If we look back a little, we find that Oedipus, Judas and
Gregorius had already been associated by the twelfth century.
The lamentations in the Judas texts may well have been
inspired by Oedipus, and may also point to the later 'Com-
plaint of Dr Faustus' (*Doctor Fausti Weheklag*). The Oedipus
story was known to the twelfth century through Statius'
Thebais and the Old French *Roman de Thebes* (1150). There is a
Latin 'Lament of Oedipus' from this period which can be
associated with the Lives of Judas and Gregorius.[81] After
blinding himself ('the wound in my heart I brought to light /
when my hand pricked out both my eyes'[82]), Oedipus delivers
this speech on his own fate:

> Fessus luctu, confectus senio,
> gressu tremens labante venio:
> quam sinistro sim natus genio,
> nullo capi potest ingenio.
>
> (lines 2–5)

Wearied with grief, worn with age, I come trembling, with halting
step: no mind can comprehend the terrible fate to which I was born.

The lament ends with an allusion to the oracle:

> Quod petebat vox detestabilis,
> complet ira deorum stabilis.
> cruciatus est ineffabilis
> quem patimur gens miserabilis.
>
> (lines 21–4)

What the accursed voice sought, the implacable wrath of the gods has
brought about. Unspeakable is the torment which our miserable race
endures.

Even before 1200 Oedipus, Judas and Gregorius stood
together – having appeared, doubtless, in that order. Antiquity, Old Testament, Age of Grace; Fate, predestination,
election; tragedy, wasted life and legend: each depends on the

others, influences the others, in a complex creative process which brings out the true characteristics of all of them. And between the ancient hero and the holy sinner stands Judas the unhappy.

CHAPTER 2

The despair of Judas

In his *City of God*, Saint Augustine pronounces a judgement on Judas which is echoed by a chorus of medieval voices: Judas' death by hanging did not atone for his crime but augmented it. He despaired of God's mercy, and so his repentance, instead of healing him, killed him: 'quoniam Dei misericordiam desperando exitiabiliter paenitens nullum sibi salubris paenitentiae locum reliquit'. (For by despairing of God's mercy he repented to his own destruction and left himself no room for saving penitence.)[1] Gregory the Great says of Judas' death: 'pejus de peccato poenituit quam peccavit' (his repentance of his sin was worse than the sin).[2] By adding despair to his other sins, Judas put himself beyond the reach of grace. His conscience judged him, too soon, too hastily, and led him into damnation. The worst sin of all is to withdraw from grace. If Judas had sought grace, he would have found it – or such was the medieval opinion. His despair, and not his treason, was the worst thing about him, the sin against which we find warnings in theology, sermon and poem.

In the *Jüngere Titurel*, Albrecht von Scharfenberg speaks of the Grail and of the Last Supper, after which Peter and Judas betrayed Christ; but each repented thereof in his own way. Judas' evil repentance, compounding treason with despair, brought him damnation and the pains of hell. The genuine repentance of Peter opened the joys of heaven to all those who follow him. Both repentances are exemplary: one is to be avoided, the other imitated.

> Ir zwene brachen an im sit die trewe.
> Sande peter erwarp die hulde   menlichen mit
>   der waren lvtern rewe.

Jvdas der verzagete   mit zwifel svnden boste,
Da mit er flvch beiagete.   der rewe sand peters
                                      ich mich troste.
Vnd alle die tovf nach tragen vnd svnde,
Den ist die selbve rewe   ein frevden hvg ein
                                      seliclich vrkvnde.

Swer nach die spise frone   an lvtter rvwe enpfahet
Der wirt von gotes throne   geworfen vnd mit ivdas
                                      gar versmahet
Mit svlcher not die nieman weiz mit sagene,
Ir freis ir marter qvale,   die sie zvr helle hant ewiclich zv
     tragene.

(verses 6169–71)

Thereafter both of them broke faith with him. Saint Peter bravely
obtained grace through his true and pure repentance. Judas did not,
but added despair to his sins, and so was damned. I am consoled by
the repentance of Saint Peter. For anyone who, after baptism, has
sinned, that same repentance is a joy and a sign of blessing. Anyone
who takes communion without true repentance will be cast away
from the throne of God and accursed along with Judas, in such
suffering that no one could describe it; their fear, their torments, they
will have to endure forever in hell.

If you come to communion after 'repenting' in Judas' way,
then you condemn yourself. In the *Alte Passional* (*c.* 1300), the
treacherous Judas not only despairs –

> sin zwifelunge in virschriet
> an also boser rue,
> das der vil ungetrue
> sich selber hienc an einen stric

(lines 318–21)

his despair brought him to such evil repentance that the faithless man
hanged himself with a rope

– but, as a traitor, also literally *bursts*. This means that his soul
can escape from his body without passing through the mouth
which Jesus kissed; and that the throat is strangled through
which issued the voice of betrayal. He hangs forever between
heaven and earth so that the evil spirits of the air can torment
him, for he has cut himself off from God and man.[3]

In her great work *Das fliessende Licht der Gottheit* (The flowing light of divinity), Mechthild von Magdeborg describes Hell as being built out of stones of sin. Lucifer laid the foundation stone, which was Pride (*superbia*). Adam contributed four more blocks of sin, and Cain three. Judas delivered four more: lying, treason, despair and suicide: 'With these four stones unhappy Judas also slew himself.'[4]

In the fourteenth-century *Kreuziger* (The crusader) of Johannes von Frankenstein[5] we read:

> was âne hoffenunge trôst
> er gedâhte: ich mac durch nicht erlôst
> werden. sust er verzeit
> an gotes barmherzikeit,
> zû anderm sînen unheil
> erhînc er sich an ein seil.
> Jeronimus stêt ûf dem punt
> Jûdas habe mêr gesunt
> mit sîner verzagnis
> den an Christs verrêtnis:
> wan als er Christ verkouft,
> di sunde wart alleine gestûft
> wider Christi menscheit,
> aber mit der zageheit
> begînc er grôzer schulde
> wider die gotes hulde
> under sîn barmherzikeit,
> ouch dâ mit er widerseit
> dem heiligen geiste,
> des wart di schuld di meiste.[6]

(lines 5625–44)

When without the consolation of hope he thought, 'I cannot be saved.' Thus he despaired of God's mercy, and to his further damnation he hanged himself from a rope. On this point Jerome says that Judas sinned worse by despairing than by betraying Christ: when he sold Christ, the sin was aimed only at Christ's humanity, but with the despair he committed a greater sin against God's grace and mercy, and he also turned away from the Holy Ghost, which was the worst offence.

Judas' repentance, which led him not into prayer but into graver sin and suicide, was seen by God as being worse than his treason.[7] Judas, like a spider, spun the web in which he himself was ultimately to hang.[8] His ears, deaf to the words of Christ, will yet hear the Last Trump of the day of judgement.[9]

Heinrich der Teichner (fl. post 1350) wrote hundreds of didactic poems, of which two (no. 10, 'On human despair' and no. 311, 'On desperation') are devoted to the theology of despair.[10] The first is a warning against receiving communion 'with divided belief', lest one eat, like Judas, to one's own damnation:

> Judas nam goz leichnam
> von got selb und ward verwazzen,
> zweiflår auch als wenig sazzen
> in dem himel sam die gaist
> die Luzifer mit voller laist
> an zweifeln haln mit.
> got hat noch den selben sit
> daz er zweifels nicht wil han.[11]
>
> (lines 160–8)

Judas received the body of God from God himself and was damned. Those who despaired had no more chance of seats in Heaven than those spirits whom Lucifer loaded with despair and dragged down with him. God still maintains this principle: he will not accept those who despair.

Poem 311 deals with the sin against the Holy Ghost, which is clearly identified with despair (*desperatio*) in the opening lines:

> Die werlt ein altz sprichwort hat,
> ez wurd nie eins zagen rat;
> daz ist, der an got verzait.
> unsers herren parmchait
> wigt über aller sunden lot.
>
> (lines 1–5)

There is an old saying in the world: no help to those who despair; that is to say, those who despair of God. Our Lord's mercy outweighs any amount of sin.

A man may fail to turn from the world, or he may give up without a struggle, but the worst sin he can commit will be to despair of salvation when

er gendeckt in seinem mût:
'mein wirt noch nymmer rat',
daz ist dw obrist missetat.

(lines 50–2)

he thinks in his heart, 'Never will help be mine.' That is the worst misdeed.

When a man's sins are weighed in the balance, God's mercy can always outweigh them. No one should despair of that ('da sol nieman verzagen pey').[12] But God's grace cannot be obtained by force:

gotes gût dw hat dw chrafft
daz seu nicman mag ergahen.
suecht mans ferr, so ist sew nahen;
seucht mans hoch, so ist sew nider;
seucht mans in der teuf her wider;
so iz ob allen himeln hoch.

(lines 82–7)

God's goodness has this power, that no one can find it. If you seek it afar off, then it is near; if you seek it high, then it is low; if you seek it again in the deepest abyss, it is above all the highest heavens.

The nature of election is unfathomable. Why did God call the Penitent Thief to him and let Judas fall, though 'both stood in the hollow of his hand' ('si stunden paid in seiner hand', line 91)? Teichner returns again and again to that question. In 'Dass Gott einen Guten fallen lässt und einen Bösen zu sich nimmt' ('That God lets a good man fall and takes a wicked man to Himself'), he comments that God's ways are so unfathomable that many a man has been lost in the attempt to plumb their depths. God may reject a hermit and elect a murderer. Grace cannot be earned:

war umb got nicht geben well
aynem als dem andern sein genad,
daz ist ein verborgens phad.
er wil got zu haimleich wesen
der iz allez wil derlesen,
Judaz val und des schacher steygen.

(lines 446–51)

Why God will not give his grace to one, as he does to another, that is a hidden path. He who wants to know all about Judas' fall and the thief's salvation is trying to know God too well.

Why do God's children, created equal, suffer such dissimilar fates? Another of Heinrich's poems, 'Von der Erwählung' (On election) wrestles with this question in relation to Peter and Judas:

> si waren ainvalticleich geporen.
> daz der Judas ward verloren
> und was doch ein zwelfpot,
> daz waz da von daz in got
> liez der rechten tugent ploz.

They were both born equal. If Judas was damned, although he was an apostle, it was because God did not give him the right virtues.

God bears the responsibility for Judas. No one could have foreseen

> daz der Judas was verlorn
> und der schacher wurd der pest
> mit der ainn rew ze lest.[13]

that Judas was damned and the thief became the best man with his one act of repentance.

Gregorius' final election to the Papacy is not meant to recall any of the real popes of that name. Rather, it reminds us of the election of another once-fallen soul to the same high office: Peter, whose repentance was always coupled, in the Middle Ages, with the despair of Judas. His load of sin – his flight and denial – was little less heavy than Judas' with his treason. Repentance and despair: Peter, the elect, and Judas, the rejected, were a favourite pair of exempla. According to Matthew, the traitor hanged himself the morning after the night of Peter's denial.[14] In the fourteenth-century religious poem 'Die Erlösung' (Salvation), Judas' repentance follows immediately after Peter's: 'Judam ouch, den bôsen wiht, / rou vil sêre die geschicht' ('that evil creature, Judas, also sorely rued what had happened', lines 4957–8). But his repentance is unsure, because he is so full of bitterness that he even tears his

hair out. There follows a lament over the place in hell which
Judas secured for himself:

> vor rûwen bitterkeite
> hing er sich an einen ast.
> Der ungedrûwe dâ zubrast.

Out of bitter grief he hanged himself from a bough. There the traitor
burst asunder.[15]

According to Rupert von Deutz, the differing outcome of
Peter's and Judas' repentance depended on Jesus' attitude
towards them: he looked on the one with mercy, on the other
with judgement. It was the same face that looked: upon Peter,
and awoke him to healing repentance; upon Judas, and drove
him to repentance in death.[16]

In Lent, 1460, the Viennese theologian Paul Wann, a
famous preacher, gave a series of sermons in the cathedral in
Passau. The subject was Peter and Judas, and the words touch
the heart.[17] God let Peter fall and led him back to repentance,
'so that no sinner should despair, for he ought to tell himself
that Peter, however low he fell, was raised by Our Saviour to
the highest position of trust on earth, and was called to keep the
keys of heaven'. Peter was one of the elect; therefore his
repentance was no spontaneous act of merit, but the workings
of grace springing from Jesus' glance, which was described thus
by St Augustine: 'this glance came not from his earthly eyes,
but from the tender heart of the Saviour, and it brought
efficient grace'.[18] Paul Wann describes this working of grace:
'And this grace penetrated the soul of the fallen disciple and
shook it . . . and now his heart grew warm; it melted under the
gaze of his master like wax in the sun's rays. He felt his whole
body tremble and could no longer restrain himself, but wept.'
Peter took this gift of repentance to himself and (unlike Judas)
continued in it, doing penance, to his life's end. His legendary
biography brings out the theological implications: Peter
cooperated with the work begun in him by grace and accepted
by him:

from then on, Peter watched, prayed and wept every night from the
first crow of the cock until morning, doing penance for his denial of

Our Lord . . . he wept for it all the rest of his life; it is even said that he
sought out a cave near Jerusalem, to which he often betook himself,
unobserved, to shed silent tears of repentance and to beg the Lord his
God again and again to forgive him his terrible crime. But why did
the Lord let his disciple fall?[19]

There again we have the penetrating, unsleeping question of
theodicy, the attempt to understand God's acceptance. Why
were two disciples and two thieves found guilty, but only one of
each given grace? It was easy – too easy – to answer that God
willed them to be examples of good and evil for the edification
of mankind.[20] Paul Wann goes on to consider both Judas'
despair and Peter's repentance in a more dramatic way, with
some psychological insight,[21] so that the interest shifts away
from the theological question of grace and despair. But the
despairing Judas gets no more mercy from man than he did
from God. Through a thousand years of passiontide sermons,
from Leo the Great to Paul Wann, it was the same story. Here
is Wann – harsh, self-confident, reproachful – pronouncing
judgement on Judas as on an inferior:

O unhappy Judas! Through thy despair thou hast done more hurt to
thy lord than through thy treachery. In thy treachery thou sinnedst
against his humanity, but in thy despair, against his divinity and his
divine mercy. If thou, like Peter, hadst wept for thy sin, thou like
Peter wouldst have had thy part of grace and forgiveness.[22]

CHAPTER 3

The penance on the rock

What are the sources of the story of Gregorius' penance upon the rock? Is it possible to trace the possible or probable footsteps of the first author ever to bring his creative imagination to bear on that story? In this chapter we shall consider some traditions which may help us to situate this episode of the Gregorius story in history, and within a narrative tradition of penances performed on a crag in the midst of the sea.[1]

The first people to perform such a penance were the father and mother of us all, Adam and Eve. There is a multilingual and very extensive apocryphal literature (Jewish, early Christian and medieval) on their life and penance after the Fall and expulsion from paradise. We can do no more than glance at it here, in search of traditions which are of interest in connection with the motif in *Gregorius*.[2] After their guilt becomes plain, Gregorius' mother is inclined to despair, whereas her son prudently advises a penance. Many versions of the Adam legend tell that after the Fall and expulsion Eve longed only for death, while Adam advised doing penance upon a rock. The following account is from the possibly fourth-century Latin *Vita Adae et Evae*[3] (also known as the *Paenitentia*), which was probably the best-known version of the Adam legend in medieval Europe:

'Let us do great penance: perhaps the Lord God will forgive us, have mercy on us and give us something to live on.' And Eve spoke to Adam: 'My Lord, tell me: what is penance, and how should I do penance? Let us not lay upon ourselves some task which we cannot perform, or the Lord will not hear our prayer, and will turn his face from us, because we have not kept our promises! My Lord, how much

43

penance do you intend to do? I have caused you so much pain and
trouble!' And Adam spoke to Eve: 'You cannot do as much as I; but do
as much as your health will allow. I shall fast for forty days. But as for
you, arise and go to the Tigris: take a stone and stand upon it, in the
water up to your neck, where the river is deepest. And let no speech
come forth from your mouth; for we are unworthy to pray to the Lord;
for our lips are unclean from doing the forbidden thing and ... tree.
And you must stay standing in the river for thirty-seven days. But I
shall spend forty days in the waters of Jordan. Perhaps God will then
take pity on us.' And Eve went to the Tigris and did as Adam had told
her. Likewise Adam went to the Jordan and stood upon a stone up to
his neck in the water. And Adam spoke: 'I say to you, water of Jordan,
grieve with me and gather to me every swimming thing that is in you,
to surround and lament with me. They must not strike themselves [as a
sign of grief], but strike me; for it is not they who have sinned, but I! At
once all the beasts came and surrounded him, and the water of Jordan
stood still from that time onwards, flowing no further.[4]

Another of the many versions of this story is found in the *Vita
Adae et Evae* in the *Magnum Legendarium Austriacum* (*c.* 1190),[5]
which was the source for the same motif in the Middle High
German verse *Adam and Eve* by Lutwin (post 1300).[6] It was in
fact widely known in German from the thirteenth century
onwards, as is evidenced by its interpolation in eight manuscripts of Rudolf von Ems' *Chronicle of the World*,[7] and by a
continuous German tradition stretching from the fourteenth to
the sixteenth century.[8] The oldest version tells how Eve, despairing of grace, begs Adam to kill her, but he advises her to do
penance and pray for mercy:[9]

43 '... daz er uber uns arme
     sich gerûche erbarme
     und vergebe uns unser schulde
     und wider lâze uns sîne hulde'
     Eva die getriuwe
     sprach mit grôzer riuwe:
     'dehein bûze kan sô grôz sîn,
50 dâ mite ich bûze die sunde mîn;
     die sint vil grôzer den die dîn.
     Doch bin ich, lieber herre mîn,
     dir vil gern gehôrsam.'
     dô sprach der wîse Âdam:

'an gote dû nicht verzage,
merke vol waz ich dir sage.
ein wasser heizet Tîgrîs,
daz fliuzet ûz dem paradîs;
dar in solt dû nackent gên
60 und solt ûf einem steine stên
tief unz an dîn kinne.
die wîle dû stêst darinne,
sô solt dû got nichtes bite,
daz dû in nicht erzurnest mite;
wan dû des nicht wirdig bist,
daz dû in der selben frist
in icht manest umb dîne nôt,
wan dû tête daz er dir verbôt.
nû merke wol waz ich dir sage:
70 alsô stant dâ drîzig tage
sô wil ich in dem Jordân trage
die selben bûze vierzig tage.
so ist unser herre sô gût,
daz er uns lîchte gnâde tût.'
Dô sô geriet her Âdam
und daz Êva wol vernam,
dô gie die arme sâ zehant,
dâ si daz selbe wazzer vant,
unde tet daz si nicht liez,
80 daz si her Âdam tûn hiez.
Âdam was ouch dô bereit,
gein dem Jordân er dô schreit;
zû der bûze was im gâch;
si sach im iêmerlîche nâch,
dô er in daz wazzer trat,
vil iêmerlîche er dô bat,
zû dem wazzer sprach er sân:
'ich bite dich, sûer Jordân,
und die vische, die hinne sîn,
90 und in den luften iuch vogelîn
und iuch tier al gemeine
daz ir mir helfet weine
und mînen grôzen kummer klage,
den ich von mînen sunden trage.
ir sît unschuldig dar an,
ich binz der dâ gesundet hân.'
dô her Âdam diz gesprach,

vil schiere er umbe sich sach
die tier und ouch die vogelîn,
100 daz wazzer lie sîn fliezen sîn,
die vische gebârten zû sîner klage
trûriclîchen achzehen tage.

that he will graciously have mercy upon us, unhappy as we are, and forgive us our sins and give us his grace again.' Good Eve spoke with great contrition: 'No penance can be great enough to atone for my sins: they are much greater than yours. And yet, my dear husband, I will most willingly obey you.' Then spoke wise Adam: 'Do not despair of God. Hearken well to what I tell you. There is a river called Tigris which flows out of Paradise: into it you shall go naked, and stand upon a stone up to your neck. While you stand there, you must not pray to God for anything, lest you anger him, for you are not worthy in that time to draw attention to your need, because you did what he forbade you. Now mark well what I tell you: stand there so for thirty days, and so will I endure the same penance in Jordan for forty days. Our Lord is so gracious that he will readily grant us his mercy.' Thus did the Lord Adam advise Eve, and she hearkened well: then the unhappy woman went and found that very river, and did not fail to do what Adam had told her. Adam was also ready, and turned his steps to the Jordan. He was intent on his penance. She looked sadly after him when he entered into the water; there he prayed, lamenting. He spoke to the water, saying, 'I pray you, sweet Jordan, and the fishes that are in you, and you birds of the air, and you animals each according to his kind: help me to weep and lament my great misery which I bear because of my sins. You are guiltless in this: I am the one who has sinned.' When Lord Adam said this, he saw crowding round him the animals and the little birds; the water ceased its flowing, and the fish added their laments to his for eighteen days.

The devil, fearing a reconciliation between God and the human pair, falsely tells Eve that God has already forgiven the repentant Adam, and so induces her to abandon her penance. Adam, however, sees through Satan's tricks and once more prays to God for mercy (lines 209–32). God hears him and frees him from the devil, so that he is able to complete his forty days' penance – whereas Eve, vanquished for the second time, leaves Adam and labours with her child all alone, for God is deaf to her pleas for mercy. But the sun and stars call Adam to her aid, and he comes and intercedes for her. 'Gott liez Evam erbarmen sich; / zwelf engel herlich / sante er ir zu helfe do' (God then had mercy on Eve: he sent twelve glorious angels to her aid', lines 351–3). And so Eve, when she brought Cain into the world, had midwives which any empress might have envied!

The gathering of sinless creatures around the first man in his penance, the river ceasing its flow, must be understood as a kind of intercession. This is clearly shown in the great Irish epic poem *Saltair na Rann* (*Psalter of Quatrains*, end of the tenth century):

> Then Adam sought a mighty boon
> upon the river Jordan;
> that it would 'fast' with him upon dear God,
> with its multitude of creatures.
>
> The stream stood still
> in its course, in its onward motion;
> the kingly stream paused from its flow
> that He might give forgiveness to Adam.
>
> Then the steam gathered together
> every living creature that was in its womb
> until the whole number of living creatures
> were round Adam.
>
> All of them prayed . . .[10]

While Eve, the weaker of the two, is tempted by the devil a second time and abandons her penance on the rock in the Tigris, God is willing to hearken to the creatures' intercession on behalf of Adam:

> God gave to His grades
> full pardon for the sins of Adam,
> and the habitation of earth at all times
> with heaven, holily noble, all-pure.
>
> And he pardons after that
> their descendants and their peoples,
> save him alone who acts unrighteously
> and transgresses the will of God unlawfully.[11]

Adam's penance, coming after the Fall and the Expulsion from Paradise, already points the way forward to redemption.

'Beside the two great literary Adam traditions – the *Vita*, with its concept of penance, and the *Descensus* with its theme of redemption there is a mass of liturgical and cult material which presents the first parents of mankind to the faithful as the most blessed of all holy sinners, even the most worthy of honour.'[12] Ireland, with its rocky, hermit-tenanted offshore islands, may also have given the world the slightly less ancient legend of Judas' sufferings upon a stone, up to his neck in the stormy sea, and of how Saint Brendan interceded for him and brought him some relief.

We hear no more about Adam's penitential stone in the Jordan, unless it inspired a clutch of late medieval, mainly Slav traditions concerning another Adam-stone in the same river. The situation is similar, but after the expulsion from Paradise Adam and Eve have no time to do penance on stones in rivers: they have to till the ground, lest they die of hunger. So they once more fall victim to the devil, who claims that the earth belongs to him, and will not allow Adam to cultivate it unless he signs a pact with him. In all other stories about pacts with the devil it is the unfortunate victim alone who pays – with his soul. But Adam's pact signs over the whole human race, right up to the Redemption. Curiously enough, this pact, subjecting the human race to the devil's power, was written upon a tablet of stone, which Adam signed. The devil then threw the stone into the Jordan, where it lies to this day.[13] As well as the Slav evidence, there is an apocryphal account of this diabolical pact in the Gnostic Armenian version of the expulsion from Paradise:

But Satan brought a stone, laid it before Adam and said: 'Lay your hands upon the stone and speak as follows: "All my descendants will be your servants." And if you do not so speak, I will bring deep darkness upon you.' But Adam laid his hand upon the stone and spoke: 'Until the barren woman give birth and the undying die, I and all my descendants will be your servants.' And he took the stone, bore it away and sank it in the river Jordan. Thus did the bond of Adam come into Satan's hand.

That bond is to be redeemed through Christ: such is God's promise to those whom Satan deceived.[14]

If we compare both versions (and the Slav one also refers to Adam's penance upon the stone in Jordan) we find that in one it is Adam's penitential stone that lies in the Jordan, and in the other, the stone bearing his pact with the devil. It is clear that, from a theological point of view, the stone recording Adam's contract with the devil was invented to counterbalance the idea that Adam would be forgiven his sins after his penance on the stone. The two stones in the Jordan stand for man the redeemable, and man the damned until the hour of redemption. In that hour the history of the recording stone in Jordan takes yet another turn. Pictures from the eastern Balkans (single icons, iconostases, frescoes, etc.) show Jesus at his baptism standing on a stone in the Jordan; their iconography – for instance, the seven snakes which creep out from under the stone – indicates that it is the stone bearing the bond of Adam and his descendants.[15] By standing upon this stone of shame, Jesus erases the signature on the devil's pact (see figures 5 and 6). The old Adam condemned the whole human race to Hell; the new Adam quashes this condemnation. Thus Christ's baptism upon Adam's stone of shame initiates the process which is to be completed at the Harrowing of Hell, when Christ leads Adam forth. The story of Adam and his stone in Jordan is really about the history of salvation: about mankind's life with guilt, his damnation, and his election.

There is no penance in the *Life of Judas* to compare with Gregorius' penance upon the sea-crag. But Judas' penance upon an island in the sea was recorded independently of the *Vita*, and two hundred years earlier than the *Life of Judas*, in the *Navigatio Sancti Brenduni*, the story of the Irish saint's journey to the Otherworld. This was one of the most popular of medieval legends: it circulated throughout Europe in a hundred different versions, some of them in the vernacular, written and also printed.[16] As early as the tenth century, a version of the Brendan legend has Judas suffering a part of his posthumous torments on a crag in the sea.[17] In the course of his sea-voyage St Brendan comes upon a storm-battered rock, bare when the waves retreat, almost submerged when they advance.

Plate 5 The baptism of Christ: Christ stands on the stone on which Adam recorded his enslavement to the devil. Nineteenth-century Romanian (Wallachian) icon.

Plate 6 Christ's baptism upon the stone of the serpents. Part of an iconostasis from Tirgoviste, Romania. End of the seventeenth century.

On it sits an ugly, unkempt-looking man who when questioned reveals that he is 'infelicissimus Judas' – Judas the most unhappy. A cloth flaps before his eyes and face, advancing and retreating to the rhythm of the waves. Judas spends most of his time in a bath of molten lead in Hell, along with Herod, Pontius Pilate, Annas and Caiaphas, who share the guilt of Christ's death. But through the mercy of Christ, he is privileged to spend every Sunday from Christmas to Epiphany and from Easter to Pentecost, as well as Candlemas and the Assumption of the Virgin, upon the rock and tormented by the cloth: to him this seems like Paradise. The reason is that once, when he was still Jesus' disciple, he gave a cloth to a leper – but as the cloth was not his own, it still has to hurt! The rock is a stone which he once laid over a ditch to serve as a bridge, in the time before he became a disciple. When the devils come on Sunday evening to fetch Judas back to hell, St Brendan procures him an extra night out of Hell, over and above the time allowed by God; and Hell is not allowed to punish him further for this. In the morning, as Brendan sails away out of sight of Judas, the devils fetch the latter back to Hell (see figures 7 and 9).

This story shows that Brendan feels some sympathy for Judas. Moreover, the saint has the power – a power beyond the ken of theology – to prolong the damned soul's respite beyond the limit appointed by God (if only for one night), because even Judas had once done some small good works. Gregorius' penance upon the sea-crag is long, but finite, and it leads him to salvation; whereas Judas, damned for eternity, can only enjoy the same penance as a short holiday from Hell. Both are in the same situation, but the elect is granted something denied to the damned. And yet the respite, granted to Judas through Christ's mercy and extended on the prayer of the saintly witness to his sufferings, exemplifies a kind of theology quite different from that taught by the medieval Church: a theology of compassion. It may seem surprising that it is directed at the man the Middle Ages most loved to hate; but people never quite forgot that God had intended Judas to bring about salvation through his sin. Thus literature offers hope even to the hopeless.[18]

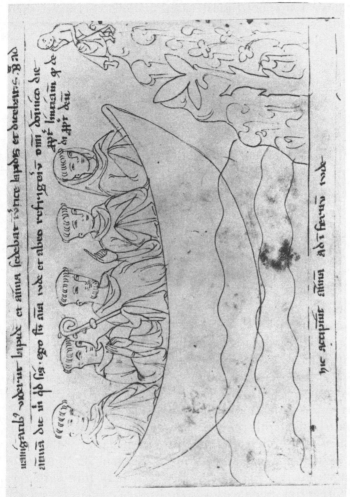

Plate 7 Saint Brendan takes pity on Judas, in torment on a rock in the midst of the sea. Krumauer Bilderkodex (post 1358).

In the German verse *Voyage of Brendan* (post 1300),[19] Judas' sufferings on the rock are intensified. One side of it is boiling hot, the other freezing. Judas identifies himself ('ich bin ez der arme Judas', 'I am poor Judas') as the man who betrayed, then despaired:

> wen dô mich ruwen solden
> mîne sunde ûz der mâzen grôz
> von der wegen ich got verlôs,
> in einem zwîvel ich dô besaz:
> mir geriet der tûvel daz
> daz ich mir selbe tet den tôt.
> des mûz ich immer lîden not.
> hêt ich gehabet rûwe,
> got der ist sô getrûwe,
> er hette mich entphangen drât.
> alsus entwirt mîn nimmer rât.

(lines 970–80)

When I ought to have repented my sins, great beyond measure, through which I lost God, I fell into despair: the devil induced me to kill myself. For this I must suffer torment forever. If I had repented, God is so faithful that he would have received me. Now I am unfit ever to be helped.

Judas hopes for nothing from Brendan's sympathetic intercession, for God will never have mercy on him (line 1000); nevertheless he gets at least one night's respite. For a century critics have agreed that this Middle High German *Voyage of Brendan* is a reworking of a lost German version of the late twelfth century (or 'around 1150'). If that is correct, and we can further assume that the German *Voyage* is not a free adaptation of the tenth-century *Navigatio* but derives via a long independent tradition from a precursor of the latter,[20] then our interest focuses on a second scene in the German version which is missing from the *Navigatio*, and which may link with the motif of Gregorius' penance for *incest*. In the German *Voyage* we find a man doing penance, on a crag in the sea, for incest with his sister:[21] the scene has much in common with the *Gregorius* motif. Brendan is driven by a west wind up to a crag inhabited by a penitent hermit, who is fed from heaven alone and has seen no other human being for ten years (see figure 8):

dar nâch er einen stein sach stân:
ûf dem selben steine
saz ein mensche aleine.
rûch als ein ber der was
der ûf dem wîzen steine saz.

(lines 358–62)

'ich hân hie gesezzen wol zehn jâr.
got der hat mir daz hâr
zu einer wête gegeben.
des himelbrôtes mûz ich leben,
wend ich hie spîse nie mê irkante
wen die mir got her sante.
sint ich ûf disen stein quam
sô ensach ich noch vernam
mê keines stimme ie
dan dîne aleine, here, hie.'

(lines 369–78)

Then he saw a stone; and on that same stone sat a man alone. Hairy as a bear was the man who sat upon the white stone. ... 'I have sat here full ten years. God gave me this hair to serve as a garment. I must live on the bread of heaven, for I could never find any food here save what God sent me. Since I came upon this stone I have never seen or heard any voice here, sir, save yours alone.'

He tells Brendan that he was once king of Pampilonia (later Babylon) and lord of Cappadocia. He took his sister to wife and had two sons by her, the first of whom he killed, while the other, along with the sister-cum-wife, was struck dead by lightning. Fearing God's punishment for his sins, he renounced his crown and set out to confess to the pope in Rome; but on the way he was shipwrecked on the crag. In bad weather he hides in a little cave:

'als ich quam ûf daz mer,
ûf disen stein versigelte ich her
zû clagen mîne missetât
dem der mich geschaffen hât,
und bite sîne genâde
daz er mich von sünden irlade.
idoch hôre ich aller tegelich
den engelsanc in dem himelrîch.'

(lines 401–8)

Plate 8 A man doing penance on a rocky cliff for incest with his sister.
Block book of the *Voyage of Brendan* (1476).

...
> 'ouch sol daz mîn gebeine
> ûf disem durren steine
> des jungesten tages beiten.'

(lines 421–3)

When I came upon the sea, I was wrecked upon this stone, to lament
my misdeeds to him who had created me, and to pray for his mercy,
that he release me from my sins. And yet every day I hear the angels
sing in the kingdom of heaven ... And my bones must wait, on this
dry rock, for the Latter Day.

Twice, then, the German *Voyage of Brendan* shows us a penitent
expiating his grave sins upon a rock in the sea. It juxtaposes the
hopeful and the hopeless; the king stained with incest and
filicide and Judas, guilty of treason and despair; the man
accursed by God and himself, and the hermit trusting in
redemption. If we accept that the German *Brendan* dates from
around 1150 or a little later, it becomes less likely that the
Gregorius author independently invented his penance-on-the-
crag motif to counterbalance Judas' similar sufferings. He
could have been inspired by the king's similar penance for

incest. But we cannot exclude the alternative hypothesis: that the *Gregorius* author shaped the motif to counter that of Judas on the rock, and it was taken over by the Brendan text, which then juxtaposed the motifs of the king's penance and Judas' torment. Both hypotheses postulate that the penance upon the rock – the king's or Gregorius' – is meaningfully related to the story of Judas' sufferings. Which is the more convincing, from a literary point of view, must remain, for the moment, a matter of taste. I am inclined to believe that the *Gregorius* author is the better artist, and took his inspiration here, as elsewhere, directly from the Judas story.

In the Anglo-Norman verse tale of Judas (thirteenth or fourteenth century), there is a description of Judas' eternal punishment which, while generally following the Gospel account, draws on the Brendan story for his sufferings on a rocky island.[22] This tale culminates in the warning against despair which follows Judas' death upon the tree. The last third of the poem is composed of warnings and exhortations to sinners. If Judas had cried for mercy before his death, he might have had God's forgiveness:

> Kant Judas, li traitre, se purverti,
> De sun eindegré a un laz se pendi.
> Mes si il eust crié, 'Merci', uncore avereit pardon.
> A de ceo ke il avoit fet avereit remission.
> Kar, seignurs, entendés bien ceo ke dirom:
> Nos ne devum pas desesperer absolution.
> Jesus, nostre Pere, ne vout pas la mort
> Del chaitif pecheor se il li fet tort,
> Mes il veut ke li pecheor vers li s'acord
> E encontre le diable soit vigrus e fort,
> Kar si li pecheres a lui veut venir,
> Il est tut prest de recoillir.
> Pur ceo deussum nos toz al lui convertir
> E nostre culpe batre e nos pechez repentir.
>
> (lines 164–77)

When Judas, the traitor, betrayed himself, he hanged himself from a noose by his own will. But if he had cried 'Mercy', he would still have had forgiveness. He would have been pardoned for what he had done. For, my lords, hear well what I shall say: we should not despair

Plate 9 Judas, wearing the black halo of the damned, is still on his crag, but has some relief from his torments. Block book of the *Voyage of Brendan*.

of getting absolution. Jesus, our Father, does not desire the death of the miserable sinner who has done him wrong, but wants him to be reconciled to himself and be vigorous and strong against the devil. For if the sinner will come to him, he is most ready to receive him. Therefore we should all turn to him, and say our *mea culpa* and repent our sins.

The sin and penance of St Metro of Verona was recounted by Rather of Verona (died 974).[23] In his youth, God allows the saint to be beguiled by the devil through worldly ambition. Later he renounces the world and lives entirely for God, seeking his mercy for some unwitting sin of the flesh which Rather does not describe in detail, but which is evidently incest with his daughter. This sin is not spelt out until we come to a (possibly) late medieval Veronese lectionary, which mentions Metro's penance 'ob incestum cum filia, priusquam esset clericus, inscienter tamen admissum' ('because of incest with his daughter before he took holy orders; but it was committed unwittingly').[24] Rather's tenth-century version does, however, describe in detail the 'unheard-of' (*inaudita*) penance the saint took upon himself:

Plate 10 The saintly penitent upon a clod of earth drifting on the sea.
Block book of the *Voyage of Brendan*.

He fastened a chain round his foot and attached it with lead to the huge rock which still stands before the church door,[25] locked the deadly ring about his foot with a door-lock, and threw the key into the Etsch, a well-known stream nearby, on whose banks the aforementioned church stands (I am telling this simply, so that it is easier to understand).[26] Fervently he prayed that God in his mercy would not let him see the key again until the grace of the Almighty had forgiven him the sins which he had undertaken to lament. Therefore I speak with caution, since, although I have obtained no written report of it, I have been told in a marvellous way that this is what, with God's permission, happened to him. They say that he spent seven years in the open, chained to the stone, until God in his mercy chose to end the suffering which attached to his penitence, and raise his martyr to the highest honour. Some fishermen sent a fish to the bishop, and in its belly the saving key was found, showing that all his misdeeds were forgiven. When the key was recognized, the bishop loosed the fetter round his foot. The blessed man was washed, clothed, restored to the church, and refreshed by partaking of the Lord's blessed body and blood. This most welcome victim to the Lord forthwith breathed his last and was carried to heaven on angels' wings: thus no one with the understanding even of a child can possibly doubt that the saint, having vanquished the one who had vainly boasted of having overcome him in battle, had gained the palm of victory and the martyr's crown in heaven. His bodily remains were buried, but in no way ceased to witness to his victory by working miracles.

(Rather goes on to say that Verona ought to have considered itself fortunate, but had let the knowledge of the story fade away, and had failed to retain such a jewel of a patron saint. The poets and writers of proud, worldly Verona ought to have recorded his deeds and miracles to keep his memory green.)[27]

Metro's place of penance – in front of the church on the bank of the river, which is so close by that he is able to throw the key in it – is no island, but it is certainly a stone *by* a river. The incest, the chaining to the stone, the throwing of the key into the water, its miraculous rediscovery in the fish, God's acceptance of the penance and the raising of the saintly sinner to temporal and spiritual glory as a martyr of self-castigation: Metro's story is so close to that of Gregorius' guilt and penance that the two seem to be related. His legend may well have been one of the images which the Gregorius author had in mind, along with Adam's riverborne penance and Judas' sufferings in the midst of the sea, when he devised Gregorius' penance on the stone.

The Gregorius legend lived on, somewhat diminished, in later *Volksbücher* (chap-books); just as important, it served as a kind of leaven in unrelated materials.[28] From the fourteenth to the seventeenth century Spain produced a series of romances, from *Amadis* to *Don Quixote*, in which the heart of the modern novel begins to beat strongly, but without denying its parent genre – the courtly romance – or its ancestor, the saint's life. The life of Amadis is surprisingly similar to that of Gregorius in the *Vita*. The penance upon the rock appears, but impoverished by removal of the incest intrigue, so that it requires a fresh motivation: Amadis mounts the crag 'no por devocion, mas por gran desesperacion' (not out of devotion, but in great despair). Thus the motif is inverted. There is the penitent, on his crag betwixt earth and heaven, but it is not God's forgiveness he seeks, but his mistress's – and not for a real sin, but one dreamed up by Oriana. Gregorius does penance for his sins and thus earns the grace of God. Amadis' penance, which is quite undeserved, is mere defiance and bravado: he has despaired of gaining his lady's favour and hopes to mollify her. One is serious, the other a jest; one a drama of salvation, the other, pure operatics. Over the centuries, a range of possible experience and expression of love for God was passed on to the love of women; this new love received the legacy, increased it and restored it to the old, so that eventually the two loves became interchangeable – verbally, and even in action, through a whole gamut of tonalities from the serious to the lighthearted.[29] The guiltless penance of the swashbuckling hero abolishes the opposition of Judas and Gregorius. His desperation, real or calculated, softens Mercy's hard heart. The lady is human.[30] But God is always God.

CHAPTER 4

The 'Mathematicus': *putting the blame on Fate*

The parents of the young Judas sought to prevent the evil prophesied for him by setting him adrift. They merely succeeded in setting him on the path already laid for him by Fate. There is another way of forestalling one's fate: by suicide. A man to whom it is prophesied that he will kill his father takes his own life: this is a case discussed in a model speech before the Roman Senate in about 100 AD, the point being that a premeditated suicide has to be justified before the Senate if the perpetrator is not to remain unburied.[1] Underlying this ancient speech is the idea that a man receives his future when he receives his own life, and can thus avoid committing a predestined crime by committing suicide instead. This problem of Fate was deliberately obscured in Christian thinking, but in the twelfth century it emerged again, and was given a fresh treatment by Bernardus Sylvestris in his *Mathematicus* ('The Astrologer'), a poem in 450 distichs.[2] A woman is unhappy because she has no child; an astrologer prophesies that she will bear a son (to be given the apotropaic name 'Patricida'), and that he will be king of Rome and kill his father. Happy and terrified over her longed-for and feared child, the mother is torn between love for him and love for her husband. The latter orders her to kill the child, but she deceives him and gives the boy to foster-parents. Patricida becomes a model of perfection: he frees Rome from the Cathaginians and becomes king. The mother, torn once again between joy and grief, confesses to the father, who is proud of his son, the glory of Rome, and is willing to die at his hands. The *Mathematicus* is a classic of oxymoron:[3] the father, the

mother, and eventually also the son live in full awareness of the
prophesied evil, and, tossing between married, filial and
parental love, are tormented by a confusion of feelings. A
blameless family, they fall into a dilemma which demands the
sacrifice of a life. The decisions they make emerge from a clash
of loves; half of their heart deals wounds to the other. The
wife's dilemma: husband or child? She must take guilt upon
herself and may give the greater love to her child. Father and
son treat each other with magnanimity and decide against
themselves. In frank, impressive speeches, the three of them
reveal to one another the nature and reasons of their human
and moral choices, with mutual warmth, deep feeling and
magnanimity. Here is part of the father's speech to Patricida:
'My son, you do no wrong: I do not believe that he does wrong,
who does someone wrong because he can do no other' (XI,
60–1). To the son, the evil foreseen outweighs all that is good in
him; he wants to forestall fate: '"Fata necemque patris praeve-
niemus," ait' ('I will forestall the fate and the death of my
father', he said). Private affairs impinge on public ones when
Patricida, who as victor is entitled to have a wish fulfilled, asks
Rome for the freedom to dispose of his own life. He is resolved
to avoid parricide ... but at this point the poem breaks off: the
ending remains, perhaps intentionally, inconclusive.[4] The son
is bound to sacrifice his own life, because he, unlike his parents,
is able to accept the tension between his own will and universal
law, between the limitation and the exaltation of existence: he
is as if grasped by a cosmic power which raises him to a
universal perfection.[5] The *Mathematicus* story, set in the non-
Christian mental universe of pagan Rome, gives another focus
to the question of living with guilt. It means not one's own
guilt, but that of Fate: 'Cogeris esse nocens, manifestaque
culpa deorum / Est' (You are compelled to do wrong: obviously the blame belongs to the gods).[6] Man must either live
with the guilt of his fate, of predetermined action, or else
exercise his moral freedom to distance himself from the guilt of
the gods. Suicide can prevent a wrong done by the gods, who
will not spare even the most perfect man some share of guilt.
Natura creatrix never does a sinless act: she does wrong to every

human being as soon as she brings her forth as a mere woman. This idea is emotively expressed in the mother's speech (initially a monologue) to the father revealing that her son has survived.[7] The *Mathematicus* presents the problem starkly enough. In his conclusion, the author recommends, with intent, a stylistic ideal: the plain, naked, unadorned word.[8] The work faces squarely up to a discovery which can be understood, ultimately, only in biological terms: that a man is bound, from birth, by circumstances of sex, endowments and constitution, historical place and time, to one particular life. Such space as he has for moral freedom, and escape from the guilt of Fate, is doled out grudgingly indeed.

Hartmann identifies Fate with the devil, his guidance a misguidance, turning the guilt of Fate into a human sin.[9] A man has to take to himself whatever has been decided for him; whatever God in his mysterious way has allotted to him; whatever he in his blindness has experienced. He has to answer for it all, even do penance for it. God grants no freedom to self-murder: it is the blackest evil. Gregorius' sin, unlike Patricida's, is not foreknown; it cannot be forestalled, and there is no way to turn aside from either its performance or its consequences. To escape into death would be to elude the grace of God. What is known in advance, by revelation, is not guilt, but grace: the hero must trust in its endless abundance. Only by slaying himself through despair could Gregorius elude divine grace; whereas, in the *Mathematicus*, it is only by a freely chosen death that Fate can be forestalled.

In the *Mathematicus*, it is evident from the beginning that the fate of the characters has been predetermined.[10] One by one they are called upon to make a clear decision in full awareness of the circumstances, and of the involvement of others. This is wholly opposed to Gregorius' search for his own identity in a world of appearances. The search brings him down from his high office and apparent perfection into the abyss of his own dark past and the wretched identity which springs from it. Both must be accepted. Oedipus as king in Thebes, Patricida as king of Rome, Gregorius as lord over his father's – and later his mother's – country, all exhibit a perfection which distorts the truth. Each falls from his high position, yet their kingdoms apparently suffer no harm: *ecce homo*! King Oedipus leaves his country as a blind man; King Patricida leaves his throne in search of death; Gregorius goes forth into the wilderness, and by devoting his life to penance answers for the guilt laid upon him. Oedipus and Patricida, by their blinding and suicide, pass beyond the ken of gods and men. Gregorius, far from the eyes of men, chains his poor human body to the naked rock of the barest existence which God will allow. His flight into the wilderness of nature removes him from the world of men, but makes him visible to the eyes of God. Expiation opens the way to reconciliation, makes room for grace. And the miracle of God's election raises him from his humble self-abasement to a height far above any kingship, to the throne of St Peter in Rome.

CHAPTER 5

The 'Vorauer Novelle': 'one shall be taken and the other left'

Our comparison of the Judas *vita* and the Gregorius legend has nothing particularly startling about it. After all, the Judas of the Bible, the despairing and damned sinner, had for centuries been contrasted with other biblical figures, repentant and redeemed sinners such as Peter, the Good Thief, and Mary Magdalene. The contrast served as a warning and a guide. It was only natural that as soon as Judas had been endowed with an extended *vita* (in the second half of the twelfth century), another biography, involving a similar fate but ending in redemption, should be paired with it in order to provide the customary comparison. Since Peter, the Good Thief and Mary Magdalene had no biographies, they would have to be invented along with the *Vita Judae*.

At about the same time – towards the end of the twelfth century – there appeared an analogous 'double' story, based on the same contrast between two sinners, one despairing (and therefore damned), the other repentant. It is contained in a French manuscript from the Cistercian monastery of Reun, near Graz, and was written, by an author steeped in the Bible and classical texts, probably between 1185 and 1200, and probably for reading to a monastic community. It is the 'historia miraculosa' of two friends, one of whom was justly damned, the other mercifully redeemed, although they lived the same life ('ex consimili vita unus juste damnatus, alter misericorditer salvatus').[1] They had but one heart and one soul, and were also alike in worth; but God's unfathomable predestination had singled one out for damnation, the other for election.[2] That the former suffers from a predestined handicap – which does not

66

make him any the less responsible for his own actions – is
revealed when the two friends commit the same grave sin, but
suffer different consequences. They flee from the hard training
of the cloister into the freedom of the city and take up the study
of necromancy, the science of the devil whose textbook is
entitled *Incipit mors animae*, 'Here beginneth the death of the
soul.' They sign a pact with the devil and wallow in sin – but to
what end? Both inherit God's anger, abusing his patience in
their reluctance to repent; both deserve the same death. But in
them the word is fulfilled: 'Then shall two be in the field; the
one shall be taken, and the other left' (Matthew 24:40). The
one dies of a sickness, as he deserves, but God takes the other to
himself so as to display his goodness towards him.[3] As the one
lies dying, he and his companion quote endless scriptural
instances of God's threats and promises to sinners, but all in
vain: even with death staring him in the face, the doomed man
is unable to escape from his unbelief into God's mercy. This
self-advertising, self-destroying interchange shows us the lost
one being sucked into the maelstrom of sin, sin against the holy
ghost: the loss of all hope, followed by unforgivable despair, the
belief that God cannot pardon him. Determinedly impenitent,
he counters all his friend's instances of biblical promises with a
sombre and decided 'desperavi, apostatum me novi' (I have
despaired, I know myself apostate).[4] God's pronouncements
are so contradictory, he says, that they must be false. Then his
friend realises: 'Who can make that straight, which he [God]
hath made crooked' (Ecclesiastes 7:13; 7:14 in the Vulgate).
The sufferer dies in unrepentant despair, but first he promises
to appear to his friend thirty days later, upon a bare mountain-
top in the wilderness, and tell him what things are like in Hell.
The friend, knowing himself elect, makes his confession, and
the priest accepts him in his penitence like the good Samaritan
who healed the sinner's wounds with oil and wine. He fors-
wears the black arts, returns to the bosom of the church, and
leads a harsh life there. 'If God gives him time, he will also
grant the fruits of repentance, and take to himself the sinner
who is reconciled and hopes in him.'[5] After thirty nights his
friend appears to him on the bare mountain peak in the

fearsome wilderness, and gives him an unforgettably graphic picture of his experiences in Hell, exhorting him to repent and do penance while there is still time, so that he may escape a similar fate in the next world. At that moment the damned man is attacked by a ravening host of devils: as a punishment for having become 'a master, apostle and a teacher of the people' – a second St Paul – and having snatched a soul from their clutches, he must himself suffer some of the hellish torments meant for his friend. 'Raving in their mad fury, they cruelly tore, gashed and tormented him' ('quadam furiali indignatione bacchantes illum lacerant, discerpunt et cruciant').[6] The 'Bacchic' tearing of the devil's faithless follower, and its setting on a bare mountain-top, recall the tearing to pieces of Orpheus by the Thracian Bacchantes one night in the mountains of Pangaia.[7] Life and suffering beyond the grave are endless: the damned are not consumed by the flames of hell. So the victim will feel his hurts for ever. After the hellish apparition has left the mountain, his still-living friend stands alone and trembling on the height, repentant, appealing for mercy: 'Thou to whom nothing is impossible, save not to have mercy on him who hopes in thee, take gently and kindly unto thyself this adversary of the light, this renegade from the law, this fallen slave, who now, as thou seest, repents.'[8] In the greyness before dawn, the 'true Lucifer' (Lucifer, 'the light-bringer') dawns in his heart; bathed in the morning light of hope in God's mercy he comes down from the mountain. As supporting evidence for his description of his hellish night, he shows his confessor his hand, burned through by a drop of the hell fire which fell from his damned friend's vitals on to the earth. The confessor sends him, a changed man, to a Cistercian abbey, where he excels himself in penitence and virtue, becomes abbot, and dies in odour of sanctity. 'See, reader, how terrible are the decisions of God upon the sons of men, how truly unfathomable his judgements, how mysterious his ways.' Same beginnings, different endings. 'I will sing of mercy and judgement: unto thee, oh Lord, will I sing' (Psalm 101:1). This is the end. The story is dominated by thoughts of the inescapability of predestination: the guilty must live with their guilt and settle with it before death, as if they had some say in the matter. The story is unmistakably related to the early Faust legends: renunciation of God, devotion to necromancy, pact with the devil, a life of sin, the horror of death, the struggle over the despairing sinner and finally his tearing to pieces. Faust's story has ancient roots, he also is torn by the devil.

There is a Middle High German verse reworking of the Reun version (which came originally from France). Written by an Alemannian author a generation after Hartmann von Aue, Wolfram von Eschenbach and Gottfried von Strasburg, it is one of the best products of thirteenth-century German literature.[9] Polished but lively, full of skilfully constructed images, it has a light touch for weighty matters and confidently aims high, with many echoes of its great literary predecessors.[10] It is openly and directly didactic, but is also a genuine work of art; it by no means shirks the horror of the deadly struggle, for the dying man bites through his tongue in his last agony. A little work, whose far from inexperienced author consciously uses all his literary powers to give a convincing warning against theological despair. The weighty, learned Latin prose gives way to an easy flow of narrative, and with it goes the overwhelming oppression of inevitable Fate. And to the extent that this burden of unfathomable predestination is removed, the two young friends are obliged to stand on their own two feet, and decide against God 'in the freedom of their hearts' ('von vrîheit des herzen', line 169). The poem turns on the (greatly extended) conversation between the dying man and his healthy companion (lines 320–509). The former cannot be budged from his belief in God's inescapable judgement, which he perceives as a curse[11] laid on him as punishment for his freely committed (as opposed to predestined) sin. His friend pleads with him as only a friend can, but he is deaf to warnings and promises alike. The theological argument is incorporated into a tale of human anguish, of the struggle to preserve a soul and a friendship: the attempt to free the sufferer from his obdurate despair belongs to real life, not to discursive theology. Because the sufferer will not believe in God's power to forget sins ('wan mîner swæren sunde / enwil got niht vergezzen', lines 392–3), God cannot in fact do so – though, as the confessor pledges, he willingly does forget the sins of a penitent, as the father confessor promises:

> vürhte dir niht, vil guotez kint!
> swie swære und grôz dîn sünde sint,
> der müeze got hiute vergezzen.[12]
>
> (lines 599–601)

Fear not, my good child! However heavy and gross your sins may be, God must today forget them.

No human or theological help can reach the poor man, hardened and bent on despair; he refuses to continue the discussion:

> an dirre veigen stunt
> bin ich an Jêsu Krist verzaget.[13]
> daz sî dir offenlîche gesaget.
>
> (lines 496–8)

in this harsh and evil hour I have despaired of Jesus Christ: I say it to you openly.

And immediately the death-stroke cleaves his heart: 'dô kom des grimmen tôdes slac / und zarrete im daz herze enzwein' (lines 528–9). Since he dies a desperate man, he is buried in the open field, un-prayed for, unblessed. But his downfall is a help to the friend who could not help him: grieving deeply in his heart ('ûz leides herzen grunde'), he goes repentant to the confessor, who absolves him. Thus the two friends' path of life leads from the gates of heaven to the gates of hell (through which one must pass), and back again:

> Von der himelischen tür
> wâren si gesprungen
> und in die strâze gedrungen,
> diu dâ leitet in den tôt.
>
> (lines 100–3)

From the heavenly gate they sprang down and entered on the road that leads to death.

But because the survivor repents from the heart, he is raised up to the very gate of heaven ('sîns herzen bîhte ûf hôhe enbor /

unz an daz himelische tor', lines 641–2). The despairing friend
is accursed by an avenging God:

> sît ich an gote verzaget bin,
> der muoz sich hiute rechen
> an mir und ûf mich sprechen
> ein urteile alsô grimme,
> diu mit des vluoches stimme
> gemenget ist sô vaste,
> daz von des vluoches laste
> mîn herze sich muoz zerren
> und daz sich ûf muoz sperren
> diu helle gein der sêle mîn.

(lines 480–9)

Since I despaired of God, he must today be avenged on me and
pronounce a fearful judgement upon me, in such a dreadful voice
that my heart must break with the weight of the curse, and that the
gate of hell must open to receive my soul.

The repentant friend – the elect – is rejuvenated by penance.
He is like the aged eagle, which flies up into the flaming clouds
to burn its wings away, and so falls into the lake and there
wholly renews its splendid nature before flying up to the gates
of heaven. The lake is the tear on the sinner's cheek. This
interpretation of the great eagle-simile ends our text (lines
615–49). Only the dying man's promise to meet his friend on
the bare mountain after thirty days (lines 519–27) suggests that
this early thirteenth-century 'Vorauer Novelle' is incomplete.
Had it survived entire, it would not have lain forgotten for so
long.

CHAPTER 6

Judas and Everyman

The New Testament gives few biographical details about its characters. From the earliest days of Christianity, and through the Middle Ages, these details were supplemented from legends and apocrypha until they assumed the proportions of full-scale *Vitae* like the *Life of Mary*. Later on, series of *Vitae* were put together to produce even longer works. They were an example of an inflationary tendency – sometimes manageable, sometimes uncontrollable – which characterised much of the literature of the time. In narrative, it produced the vast 'Prose Lancelot' (pre 1230) and the great cycles of *chansons de geste*, legends and romances, which are contemporary with the theological *summas* and the great cathedrals; it also affected the religious drama of the later Middle Ages. It gave a new place and a new function to the Life of Judas by incorporating it in the narrated or dramatised Life of Christ. 'Lives of Christ' which include the Life of Judas were widely disseminated in fifteenth-century France: from 1485 they began to be printed, and they endured right up to the eighteenth century.[1] For example, the richly elaborated *Life of Judas* found in a Paris incunabulum of 1485 is part of the *Vie de Jesu Christ* by Jehan Cres and Robin Foucquet.[2] The life of Christ, from the Nativity to the Resurrection, is preceded by the creation of the angels and the Old Testament story up to the parentage of Mary. The life of Judas, as far as his assumption of the biblical role of betrayer, is inserted just before the Passion. Judas disappears after the arrest of Jesus: his repentance and death are not recounted.

It was via such works that Judas found his way into the

72

Passion Play. Initially he was confined to all or part of his biblical role; later he was given more space. In many plays Judas' final lamentation, which can come either before he returns the blood-money or before his suicide under the tree, points out the inevitability of his damnation. Here follow some examples from various plays which use the biblical material on Judas, showing his bitter contrition and the resulting despair previous to his suicide. In one of the oldest French Passion Plays (mid fourteenth century),[3] Judas foresees his death from despair ('je mourree par desesperance', line 1686) after the devil has prompted him to betray Christ, but before returning the blood-money. So crushed with guilt is he that as he dies on the tree, he commits his soul to devils:

> J'ay pechié trop fort mallement.
>
> (line 1691)

> He! Mort felonesse et obscure,
> Pren moy, je suis faulz et trahistes!
> A cent dyables je me rent quites.
> Quant j'ay osé mon seigneur vendre,
> Sanz remede je me vois pendre.
> Diables, prenez mon esperit!
>
> (lines 1720–5)

Most foully have I sinned ... Ah, dark and dreadful death, take me: I am a false traitor! I surrender myself to a hundred devils. Since I have dared to sell my lord, I am going to hang myself: there's no help for it. Devils, take my soul!

In the fifteenth-century Augsburg Passion Play Judas flings the money at the Jews' feet:

> ich will yetz von euch hin dan gan
> Vnd mich erwirgen an aim sail;
> also ist mir mein leben fail.
> Ich mag doch nit behalten sein;
> tewfel, nem hin die sele mein!
>
> (lines 1023–7)[4]

Now I will leave you and strangle myself in a rope: so vile is my life to me. So I cannot be redeemed: devils, take my soul hence!

In the Donaueschingen Passion Play Judas makes a great lament under the tree:

> O ir mensche vernänd min clag,
> die ich uff dissen hütigen tag
> vor aller welt clagen müss.[5]

O you people, hear my lament, which I must lament before the whole world this day.

In the end Judas, seeing no hope of salvation, delivers himself up to the devil:

> küm, tüffel, min clappern is vmb sus:
> ich will mich selb ze tod erhencken
> vnd dir hie lib vnd sele schencken!
> kum bald, hilff mir der marter ab,
> sid ich so vbel gesundet hab,
> wann hie ist kein erlösung me:
> zitlich gût, du tûst mir we!

(lines 2491–7)

Come, devil, my chatter is in vain: I will hang myself to death, and give you my body and soul! Come soon, help me out of the torment I have endured since my vile sin, for there is no more salvation for me. Worldly goods, you give me pain!

The lamentations of Judas find echoes in those of Faust. Judas sees that by betraying Christ he has sold himself to the devil, just as Faust sold himself when he betrayed God and made a pact with Satan. The devils receive Judas into hell as one who had committed himself to them whilst still alive:

> er mûss ietz tantzen vnsern reigen,
> wann er hat sich an vns ergeben,
> die wil er dennocht was in leben.
> Lucifer, lieber here min,
> enpfach Judas, den diener din!

(lines 2511–15)

Now he must dance to our measure, since he gave himself to us whilst he was still alive. Lucifer, my dear lord, receive Judas thy servant!

In the Eger Corpus Christi Play, Judas sees the soldiers who have arrested Jesus mocking and scorning him, and as he returns the money he bitterly laments his self-forgetfulness in betraying Christ, and acknowledges that God's grace cannot extend to him:

Ich hab gross sundt begangen,
Das er ist worden gefangen;
Darumb wirt mein nimer rat
Umb mein grosse missetat,
Wan mein bosheit vil grosser ist,
Wan mein gnadt zu diser frist.
Dar umb wil ich im nit mer genahen,
Ich wil gen mich selbert hahen.

(lines 4978–85)

I have committed a great sin, since he has been arrested; therefore I shall never have help because of my great misdeed; at this moment my wickedness is much greater than my [right to] grace. Therefore I will not go near him again, I will go and hang myself.

As usual, the Jews will have nothing to do with Judas, fail to understand his feelings of guilt, and let him go, 'shattered', to the tree, where he utters his dying lament:

Ich kan nimer selig werden
Weder in himel noch auff erden;
Darumb wil ich mich hie hahen,
Die teufel mein sell enppfahen.
Ich muss ewig verlorn sein,
Brinnen und bratten in der helle pein.[6]

(lines 5026–31)

I can never be blessed, either in heaven or upon earth; therefore I shall hang myself here: may the devils receive my soul! I must be lost forever, and burn and roast in the torments of hell.

Judas is the 'despairing evildoer', and Lucifer rides him for sport, like a dog, in hell.

Judas has some kind of inner awareness of the relentless destiny which rules him, and which tells him how he might have avoided disaster. So in the Sterzing Passion Play:[7]

Und hiet ich rew enpfangen,
So wär es mir leicht pass ergangen.
Des hab ich layder nit getan!
Des mues ich in der helle stan.

(lines 1623–6)

And if I had repented, then things would easily have been better for me. Alas, I did not do so! So I must go to hell.

If Judas knows this, why then does he not repent on the spot?
It is the devil, seeing him on the brink of salvation, who kicks
him away from it – just as he will do later to Faust. Judas curses
God and the earth, the father, the mother, the day and the
hour which brought him into this life, and then, screaming and
howling like one in despair ('ad modum desperantis'), he runs
to the tree and hangs himself.[8] It is not clear whether some
more or less predestined impediment forestalls the repentance
which Judas knows to be necessary, or whether he actually
points to himself – Ecce Judas! – to focus the spectators'
attention on his value as an object lesson.

In the Frankfurt Passion Play (1493),[9] Judas is without
mercy *on* himself because he sees no mercy *for* himself. On his
way to the tree his lament rises to a curse on his existence –
guilt, nothing but guilt – and on the world, the sun, moon and
stars, the throne of heaven, the angels, and his own birth. It
culminates in a willed forgetfulness of God: 'ich wil gen und
mich selber hencken / und gottes nummerme gedencken' (I
will go and hang myself, and never again think of God, lines
2669–70). The devil fetches his soul out of his body. Space
empties itself round the lonely figure of Judas ('see thou to it',
Matthew 27:4) as with a curse he casts off God and the world,
goes to his last earthly requisite, the tree, and hangs himself.
This wilful rejection of God and the world leaves the stage in a
brooding silence. Into that silence comes a voice which is to
lead us out of mystery, placing the unfathomable and isolated
event against a background of life and its possibilities. Enter
Augustine, creator of the theology of Judas' despair, to point
out the warning inherent in the scene:

> By Judas sij uch kunt gethan,
> das ir alle sullet ruwen han
> umb uwer sunde und missfellen,
> das ir nit komet in die hellen!
> kein sunder nicht vertzwifeln sol:
> got ist so grosser gnaden fol,
> das er ime vergit sin sunde!
> het sich Judas nit in der stunde
> vor grossem leide erhangen,
> *got het in gerne entphangen.*[10]   (lines 2671–80)

By Judas you should learn that you should all repent of your sins and misdeeds, so that you come not to hell! No sinner should despair: God is full of such great mercy that he always forgives his sins! If Judas in his great grief had not hanged himself on the spot, *God would gladly have received him.*

Augustine beholds the scene through the hieratical eye of the theologian, which sees what Judas himself could not see. Medieval people had no sympathy for Judas. They endowed him with a complete life story, but omitted to provide him with a burial. He is assisted only by devils, who in some of the plays trespass on his lonely death, offering a noose and some encouraging words before they take him off to hell. This scene is sometimes quite extensive; the briefest version is in the Alsfeld Passion Play, though it does contain a chorus ('Alas, poor Judas'), which is sung as Judas hangs himself, after his great lament on the way to death:

Et sic omnes demones conveniunt portando funem. Sathanas dicit:
    Judas, wollestu dich hengken,
    Ich wyl der eyn strick darzu schengken!
Sic Judas cum eis decedens laqueo se suspendit. Chorus cantat:
    Ach, du arme Judas etc.
quoadusque facta sunt omnia illa. Post hoc diaboli ducunt cum ad Infernum cum magno strepitu.[11]

And thus all the demons come together carrying a rope. Satan says, 'Judas, if you want to hang yourself / I will give you a rope!' Thus Judas, going with them, hangs himself from a noose. The Chorus sings: 'Alas, poor Judas' etc. until all this has been done. After this the devils lead him to Hell with great noise.

The first line of the chorus is from the last verse of the fourteenth-century Passiontide hymn *Laus tibi, Christe, qui pateris* (Praise be to thee, Christ, who dost suffer ...'),[12] which was also widely known in German:

       O Du armer Judas, was hastu gethon,
       das du deinen herren also verrathen hast!
       Darumb so mustu leiden in der helle pein,
       Lucifers geselle mustu ewig sein.
          Kirie eleyson.[13]

Alas, poor Judas, what hast thou done, that thou hast thus betrayed thy lord? Because of it thou must suffer in the pains of Hell: thou must forever be companion to Lucifer. *Kyrie eleison.*

This verse is preceded by three verses in the Latin (ten in the German), all ending *Kyrie eleison* – which implies they are asking for mercy on the audience, not on Judas. As in a classical tragedy, the chorus communicate an intelligent and perceptive view of the action. They reproach Judas rather than sympathising with him. Alas for poor Judas: he is lost.[14]

The Autun Passion Play offers an unforgettable version of Judas' death.[15] Even before returning the blood-money he knows himself to be beyond redemption: this recognition is the culmination of his lament. He knows that he ought to beg for God's mercy, but in view of the enormity of his guilt, he cannot:

> Jamès ne puis avoir marcy.
> Helas! on le mainne par cy,
> Certes ce marcy ly crioye
> Trestout outrecuidier seroie,
> Ma culpe est sy grant et sy orde
> Qu'el ne desert misericorde.
> Honny soit quil vers ly ira,
> Ne quil marcy ly cryera!
>
> (lines 6613–20)

Never can I have mercy. Alas! They are taking him away. Certainly if I were to beg him for mercy it would be great presumption: my sin is so great and so vile that it deserves no forgiveness. Cursed be he who goes near him or begs him for mercy!

He goes and throws the money at the Jews' feet; they tell him: 'You know that none of us asked you to betray him.' An innovation in this play is that the wretched Judas also tells Jesus he is damned:

> Sire, je ne vous sçay ou querre.
> Las chetifs, com suis esperdu,
> De pechier mort et comfondu!
> Jamais n'aray par nul acorde
> De mon pechier misericorde:
> Oncques culpe ne fut pareille.
>
> (lines 6638–43)

Sir, I know not where to seek you. Alas, wretch that I am, how I am lost, dead and confounded in sin! Never by any means will I have forgiveness for my sin: never was there such guilt.

Mary, overhearing this, laments the betrayal but does not prevent Judas from appealing to her son for mercy; she assures him of redemption:

> Tu as vendu mon filz le Dieu parfait,
> Crye le mercy en ton couraige.
> Je te prometz, pardon te sera fait,
> Car nous cueurs tient en amoreulx servaige.
> Par repentance peulx avoir sauvement.

> (lines 6644–8)

You sold my son, the perfect God. Cry to him for mercy in your heart: I promise you, you will be pardoned, for he holds our hearts in loving servitude. By repentance you can be saved.

Why does Mary speak but not Jesus? Why does Judas not heed her (just as, later, Faust fails to heed the same comfortable words from his good angel)? The answer lies in God's inexorable, incomprehensible providence, which allows Judas no escape on to the way of salvation – which indeed makes him reject it of his own will.[16] Jesus is silent. Mary, unaware of the fate hanging over Judas, offers him salvation. Judas, as his fate requires, is deaf to the offer:

> Pierre de marbre et coronne d'ayment
> Est mon faulx cueur. Que me voix tu disant?
> Je dois aler a male destinee,
> Fuy toy d'icy, car tu m'es trop nusant.
> Quant je reguard ton tresdoux viz plaisant,
> Ta douce face que j'ay descoloree . . .

> (lines 6652–7)

Marble stone and crown of adamant is my false heart. What are you saying to me? I must go to an evil fate. Away from here! You pain me too much. When I look on your gentle sweet countenance, your sweet face pale because of me...

In Mary's goodness, in the tormented face of the mother of his betrayed lord, Judas sees his own guilt and is turned to stone. Knowing that it is by his fault that her son is pierced and

Plate 11 Judas and Christ both die on a tree. Italian ivory casket, early fifth century.

Plate 12 Judas on the tree close to the cross of Redemption.
Drawing by Annibale Carraci (post 1600).

nailed to the tree, he asks the devil for help and advice, which is forthcoming in the form of death upon the bough. Judas' Passion anticipates that of his lord. His damnation is the price of salvation. Judas and Jesus both hang upon a tree, but what a difference! One fallen, the other standing fast; one alone, the other surrounded; one damned, the other the Redeemer (see figures 11 and 12).

Late fifteenth-century France saw the production of two enormous Passion Plays, by Arnould Greban and Jean Michel,

in which the Judas *vita* figures more extensively, and with
inclusion of non-biblical elements. In both plays the Judas
scenes are detailed and powerfully memorable. Greban's
Mystere de la Passion uses the early part of the *vita* (up to the
discipleship of Judas) in only one place, when Judas looks back
on his sinful life in a monologue: the murder of the king's son
and of his own father, and the marriage with his mother, impel
him to beg Jesus' forgiveness.[17] I shall quote the scene of Judas'
death in James Kirkup's striking modern adaptation of
Greban's work. This abridged translation was performed in
Bristol Cathedral in 1961, and has also featured on stage, radio
and television. After the betrayal, Satan summons up against
Judas all the hellish powers of self-annihilation. Despair in
person attends him, pitilessly, to his death on the tree, and
dismisses his trembling hope of a sympathetic hearing if he
made a last appeal to Christ. Despair seals Judas' damnation
by falsely assuring him that no prayer can bridge the distance
between him and God. Let Arnould's version of the death-
scene serve as a typical example for the Passion Plays:[18]

> *Part Four, Scene Three: Despair*
> *Thunder and lightning. Satan leaps up from below.*
>
> *Satan* Listen to me, you down below. Allow me, dear
>   Fellow-devils, a few words in your ear.
>   Come, Care, and Melancholy, Fear, Disgust and Pride,
>   Self-pity, too, and Accidie, Remorse and Suicide!
>   You have heard of late, have you not,
>   Of our good friend Judas, named Iscariot?
>   Well, I've overheard him talking to
>   Himself – always a silly thing to do.
>   *Enter Judas, muttering and groaning, and carrying a noose.*
>
> *1st Woman* Judas! There he is again, the dirty villain!
>
> *2nd Woman* Drunk again.
>
> *1st Citizen* Drunk again.
>
> *2nd Citizen* Fetch the constable!
>
> *Carpenter* Leave him alone.
>   Let him get on with it.

Satan Poor Judas, our long-lost brother,
   Now finds that he is full of horror
   And even remorse for what he's done:
   Just imagine! he goes round calling on Death to come!
                              Diabolical laughter.

   Ha! Only an amateur could be so easily demoralized!
   Poor Judas! He's sensitive. He feels despised ...
                              Diabolical laughter.

   We'll help him in the shortest time we may
   To put himself away.
   He'll hang himself up high
   Upon a holly-tree, against a blood-red sky.
   Now who have we got here who'll
   Relieve the wretch of his immortal soul?
                              Diabolical laughter.

   Yes, I know, you scoffers,
   He's not much of a catch. Well, any offers?
   Ah, yes, a practised hand. Despair.
   How are you dear?
   Step forward there.

Despair I am Despair.

                 Judas Despair!

                              Despair Despair.

                 Thunder and lightning. Satan vanishes.

Judas. Despair. O terrible avenger,
   O, beautiful stranger,
   O, ineffable danger,
   Come to me, come close, and closer, closer yet.
   Give me your hand, and cast your net
   Around my bones: these ropes of flesh
   Make for my soul too small a mesh.
   How shall it escape?

Despair Let me lay the rope around your neck.
   So ...
                              She puts the noose over his head.

   Now I am ready, Judas dear,
   To snatch you swiftly away from here.

Judas A moment more, and then I'll let it be.
    Despair, is there no hope for me?

Despair It is so easy, dear; don't be afraid.

Judas But if just for a little while I prayed
    To my Master, say, would he
    Still forgive my treachery?
    Would my sins be all forgiven
    And I live with him in Heaven?
    That would be Hell enough, to live each day
    In the love of the friend I did betray.

Despair, a soft, warm laugh It is no use. For you have gone
    Far beyond the reach of prayer. What you have done
    Deserves no mercy, because you offered none.

Judas What must I do? I know I'm allowed to
    Sell my soul to the devil, but I've never known how to.

Despair Poor innocent boy! It is already sold.
    And only for silver, too. Not even gold!

Judas The day grows very cold.

                                          A slow bell tolls.
Despair Son, it is time.

Judas, going towards tree Deep into hellish dark I climb.

Despair You must swing high, you know,
    If you would find yourself below.

Judas Black are the leaves,
    The berries red as blood.
    Black is the sky.
    The bough is high.

Despair First, dear, you must stand upon this block.
              Judas mounts a wooden block beneath the bough

Judas The block is underneath the bough.
    The wind will rock
    The block is underneath the bough.

Despair Just pass me the end of the rope, dear,
    I'll sling it over now.
    There! First go!
    Now let me knot it tight.
    That'll do! That's right.

Now dear, I'm ready when you are.
No hurry, of course. You haven't far
To fall.

Judas Like this? Is this how I must stand?

Despair Yes, O you look grand,
    With that big knot underneath your ear.
    Well, if you're ready dear
    I'll just kick the block away ...

Judas No, no! Not yet! A moment more, I pray.

Despair Just as you like. Wait a sec!
    The rope's not tight around your neck.
    Why, you're trembling!

Judas The world is ending.

Despair The strange thing is, it doesn't end
    Just because you into nothingness descend.

Judas Hell! Already I can feel the sharp flames biting!
    Hell! How affrighting!
    Chalky skeletons down there perspire,
    Sprigged with keen blue jets of fire!
    Their hands are grates heaped high with ash,
    Their skulls like scalding cauldrons clash;
    They rake the hottest flues of Hell
    With sooty ribs, but cannot quell
    The freezing fire that shrieks and singes,
    Shrivels fingers into ravelled fringes!
    Hell! I can feel the sharp flames biting! Quick!
    Despair! The block! Now, kick!

                 Despair kicks the block away, and Judas hangs

    Hell and despair!

Despair, she leaps down into Hell with Judas Hell and despair.

Satan below Hell and despair

Echoes below Hell and despair!

Thunder, lightning, diabolical laughter.

Jean Michel's *Mystère de la Passion* (1486)[19] contains 30,000
lines, and its performance in Angers took four days. It includes

almost the entire history of Judas. In comparison with his predecessor, Greban, Michel in his enormous work consistently extends the role of minor characters, and Judas is no exception. Michel obviously knew the *vita*, and inserts scenes from it into the great Passion narrative loosely and without regard to chronology, sometimes prospectively, sometimes retro-spectively, as if they belonged to the biblical account. Elements which previously existed mostly in isolation – canonical and apocryphal, old and new – are woven into a drama whose time-span is confined to the life of Christ, from birth to entombment.

First day: Judas, having murdered the Prince of Iscariot, is ready for any wickedness. He enters into the service of Pilate (lines 2595–724). Judas and Pilate, out for a walk, meet Reuben and Cyborea, who are agonizedly lamenting the loss of their cast-away son. Reuben's sole consolation is his orchard. Judas, stealing apples for Pilate, quarrels with Reuben, fights him and kills him. The mother laments his death and demands justice and revenge from Pilate. Pilate laments the murder and orders the murderer to marry Cyborea in compensation. The mother is most reluctant, but Judas, with an eye to her posses-sions, persuades her to change her mind (3562–891). Cyborea, torn between fear and love, asks Judas about his origins and hears his life-story. Both lament the incest, 'de tous peches le plus enorme' (grossest of all sins, line 4552) and the parricide; but since they were committed unwittingly, there is hope of obtaining God's mercy through repentance (4408–61). Judas, cursing his fate and hoping for forgiveness, throws himself at the feet of Jesus, who, hearing him repent, accepts him as a disciple (4829–89); his conversion is followed by the miracle of the water which turns into wine.

Second day: Judas as disciple (8035–8, 8295–6, 9561–4, 10,129–40, 11,792–4, 12,314–19). His scolding of Mary Magdalene is the seed of his treason (15,003–92).[20]

Third day: Judas at the entry into Jerusalem (15,588–91). Mono-logue revealing him as a rebel, like Lucifer (16,125–82). Judas isolates himself (17,162–3, 17,213). Sathan, Belzebuth and Berith urge the betrayal on him; he gives it lengthy consideration (17,400–567). The treacherous bargain with the high priests (17,620–718). Judas dissembles before Jesus and the disciples (18,064–83, 18,088–99, 18,108–9, 18,152). The Last Supper (18,291–330, 18,744–7, 18,781–2, 18,878–7, 18,976–7, 18,995–19,005). Sathan,

Beelzebuth and Berith egg Judas on (19,012–170). Judas at Jesus' arrest (19,506–89, 19,708–9, 19,738–47. 19,755–6, 19,084–27, 19,840–6, 20,174–5, 20,216) and before Caiaphas (21,913–31).

Fourth day: begins with Judas' repentance (22,867–937), which is repeated before the Scribes and Pharisees (23,394–448); return of the blood-money (23,449–92). He disbelieves in forgiveness and summons all the devils of Christendom and Antiquity (23,557–694).

Lucifer condemns Judas to death by despair. 'Desesperance' leaves Lucifer's entourage, comes to Judas and introduces herself, explaining her origins in the lowest depths of hell. She assures Judas that his sins are beyond forgiveness, his hope in God and Mary vain: he must die. Judas spends his last hour wrestling with Despair. Has Judas acknowledged his sins, done penance by returning the pieces of silver, quivered with remorse till his heart well-nigh broke? 'No use!' says Despair, 'ta grace est passee': it is too late for forgiveness (line 23,776). He must open his heart to Despair and hang himself. In this last extremity Judas, taking refuge in a pyrotechnic display of verbal, metrical and rhyming dexterity (in this he is an ancestor of Adrian Leverkühn),[21] accepts the noose from the hands of Despair and voluntarily renounces all hope of God. Desesperance attends him to his hanging and even climbs the tree with him, while the devils wait underneath. Sathan hears Judas' last wish: he allies himself with the devils, abjures grace, commends his soul to Lucifer and his body to hell. Sathan: 'Enough! Do you abjure forgiveness and all hope?' Judas' last words reiterate his resolve on suicide 'sans espoir de misericorde' (without hope of mercy, line 23,920). Heavy with this resolve, he casts himself from the heights of despair into the abyss of hell. There is a small element of comic relief: the devils are worried because they cannot find the soul, and are relieved when the corpse bursts asunder and the soul emerges. It could not escape via the mouth which had betrayed Christ with a kiss. The despairing soul, freed from the body, calls on the devils for revenge on God, who created and then damned it. Despair cuts Judas down from the tree, and amidst a hellish noise the devils take his body and soul down to torment. Lucifer has the last word:

Traistre renoncé
larron, cabasseur de peccune,
desloyal remply de rancune,
ministre de perdicion,
occis par desperacion,
privé de grace et de tout espoir,
va t'en au lieu de desespoir,
au lieu de mort aspre et vilaine,
porter interminable peine,
sans jamais espoir de salut.
Et au desesperé palut
seras des grands dyable affin
tant que Dieu durera, sans fin:
si sçauras combien peché nuyt.

Ycy se faict tempeste en Enfer.

(lines 24,058–71)

Abjured traitor, thief, money-grubber, faithless man filled with
rancour, minister of perdition, slain by despair, bereft of grace and of
all hope, get you to the place of despair, to suffer endless torment in
the place of bitter and shameful death, with never any hope of
salvation. And in the slough of desperation you will be in the
company of the great devils endlessly, as long as God endures: thus
you will find out the harm done by sin. *Here a tempest in hell.*

From Judas' first words in the play, 'Ha, Judas, ha povre
Judas' (Alas Judas, alas poor Judas, line 2595), his story is one
plaintive lament, forever reiterated by all those involved, and
expressed in his own mouth through a gamut of different
emotional tones, up to its deliberately shrill climax in his
renunciation of salvation. Judas' fate is sealed before the other
Passion, that of Christ whom he betrayed, has even begun.
Judas dies before Christ's death has redeemed those who
believe in him.

By the sixteenth century the Passion Play had extended its
coverage of Judas' life even further than had Greban and
Michel, to include an account of his birth and casting away,
and his youth on the island. Thus in the Valenciennes play of
1547.[22]

The 'Townley Cycle' of mystery plays goes from the creation
via Christ's passion to the Last Judgement. In about 1500 a

strophic lament of Judas for his own life, *Suspencio jude* ('The hanging of Judas'), was appended to the manuscript:

> Alas, alas & walaway!
> waryd & cursyd I have beyn ay;
> I slew my father, & syn by-lay
> My moder der;
> And falsly, aftur, I gan betray
> Myn awn master.[23]

Judas' monolgue of lamentation in the Passion Play now stands by itself as a lyrical autobiography. It must have recounted his whole life, beginning with his mother's dream prior to his birth and culminating, without doubt, in this lament, in which Judas, about to die on the tree, looks back over his life. This change from third to first-person narrative enables Judas retrospectively to assume responsibility for his life, and thus for its outcome – his suicide. Unfortunately the MS breaks off after sixteen verses, which tell how the queen who adopted the foundling Judas gave birth to a child of her own two years later. The sinful course of Judas' life remains to be traced. Most of the 'Hanging of Judas' is missing. The English 'Ballad of Judas' (*c.* 1250) is unique in giving him a sister who hastens his fate by urging the betrayal on him before the Last Supper.[24]

The devil hates perfection and attacks success. After the fall of the rebel angels, God created mankind as a replacement for the highest rank of angels. Fallen Lucifer in his jealousy plotted the fall into sin of this paragon of animals, and he succeeded. Man came into his power. Christ saved men from sin, but that did not make the Tempter give up. He attacks saints most particularly. In *Anticlaudianus*, the poetic masterpiece of Alain de Lille (*c.* 1180), the climax is the creation of a perfect, blessed, heavenly New Man, intended by God and Nature to be faultless. Thereupon Allecto summons a council of the infernal powers in Tartarus so as to entrap the *novus homo* like Adam, and ruin the New Creation; but in the ensuing psychomachia the infernal powers are defeated, leaving the New Man triumphant upon the New Earth.[25]

As far back as the ninth century a set of rhythmical verses existed in which Judas returns to destroy the growing throng of believers.[26] The author begs God's help against the envious foe of truth, whose cunning deceives with a scorpion's sting. He threatens Judas with leprosy: may the devil take his soul, and may he die a traitor's death, bursting asunder like Arius or torn in pieces! He is confident that the persevering will be numbered among the elect in heaven:

2. Iudas ecce resurrexit,   ecce venit impius,
   Proditor magistri venit   perdere discipulos:
   Ad te nostra fuga tantum   erit, dei filius.

3. Inimicus veritatis,   inimicus patrie
   Corde dolos machinatur,   accusator vulnere
   Scorpionis more ferit,   et doloso gutture.

5. Fratrum turbam dei dono   quamquam novit crescere,
   Hanc prostrare, demolliri,   hanc vult interficere:
   Cunctis simul desolatis   solus credit vivere.

7. Time, Iudas, time deum,   time dracho perfide,
   Animam a te malignus   in hac nocte auferet,
   Faciem et linguam tuam   vermes cooperient.

(verse 2, 3, 5, 7)

Behold, Judas rises again, here comes the impious one: he who betrayed the master comes to destroy his disciples: o son of God, we will take refuge only in you. The enemy of the truth, the enemy of his country, is plotting tricks in his heart: the accuser with his wounds strikes like a scorpion and with a false throat. Though he knows that the crowd of brethren grows by the gift of God, he wants to lay it low, crush it, slay it: he thinks he can live only if all others are destroyed. Judas, fear, fear God, fear, perfidious serpent! The evil one will fetch your soul tonight, and worms will open up your face and tongue.

This return of Judas was further developed in the late Middle Ages, when elements of the *vita* were included. Now Judas returns as an apostle of despair at the behest of a council of devils. In the rhymed poem by Hans Folz, 'Judas the heretical apostle' (1483),[27] which sees Judas as the arch-heretic, there are various allusions to the *vita*. Judas slew a king's son who was thought to be his brother.[28] Before becoming a disciple of Christ, he 'nam seim vater auch den leib / Und sein rechti muter zu weib' (took his father's life, and took his own mother to wife).[29]

> Und was das pöst ob diesen alln:
> Das er det in verzweiflung falln
> Und hing in der versagnüs sich.[30]

And what was worse than all that, he fell into despair, and in desperation hanged himself.

The result being that he went to hell. However, since neither persecution nor heresy can prevail against the Christian faith, the devils' council a thousand years later lets him free again, as a ghost, to deceive 'learned hearts'[31] and tempt people into sin. 'Judas was a finder of all this',[32] the instigator of a new heresy.[33] Judas the desperate broadcasts doubt:

> Er verzweifelt auch an gots güt
> Darum er eym yden gemüt
> ein sundern zweifel pflanczet eyn
> Das keiner weiss, woran sie sein.[34]

He despairs even of God's goodness, so he plants an individual doubt in every mind, so that nobody knows where he is.

Faust, who appeared on the scene a couple of decades after this poem, could be seen as a victim and disciple of Judas, the apostle of despair.

In 1552 a virulent Protestant by the name of Thomas Naogeorgus gave a new twist to Judas' 'afterlife' with his 'tragoedia nova et sacra' *Judas Iscariotes*, whose form and theme were modelled on classical tragedy.[35] Naogeorgus turns the treason motif against the treacherous avarice of Christians who deserted the newborn Protestant cause for the old Church in that time of 'turncoats and betrayers'. Naogeorgus also translated the whole of Sophocles into Latin, and two plays, *Ajax* and *Philoctetes*, appear in the same volume of his works as the *Judas*. All three works hinge on the *extrema calamitas* of suicide – Judas' and Ajax's – and show that (as in the case of Achilles, Ahab or Samson) great gifts, if uncontrolled, are no protection against misfortune. The concluding aphorisms of the chorus in the *Judas* read like an anticipation of the Job-like patience of Philoctetes:

> Felix qui medio scit in dolore
> Afflictumque animum premente culpa,

> Quo se conferat atque ubi salutis
> Sit quaerenda et mali leuamen.

Happy the man who in the midst of suffering, with guilt heavy on his afflicted mind, knows where to turn, and where salvation and relief for his sufferings is to be found.

Christendom should show itself superior to 'what is common to heathens and Turks'. But Judas knew no way out of guilt and need: they drove him to despair. The heart of this drama beats in the figure of Conscientia, always in pursuit and confrontation of Judas. Ever at his heels, loving him in spite of himself, wrestling with him and the devil for the prize of himself, she it is who pronounces final sentence upon him. In answer to his great lament, she precipitates him into damnation and despair. Conscience, if unheeded, is unmerciful. She, who loved Judas, cold-bloodedly drives him to destruction.[36] The devil leaves Judas to himself: 'Tua etenim culpa tota non mea est' (the fault is entirely yours, not mine). But the devil does not hesitate to blame Conscience for forcing him mercilessly into death. Conscience turns destructive when she renounces that which she loved, harshly enough to make the very devil shudder: 'Haec nimium acerba sunt' (that is too cruel). The devil says to Conscience: 'Do you not see to what you have brought him?'; Conscience says to Judas: 'That you must do, do quickly.' The devil handing Judas the noose seems more humane: 'Et hac in parte non te deseram' (even in this pass I will not leave you). He will not leave Judas horribly alone with 'scelesta et atra Conscientia' (dark and evil Conscience). Conscience leaves Judas no hope of mercy, and with his last breath he curses her. As Judas falls into the Chaos of despair he echoes the words of Cain, who thought his guilt exceeded all possibility of forgiveness. As he puts the noose round his neck he sees himself as the victim of Conscience, a sort of Protestant *Moira*:

> Veh mihi iterum atque iterum. Quid egi? In quod chaos
> Me criminum mersi execrandae gratia
> Pecuniae. Non est receptus uspiam.
> Maiora sunt peccata mea quam quae queant
> Remitti. Igitur hunc gutturi aptabo meo,
> Vitam hanc relinquam ut ocyus miserrimam.

Sint execrati coelites et inferi,
Et quicquid in terris agit mortalium.
Tu quoque scelesta et atra Conscientia,
Autorque subdole scelerum Sargannabe
Valete, de me sicuti meremini.
CON (*scientia*): Tu perge. Quisque sua recipiet praemia.

Woe is me and thrice woe! What have I done? Into what chaos of
crime have I plunged because of accursed pelf? There is no refuge
anywhere. My sins are so great that they cannot be forgiven. Therefore I will put this round my throat, and leave this most miserable life
as soon as I can. Cursed be heaven and hell and all mortal things
upon earth. And thou, black and evil Conscience, and Sargannabus,
treacherous author of wickedness, farewell: have from me what you
deserve. (Conscience): Away with you! Everyone will get what he
deserves.

Judas went against Conscience when he undertook the first
sin of treachery, so Conscience pushes him into the second, and
worse, sin of despair. In 1532 Luther (in his table talk) said
that the betrayal, being forgivable, was Judas' lesser sin, and
the despair of grace, being unforgivable, his greater sin. Luther
dismissed as slanderous the idea that he was preaching 'first
sin, then believe' – i.e. *praesumptio*, the calculated expectation of
grace by a bold sinner. *Praesumptio* is as unforgivable as despair:
'Sin leads either below itself to despair, or above itself to
presumption. Both are called unforgivable sins, because the sin
is either over-acknowledged or not acknowledged at all.'[37]

Despairing, lost and damned, Judas and Faust stand on the
threshold of modernity. But there has never been an age which
has utterly obliterated or neglected a whole aspect of human
potential. An extreme portrayal, which we might take as
typical of its age, always has its opposite. In the Passion Play
there is no Judas without Peter, Mary Magdalene or the
Penitent Thief. And in the sixteenth-century drama the exemplary singularity of the damned sinner is usually contrasted
with the redeemed sinner – the Prodigal Son or Everyman,
who repents and finds mercy before the grave. Naogeorgus'
1552 *Judas* is a rousing rejoinder to the optimistic plays which
had been popular for a good half-century everywhere from
England to the south of Germany, a play in which the sinner

wins forgiveness in the hour of his death, and the rich man is brought to the brink of despair and away from it again: the play of *Everyman*.[38] In the late fifteenth-century plays of *Everyman* and *Elckerlyc*, the protagonist, in imminent danger of death, finds that everyone shrinks away in horror and offers no help, and is abandoned by everything worthy of trust; his terror of death carries an aura of treason. But he does not yet bear the stamp of theological *desperatio* which marks the sixteenth century. When Judas commits suicide the devil helps him along with his 'non te deseram': this is a parody of the 'non te deseram' which Everyman hears as he trembles on the brink of the grave – a promise which is seldom to be relied on.[39] The *Everyman* plays can be seen as dramatised *artes bene moriendi* just as the Judas drama is a warning against dying in sin.[40] Macropedius (1539) and Hans Sachs (1549) both wrote plays entitled *Hecastus*, in which the hero is utterly forsaken in his fear and need, spends his last hour within the narrow confines of his conscience – between judgement and hell – and for a time despairs:

> Derhalb muß ich in dieser quel
> Verzweiffeln beid an leib und seel,
> Weil ich kein trost von niemandt han,
> Der sich mein hie wil nemen an.[41]
>
> Ich aber hab der sünden berck
> So über-schwer auff mich geladen,
> Das mich Gott gar nit kan begnaden,
> Wann er ist gar gerecht und streng.
>   Der priester spricht:
> Merck! hestu aller sünden meng
> Auff dieser gantzen erden than,
> Dennoch solt du kein zweiffeln han
> And der Gottes barmhertzigkeit.[42]
>   . . .
> Darumb kein sünder sol verzagen,
> Wie groß ist seiner sünde schar.[43]

Therefore in this torment I must despair of both body and soul, for I have no consolation from anyone who might take my part. I have loaded such a mountain of sin on myself that God cannot forgive me, because he is indeed stern and just. [The priest says:] Hearken! If you had committed every single sin on this earth, you should not despair of God's mercy. ... Therefore no sinner should despair, however great his host of sins.

The rich man believes: his sins are forgiven. The devil is disappointed in his hope of 'yet bringing him to despair',[44] and Hecastus is one of the elect at the Last Judgement.[45]

In the play of *Homulus*, by Ischyrius, the hero is forsaken – an earthly desperation – and then, nearing death, reaches the brink of theological despair when he contemplates his lot beyond the grave.[46] His is the attitude of the despairing sinner in Michelangelo's *Last Judgement* in the Sistine Chapel.[47] This characteristic attitude goes as far back as the *penser* ('reflection') of the melancholy King Arthur in the thirteenth-century Prose *Lancelot* and (somewhat transmuted) as far forward as Rodin's *Le Penseur*.[48] But Virtus, Cognitio and Confessio urge the apprehensive Homulus to confess himself: 'Homule, caue diffidas vnquam, sed cogita facitoque religiose' (Homulus, take care never to despair, but think and do what religion shows to be right', line 876). Homulus repents, confesses, prays for mercy, does penance: 'Bonae confidentiae nihil anteponam' (I will put nothing before true confidence, line 982). Seeing his salvation, the devils curse in vain. Just as Satan stood by Judas as he hanged himself, so Virtus and Cognitio stand by Homulus at his graveside when all others have forsaken him. An angel receives his parting soul as a bride of God.

Naogeorgus' play *Mercator*[49] concerns a merchant afflicted with the plague and staring death in the face. Conscience, calling for his punishment, drives him relentlessly towards despair, as cruelly as she once hounded Judas to his death. The fiercely anti-Catholic Neogeorgus gives Conscience some satirical comments on the priest who, failing to recognise the radical sinfulness of mankind, plies the dying Mercator with advice on good works:

> Durch Gottsschickung des Pfaffen Bricht
> des Kauffmanns Gwissen widerspricht;
> wirfft ihm nur d'Sünd für und Gotts Zorn,
> dadurch sein Hertz ist ängstigt worn,

> besonders da der Teufel bracht
> ein Buch voll seiner Sündn, und veracht
> des Pfaffen Narrey; wird er gar
> zu Verzweiflung trieben fürwahr.[50]

Through God's grace, the merchant's conscience contradicts the priest's teachings, reproaching him for his sins and threatening him with God's anger, so that his heart becomes troubled, especially when the devil brings a book full of his sins. He scorns the priest's idiocies; surely he will be driven to despair.

Before the merchant comes to believe in salvation through grace and mercy alone, Conscience and the devil force him to acknowledge his own imminent damnation by showing him the register of his sins, which is nothing inferior to that of Judas:

> Dein Hoffnung wird nichts helffen dich,
> irrt auch uns beide nicht durchauss,
> wann nur z'letzt wird Verzweifflung draus.[51]

Your hope won't help you: unless we are both very much mistaken, despair will come of it in the end.

Conscience rejects every consolation offered by the priest and routs him. But just as the merchant is giving himself up for lost, that same Conscience prepares a place for spontaneous grace:

> Allenthalben spür ich den Fluch,
> ich seh, ich muß verloren sein,
> d'Sünden drucken mich biß in d'Höll nein
> ...
> Hier ist kein Hilff, noch Trost, noch Gwinn;
> ich spür wohl, daß ich muß verwefflen,
> und weiß kein Heyl: ich muß zun Teufflen.
> Aber wie ein thaukühler Wind
> bläst mich an, ein Hoffnung sich findt;
> ist gleich, als käme ich vom Todt.
> Mein Hertz begehrt z'beten zu Gott;
> weil mir sonst all Hilff is versagt,
> kehr ich mich zu ihm unverzagt.
> Bissher an Gott ich nie dacht han,
> ich spür, daß mich Gotts Geist bläst an;
> Gwissen, was sagstu? Könnts nicht gschehen,
> daß mich Gott gnadig that ansehen?[52]

Everywhere I perceive the curse; I see that I must be damned, my sins drag me down to Hell … Here is no help, no comfort, nothing to gain; I perceive indeed that I must despair, and I know of no salvation: I must go to the devils. But, like a cool wind blowing on me, a hope comes: it is as if I were brought back from the dead. My heart yearns to pray to God; because all other hope is lost to me, I am bold to turn to him. Until now I have never thought of God. I perceive that God's spirit breathes upon me. Conscience, what say you? Could it happen that God gave me grace?

The prostrate sinner experiences the working of unmerited Grace. Conscience answers a resounding 'yes' to his final question, thereby emphasising, at this turning-point of the drama, the radical doctrine of 'sola gratia, quae fide apprehenditur'[53] (grace alone, which is perceived through faith). All the merchant's experiences thereafter are a mere reiteration of what has gone before.

Since the days of the early Church Fathers, the favourite metaphor for salvation had been a healing from sin, with Christ as the doctor. In keeping with this, St Paul and the doctor-saint, Cosmas, 'cure' the merchant of his erroneous belief that the infusion of grace into his soul came from his own good works and not from God's election before the world was created:

> Nein, Kauffmann, du bist unrecht dran:
> auß lauter Gnad sieht dich Gott an,
> durch welch du zu ihm bruffen bist,
> in ihm ehe der Welt Grund glegt ist.[54]

No, merchant, there you are wrong. God looks upon you out of pure Grace, through which you are called to him: you were in him before the foundations of the world were laid. [The Latin is: Nequaquam, Mercator; neque istuc sentias. / Gratuito te favore ille atque gratia / Respexit, quibus etiam in illo ipso scilicet / Mundi ante constitutionem electus es.][55]

They heal him of the 'hydropsy' of his hellish confidence in good works, which threatens to 'burst him asunder' ('rumpere medius',[56] 'in der Mitt zerknellen',[57] just as Judas 'burst asunder in the midst, and all his bowels gushed out', Acts 1:18). Suitable fate for a betrayer of the belief in salvation *sola gratia*!

Paul's 'healing speech' warns against the 'presumption'[58] of trying to 'touch heaven with one's fingers' by fulfilment of the law.[59] No indeed:

> von Natur sey keinr, so Gott gfall.
> Sünder seiens, müssen täglich
> umb Gnad bitten demütiglich,
> verlassen sich auff keine Werck,
> vernichten all ihr Krafft und Stärck,
> daß die Gnad Gotts könnt bey ihn bleiben.[60]

No man is by Nature pleasing to God. Being sinners, men must daily pray humbly for grace, place no reliance on works, count all their power and strength as nothing, so that God's grace may rest upon them.

According to the confessional polemics of the time, you cannot save yourself through works: you must let yourself drop into Grace. This is a modification of the earlier doctrine of *praesumptio*: God 'leidts nit, wann einr mit seim Traumen / ihm den Himmel wollt selbs einraumen' (will not suffer someone to dream his own way into a place in heaven).[61] The medical metaphor for grace is actualised in an extensive and repulsive scene of purgation,[62] which convinces the patient that he is the damndest of the damned, and so brings about his surrender to grace. Paul tells him: 'Zweiffle nit, und du schon selig bist' (despair not, and already you are blessed).[63] Thus converted, he finds kindness in his conscience and in God:

> Mein Gwissen sieht mich lieblich an ...
> Gotts Geist gibt deß Zeugnuß meim Geist,
> bläst mir ins Hertz nein und mich heißt
> vertraun und lieben meinen Gott.[64]

My conscience looks lovingly upon me ... The spirit of God reveals itself to my spirit, infuses into my heart, and bids me trust and love my God.

The Everyman theme concludes with the merchant's 'freely and willingly I die' at the end of the third act. The last two acts show Everyman-Mercator's superiority to a duke, a bishop and a Franciscan friar. Blindly self-righteous, these characters are mad enough to believe that the temptation to despair,[65] in their last hour, can be eluded through their own efforts. This makes them the elect of Satan,[66] and the merchant accuses them of unbelief. Well-ballasted with good works as they are, they still weigh too light in the scales of Archangel Michael.[67] Their salvation account is unbalanced; but in the merchant's case, and his alone, Satan and the Archangel can find no extra sin to charge to him. In medieval art, St Michael is often shown carrying the scales which weigh good and evil. That image inspired the fifth act of *Mercator*:[68] it consists of 'weighing' scenes which dramatically concretise the metaphor of the load of sin. Mercator is saved, while the duke, the bishop and the monk are weighed up on the Archangel's infallible scales. Whole acts of *Mercator* are, in fact, no more than images and metaphors, taken literally and dramatised with skill.[69] It is strange to see the devil and St Michael in alliance against religious hypocrisy, but this is explained by the iconographic evidence, which often shows Michael and Satan collaborating in the weighing of souls.[70] Just as Gregorius and his mother were 'zwei ûz erweltiu gotes kint' (two of the elect children of God, line 3954), so the merchant ends as 'electus Dei', numbered among the 'chosen children of God'.[71] The sinner who trusts in grace becomes Elect. The duke, the bishop and the monk are godless, damned. Naogeorgus enlarged the play of Everyman into a 'Play of the saved and the damned sinner',[72] and – as in the Passion Play with its contrasting examples of Judas and Mary Magdalene – he thereby showed two possible ways of living with guilt. The examples are played out simultaneously on the stage and constitute an 'art of dying' – *after* guilt. The merchant must feel the weight of hopelessness, but God's unfathomable election saves the merchant from the despair of Faust:

> Gar ein großen, thu ich dir sagen,
> hätt mich schier druckt zur Höllen Grund,
> daß ich kein Gnad mehr hoffen kunnt;
> wollt mich gleich dem Teuffel ergeben.
> Aber dazumaln wurd ich eben
> vons Himmels Geist anblasen gschwind.[73]

For I must tell you that a great weight would have dragged me right down to hell, so that I could have hoped no more for grace, and would

have surrendered myself to the devil at once. But thereupon the spirit
of Heaven swiftly blew upon me.

Much later, in Hugo von Hofmannsthal's *Everyman*, we find
Faith leading the hero out of unbelief into accepting that even
the guilty may be saved:

> *Jedermann* Doch weiß ich, solches kommt zugut
> Nur dem der heilig ist und gut:
> Durch gute Werk und Frommheit eben
> Erkauft er sich ein ewig Leben.
> Da sieh, so stehts um meine Werk:
> Von Sünden hab ich einen Berg
> So überschwer auf mich geladen,
> daß mich Gott gar nit kann begnaden,
> Als er doch Höchstgerechte ist.

> *Glaube* Bist du ein solcher Zweifelchrist
> Und weißt nit Gotts Barmherzigkeit?

> *Jedermann* Gott straft erschrecklich!

> *Glaube*   Gott verzeiht!
> Ohn Maßen!

Everyman: Yet I know that such a reward comes only to the good and
holy man: he buys himself eternal life by good works and piety. But
see my state! I have loaded such a heavy burden of sin upon myself
that God cannot forgive me, since he is most just. *Faith*: are you such a
Christ-doubter, and do you not know of God's mercy? *Everyman*:
God's punishments are fearful! *Faith*: God pardons without measure!

Everyman is now contrite, and kneels in prayer:

> Hier schrei ich zu dir in letzter Stund,
> Ein Klageruf geht aus meinem Mund,
> O mein Erlöser, den Schöpfer erbitt,
> daß er beim ende mir gnädig sei!

Here I cry to thee in my last hour, a cry of lamentation comes from
my mouth: O my redeemer, pray the Creator to be gracious to me at
the end!

Next, the devil is defeated, and Death accompanies Everyman
to his grave:

O Herr und Heiland, steh mir bei.
Zu Gott ich um Erbarmen schrei.

O lord and saviour, stand by me. I cry to God for mercy.

And finally comes this:

Jedermann im Grab, nur Haupt und Schultern sind noch sichtbar.

Wie du mich hast zurückgekauft,
So wahre jetzt der Seele mein,
Daß sie nit mög verloren sein
Und daß sie am Jüngsten Tag auffähr
Zu dir mit der geretteten Schar.
Er Sinkt.

Everyman in the grave; only his head and shoulders are still visible. Just as thou hast redeemed me, now protect my soul, that it be not lost, and at the Last Day may ascend to thee with the host of the saved. *He sinks down.*

The fanaticism which Naogeorgus evinces so strongly in his *Hecastus* contrasts with the Breugelian colouring and dramatic skill of another *Homulus* play, by Jaspar von Gennep (1548),[74] which preaches the doctrine of Penitence. The usual allegorical figures appear, along with God, the Angel, Mary, the Devil, Death and Sin. Here too we think of Judas, as Homulus, forsaken by all created things ('den all geschaffne Ding verlassen'),[75] contemplates suicide in his initial terror of death:

Soll ich anders kein Trost erlangen,
langt mir ein Strick, daß ich mich hangen,
so komm ich doch von dieser Marter und Pein,
die Hell wird doch mein Herberg sein.[76]

If I can get no comfort elsewhere, give me a noose, so that I can hang myself: so at least I will escape this pain and torment, though Hell become my dwelling place.

But a whore preaches Lutheranism at him, whereupon his despair tilts over into a 'Protestant' *praesumptio*:

Kann uns der Glaub allein selig machen,
Narren sinds, die Gotts Zorn groß acten,
darumb will ich nu nach meim Willen leben
und gläuben, daß mirs Gott werd vergeben.[77]

If faith alone can make us blessed, they are fools who care much for God's anger; therefore I will now live as I please, and believe that God will forgive me for it.

Pitiless Infamy – not, as elsewhere, that of his conscience or the devil, but that of Death – tries to talk Homulus out of his only hope of salvation (lamentation of his sins) and into certain damnation.[78] But at that moment a cry is wrung from him: 'O Gott im Himmel, erbarm dich mein / in der unmaßigen Barmherzigkeit dein'[79] (O God in Heaven, in thy infinite compassion have mercy upon me). He has spoken the word which bars Hell to him and opens the gates of Heaven. A 'Brother' frees his neck from the noose which sin, death and the devil had placed there.[80] Contrition, Confession, Penitence and the prayers of Mary raise him out of despair into mercy, the mercy which the devils vainly beg for themselves:

> Zwiefel nit, sobald dem Sünder sein Sünden sind leid,
> ist Gott zu Genade und Barmherzigkeit bereit:
> wer ihm vertrauet ohn all Zwifel,
> der mag nimmer verlorn bliben.[81]

> O Homule, zweifel nit an Gotts Barmherzigkeit,
> hab um dein Sünden Reu und Leid,
> ein zerschlagen Herz Gott nit verschmaht.[82]

Doubt not, as soon as the sinner repents of his sins, God is quick with his grace and mercy: who trusts in him without any despair, can never be left forlorn. O Homulus, doubt not of God's mercy, repent of your sins: a contrite heart will God not despise.

Homulus lies down to die in the 'dazzling garb of Penitence' ('blinckende Kleid der Pönitenz').[83] Everyman, the changed sinner, ends his life on the very threshold of Hell, where death appears to him with the urgency of the medieval *danse macabre*. At the last moment he escapes the devil's clutches, repents, and throws himself into the arms of Grace. Within sight of the grave, forsaken by all the world, there is still a hand reaching out to him. Before he can despair he is given the help due to the elect, encouraged, comforted – and he attains the salvation denied to Judas and Faust, who are utterly lost and forsaken at the last. The damned have their own names, but the name of the Elect is Every Man.

CHAPTER 7

Faust: saved or damned?

If we seek a comparison for Faust's dramatic fall into sin, we should initially look to Lucifer rather than Adam. Faust conjured up the devil and is willing to submit to him. He is the man who signed a pact with the devil. He falls in a world already saved: there can be no second salvation. Will he remain an outcast, like Lucifer, or return to the fold, like the Prodigal Son? Will he despair or trust in grace? It is up to him. Most authors damn him; only seldom, and only in later works, is he among the saved. Their choice of a posthumous fate for Faust depends on their own attitude towards that fallen hero and the power surrounding him. Everyone accepted that Judas was damned and Gregorius among the elect; Faust could be assigned, on reflection, to either camp. Human existence in this world offered an easily comprehensible framework of literary possibilities within which Faust's position could be changed: he could be saved, or damned. The change from one to the other fits into a clear and comprehensible shift in the literary treatment of human destiny. Few characters in literature have known such a reversal of their entelechy; most continue to follow the laws which brought them into being. Faust could be a pattern for either salvation or damnation.

An early 'folk book' of Faust (1587),[1] by a Lutheran scholar, bases its account of the hero's life on an oxymoron: Faust is 'infaustissimus', most unfortunate.[2] This is a humanistic reminiscence of the Roman name 'Faustus', meaning one born on a 'dies faustus et felix' (a fortunate and happy day): one under a favourable star, one highly favoured, but whose promised happy destiny is never fulfilled, because, through his own fault, he lives unblessed and 'infaustus'. Gifted from birth with eloquence, wit, skilfulness and luciferian imagination, he was meant to be among the elect, but in the end is damned. Forsaken of God – because forsaking of God – Faust breaks the bounds of baptism by binding himself to the devil. Through 'deliberate folly and dreadful unrepentance'[3] he forfeits God's grace: once triumphant, now accursed, he falls from presumption into despair. He who once travelled in the heavens falls into the abyss of hell. He who was once called to God is cast out by God. Thus did Faust become, for several centuries, the dreadful example of the misuse of 'splendid' talents, which with diabolical help increased beyond measure and so brought ruin upon him.[4] The pattern for such presumption was the fallen angel, Lucifer himself, who through vanity rebelled against God and was cast into Hell, and through presumption fell far from the God to whom he had once been near. Destined for the pinnacle of creation, he missed his mark – through his own sin – and fell into damnation. 'What crueller and more fearful thing could be said of a man?'[5] But it must be said of Faust, 'as a fearful pattern, horrible example, and true hearted warning to all arrogant, forward and godless people', as the title-page of the folk book puts it. The devil's intention is to induce his victims, beguiled into a covenant with him, to follow the fatal pattern of Lucifer's life: starting too high, ending all too low. The fallen angel, once so high, wants more than the fate of Adam, who was not beyond redemption. For those who signed the devil's pact with their own blood there was – reputedly – no more redemption. It certainly seems to seal Faust's damnation. He betrayed God, but keeps his word to the devil. He does revolt, but then he submits. The bloody signature is a fearful thing, equivalent to a self-chosen predestination, with no way out – just as the devil wishes. Faust and his literary biographers seem to accept it as such. The guilt which Faust lives with is that of the pact with the devil, the oath which weighs heavier than any sinful *deed* – which, once repented, would readily be forgiven.

The devil wears his beaver up. he is well-versed in theology and remorselessly orthodox: it is for him to teach Christians that in the last instance, despair is the only precondition for damnation. He puts the point quite clearly to Faust as they bargain over the pact, singing to him 'of poor Judas' and telling him,

> Dennoch mustu mit, da hilfft kein Bitt,
> Dein verzweifelt Hertz hat dirs verschertzt.[6]

Yet you must follow, no prayer will avail: your despairing heart has forfeited that chance.

And a clause in the pact, forbidding Faust to attempt any return to God, bars all other ways of escape.[7] Faust is 'stiff-necked', that is, he has a hard and rebellious heart and refuses to do penance: his *obstinatio*[8] excludes all contrition. One subject of his learned and instructive conversations with the devil is the nature of Lucifer,[9] and in that figure Faust comes to recognise himself. Thus his first lament expresses contrition, but contrition without hope:

'Thus I can hope for no further mercy, but shall, like Lucifer, be cast off into everlasting damnation and misery. Ah woe, woe! Of what should I accuse myself? I wish I had never been born!' Thus did Dr Faustus lament, but he could form no belief or hope of being brought through penance back into God's grace.

Faust is deaf to the Church's promises – that if you appeal to God for mercy and forgiveness, then you may wrest your soul, if not your body, away from the devil: 'But in all his opinions and judgements he became doubtful, unbelieving and without hope.'[10] Faust laments as he contemplates his apparently irrevocable damnation. The lament fits both the beginning and the end of Faust's period of sinful worldly enjoyment, because despair of grace opens the floodgates of immeasurable sin. This is the Augustinian 'Peccata addere peccatis' (adding sins to sins), which once barred Judas' way to salvation. Judas, like Lucifer, is an ancestor of Faust: the devil now casts Faust as Judas. Like Judas after the betrayal, Faust has a change of heart; but the chief priest (to whom the devil alludes) did not release Judas from his torment, and the devil will not release Faust. Faust complains to Mephistopheles:

'Alas, what have I done?' The spirit replied: 'See thou to that.' So Doct. Faustus went away sorrowful. ... Dr Faustus did always feel some contrition at heart, and lamented that he had endangered his soul's bliss and pledged himself to the devil for things temporal. But his contrition was the repentance and penance of Cain or Judas, which was indeed a contrition of the heart, but despaired of God's mercy, and it was to him impossible that he should come again into God's grace. Just like Cain, who despaired thus: 'My sins are so great that they can never be forgiven.' Thus also Judas etc. Thus it was with D. Faustus: he did indeed look up to heaven, but he could see nothing there.[11]

This mention of Cain completes Faust's ancestral line. He goes through the motions of prayer and looks up to heaven, but his eyes are blind.[12]

Faust is constantly urged to appeal to God's mercy by such positive antitypes as the 'holy sinners' (the Penitent Thief, Peter, Matthew and Mary Magdalene) and the repentant magician Simon of Samaria (Acts 8:9–13). He might indeed have broken his pact, but the devil steps in and forces him to renew it on pain of being torn limb from limb.[13] At that point Faust's destiny takes a sharp downturn and he sinks into dissipation. Seeing his end fast approaching, Faust puts his lamentations into words, writhing in his bonds of sin, but vainly – as he knows, because God has forgotten him: 'O despairing hope, never will you be remembered more ... Alas, alas, who will redeem me?'[14]

The prose of the folk-book is an adaptable medium. It lends itself to reporting, lecturing, exemplifying, describing endless magical marvels, even to monologues of lamentation; and it is Mephistopheles' usual means of communication with Faust. But at the beginning and end of the story, following his own scholastic logic to its conclusion, he switches to lyrical verse, enticing Faust to the final sealing of his fate: 'Es ist zu spat, an Gott verzag, / Dein Ungluck läufft herein all tag' (it is too late, despair of God: your misfortune is ever increasing).[15] 'And when the spirit had sung enough to Faust of poor Judas, he vanished away, and left Faust alone, all melancholy and bewildered.'[16] Faust, like Judas after his last interview with the high priest, is staring damnation in the face and knows no way out of lamentation into prayer. He is not tempted to suicide – though he slays his own chance of eternal life – because he knows that he is bound to die next day when his pact expires. Faust, about to meet his diabolical (but theologically licensed) executioner, watches his life trickle away through an hour-glass. It is a strange fate. To his students he bequeathes a farewell reminiscent of the Last Supper. The saint's-life-in-reverse serves as an awful warning to Christians: 'that is what you will find written of me: let my terrible end be an example and reminder to you all your days, to keep God before your eyes'.[17] His last wish is that Wagner should write the story of his life, 'for people will want to know this my story from you'.[18] The 'relics' of Faust the un-saint are written records. There is his pact with the devil. There are his records of visits to heaven and hell, which are reminiscent of medieval visions of the otherworld. (Alas, his trip into the sky left him no better informed than a cosmonaut about the true nature of heaven!) And there are his lamentations.[19]

On the evening before the last dreadful night, Faust transcends himself in care for his students. Like Judas he is contrite;[20] though damned eternally, he 'takes heart' to deal with things temporal, and wishes them good-night knowing that the devil is about to come for him:

Finally and to conclude, I affectionately bid you go to bed and sleep in peace, and be not dismayed if you hear a disturbance and crashing in the house; fear not, for no harm will come to you if you stay in your beds; and when you find my dead body, give it burial.[21]

Despairing Faust, leaving his students, bids them not to despair. When they finally learn the truth about him they wish they could have saved him. But the concerned and anxious words of his students cannot save the scholar from his scholarship. His fate is otherwise. They entreat him to pray, 'God be merciful to me a sinner.' 'To each one he promised that he desired to pray; but he could not, like Cain, who also said his sins were so great that they could not be forgiven.'[22] The scholars, weeping and clinging to one another, go to their uneasy and sleepless beds. Towards midnight Faust's screams are choked amidst diabolical tempest and tumult. The devil executes on Faust the traitor's just punishment: he is burst asunder, torn limb from limb. No horrific detail is spared in the attempt to arouse terror. In the morning the students seek Faust in his study:

They saw no Faust any more: nothing but the study all splashed with blood. The brain was sticking to the wall, because the devil had smashed him from one wall to the other. Also his eyes and some teeth were there, a cruel and frightful spectacle. Then must the students lament and weep for him, and they sought everywhere. But finally then found his corpse outside by the dung-heap, which was horrible to see, for his head and all his limbs hung loose.[23]

Faust's evil lay not in deeds but in thoughts. His sin was in his head, and his head paid the price.

This unholy death contrasts with the death of saints. Just like a saint, Faust appears after death to those who knew him: 'D. Faustus also appeared, just as he lived, to his assistant by night, and revealed many secrets to him.'[24] Like a saint's life, the anti-hagiography needed reliable witnesses to its truth: his students witnessed his death in the next room. His whole story, written by Wagner according to his last request, is to be found at Wittenberg. Thus there are fictions to vouch for the genuineness of this un-saint's life: several chapters are by his own hand; there are witnesses to his life, summoned by himself, such as Wagner, and other students witness to his end, so that the whole anti-hagiography can claim authenticity as a first-hand account. This attempt, in a fictitious saint's life, to abolish the fictionality of a fictional work marks Faust's biography as an *inverted* saint's life, replacing the saint's hope of 'living in eternal bliss with Christ' with an updated vision of horror. Times have changed: the lesson is taught not through an idealised saint, but through a bogeyman. In Faust's story 'we find the terrible example of how he signed away his soul and perished'. The work ends by quoting, for the edification of all Christians, 1 Peter 5:8–9: 'Be sober, be vigilant; because your adversary the devil, as a roaring lion, walketh about, seeking whom he may devour; Whom resist stedfast in the faith.'[25]

Like the Lives of Simon Magus, Judas and Pontius Pilate,

this folk-book is an anti-hagiography. Such heroes work wonders through the devil's power, not God's, and they go not to eternal bliss but to eternal damnation; if they repent, as Judas does, it does them no good. Later versions of the Faust legend drop the insistence on eye-witness verisimilitude, reject historicity, abandon the precise location in time and space imitated from the saint's life, and move the story to a placeless, dateless, fictional world in which poetic imagination and planned innovation are given free rein. Then the message can be inverted: Faust, foremost of the damned, can be saved; the accursed can become the elect. For a century and a half, almost up to Goethe's time, Faust was usually represented as the unblessed hero of an inverted saint's life. Goethe's *Faust*, the greatest literary treatment of his story, led Faust into the *telos* of redemption without really upsetting his image as one of the damned – as Thomas Mann's novel was to show.[26] Let us now visit a few stations on Faust's way to Goethe.

Before Goethe the greatest work of Faust, in content, form and spirit, was Christopher Marlowe's *Tragical History of Dr Faustus* (1590): for a century and a half it counted as definitive.[27] Marlowe's Faust is an Icarus who falls from salvation into magic, intoxicated by the chance of mastering the impossible to his own glory, 'Be it to make the moon drop from her sphere' (sc. III line 40). Like Lucifer, he is rash enough to risk his salvation in the teeth of damnation, and surrenders himself to despair in full theological awareness of what he does: initially, rebellion; finally, collapse. Entering on the pact, he buys supposed freedom and truth at the price of his soul and has four-and-twenty years to enjoy his guilt. Those years demonstrate the truth spoken by Mephistopheles, the fallen angel:

> Hell hath no limits, nor is circumscrib'd
> In one self place, but where we are is hell
> And where hell is, there must we ever be.[28]

It is hell for Faust also: under the tyranny of the devil's false theology he has the will, but not the strength, to repent. It is a restless tragedy with ever-shifting perspectives, weaving together classical antiquity and cosmic modernity; now winged, now crawling; now mocking a Pope and Emperor, now tolerating a clown. Now it focuses on a flea; now it surveys the world, as Faust and Mephistopheles travel space on a cosmonautic dragon's back: 'That looking down the earth appear'd to me / No bigger than my hand in quantity.'[29] Sparkling with literary and scientific erudition, venturing into the affairs of both Church and State, the play takes the measure of a world unmasked, and the revelation drives Faust to despair.

Faust, torn between contrition and despair, is tossed between two inescapable betrayals. By signing the pact he betrayed God, and in punishment for that betrayal he will be torn in pieces. By breaking the pact he would betray Lucifer and incur the same, traitor's punishment:

> Thou traitor, Faustus, I arrest thy soul
> For disobedience to my sovereign lord [Lucifer]:
> Revolt, or I'll in piecemeal tear thy flesh.
>
> (Sc. xviii, lines 74–6)

Before the fatal night, Faust looks back:

Oft have I thought to have done so [repent]; but the devil threatened to tear me in pieces if I named God, to fetch me body and soul if I once gave ear to divinity; and now 'tis too late. Gentlemen, away, lest you perish with me! (Sc. xii, lines 71–4)

He has let the devil deceive him. If he had cried to God for mercy, the pact would have been broken; betraying Lucifer, his tempter, would have set him free. Faust thinks himself bound by the contract, though by breaching it he would have obeyed God and escaped damnation. Faust cannot repent: he is in the power of despair. His last hours are a lost battle. His good angel bids him 'Remember that God's mercy is infinite' (sc. xix, line 40), and exhorts: 'Yet, Faustus, call on God' (ibid., line 54). But as the devil hounds and hammers on Faust remorselessly, the good angel must leave him: he has given himself up. He panics, and himself turns the church's teaching on its head: 'The snake which seduced Eve can be saved, but Faust cannot' (sc. xix, line 41). Still the devil drives: ''tis too late, despair, farewell!' (sc. xix, line 97). In his great dying speech, with his last breath, Faust fights the fight yet again. As he speaks his last words on that fearful night, the devils tear him to pieces in punishment for his betrayal – of God. The students find him next morning:

> O help us, heaven! see, here are Faustus' limbs,
> All torn asunder by the hand of death.
>
> (Sc. xx, lines 6–7)

Full of awe and care for their teacher, they, as good Christians, form a funeral procession: 'We'll give his mangled limbs due burial' (sc. xx, line 17). If people like Faust were less arrogant, their will and conscience would help them stop on the slippery slope to fated or chosen self-destruction, instead of speeding them on. But, bound to despair, they reveal possibilities which make the most unbiased spectator shudder. Marlowe adds a moralising conclusion, but the fearfulness of Faust's destiny is greater for him than this:

> Cut is the branch that might have grown full straight,
> And burned is Apollo's laurel bough
> That sometime grew within this learned man.
> Faustus is gone: regard his hellish fall,
> Whose fiendful fortune may exhort the wise
> Only to wonder at unlawful things,
> Whose deepness doth entice such forward wits
> To practise more than heavenly power permits.
>
> (Epilogue)

Faust, unlike Judas, is no self-murderer. He despairs and is damned, and is torn limb from living limb by the devil: so in the folk book, in Marlowe, in Mountfort and in Klinger. Lenau is the first to have Faust commit suicide, though the possibility is indicated in the farcical *Faust* of William Mountfort (1697). Here, before the hero's end, Harlequin and Scaramouche make mock of the idea of self-strangulation out of despair, acting it out together on the gallows. Scaramouche almost does hang himself, inadvertently, grasping a message which says, 'Therefore my conscience dealt me a mighty blow, and in despair I hanged myself, even as you see.' The poor folk take pity on him and decide to have him hanged by due process of

law, to prevent him damning his soul through self-slaughter –
whereby he escapes them altogether. The allusion to Faust's
Judas-like death in a noose is playfully evoked, no more.[30]
Faust himself is torn to pieces, as usual. The student finds him
in the morning, his bones torn and scattered by some diabolical
agency.[31]

The bifurcation of Faust's fate has a long literary history.
Saint-sinners of late Antiquity (such as Proterius' slave, Theophilus and Anthemius),[32] who make a pact with the devil but
achieve holiness by repenting of it and doing penance,
appeared a thousand years before the late medieval anti-saint
Faust, with *his* diabolical contract, who is obviously designed
to be damned. Each type was conceived on the threshold of a
new epoch: the first in the early years of Christianity, the
second when Christianity was in danger of fading before the
approach of modernity. In the first, a saint turns penitently to
God; in the second, a man is damned because in his despair he
turns away from God. Both the saintly sinner and his opposite,
born a thousand years later, spring from the heart of Christianity as classic exemplars of good and evil. Faust was conceived as a dreadful warning: his fascination could scarcely
have been foreseen. The story of the repentant devil's accomplice remained part of the church's repertoire, as is demon-
strated by Calderón's play *El mágico prodigioso* ('The miracle-
working magus'),[33] written for the Feast of Corpus Christi in
1637, which harks back to the tradition of the saintly sinner.
Calderón combines the fourth-century legend of the magus
Cyprian of Antioch[34] with elements of the Spanish Faust
tradition, showing whence a Faust-type legend could incline
towards salvation rather than catastrophe. Cyprian, thirsty for
knowledge and love, signs away his soul to the fallen angel
Lucifer, who kept his knowledge when he lost the grace of God.
But Cyprian acknowledges the greater power of God, wipes out
the blood of his signature with the blood of martyrdom, and so
is united with his beloved Justina, whom no diabolical art
could help him to attain.

Some of the authors in whose works Faust is saved may have

drawn on the saints' lives for purely literary motives. Others may have found the bad example of his damnation less attractive than the exemplary portrayal of a sinner saved, and so deliberately have contrasted Faust the saved with Faust the damned. Which is which must emerge from individual studies. In any case, all treatments of his legend revolve around his life with guilt, and make it clear whether he is saved or damned. This opposition can be either incarnate in two separate figures, such as Judas and Gregorius, or shown through the evolution of a single figure – here, Faust. We have only to think of the folk book and Marlowe on the one hand, and Calderón and Goethe on the other, to see how wide is the terrain of this contrasting legend. A fleeting look at some of its outer reaches will demonstrate this before we focus on Thomas Mann, who found Faust damned once again, and once again saved him.

Lessing's play *Faust* (before 1759),[35] which survives in a single fragment, caused 'anxiety bordering on fear', according to Blankenburg. Faust's passion for knowledge brought him so deep into the devil's power that the devil would have triumphed, 'were it not that the denouement brought reassurance to humanity'. In the 'most reassuring way, as everyone thought', an angel, 'an appearance from the world above', forestalls Hell's victory with this message: 'The Godhead did not give mankind the noblest of desires so as to make him forever unhappy.'[36] The disturbing factor came from the folk book; the reassurance was provided by Lessing. By saving Faust, Heaven gives its blessing to the noblest of desires, the insatiable thirst for knowledge. Did Lessing's play have any more than a trace of theology? And what was it (surely not Faust's repentance, for what sin would he repent?) that moved this angel from an Enlightened heaven to wish no one 'forever unhappy' through knowledge?

The last days of Faust were acted out, for the delectation of Prague, Vienna and southern Germany, in an allegorical play by Paul Weidmann (1775).[37] The formal unities of time and place (Lessing's play also lasts 'from midnight to midnight') do not guarantee the third unity of action. In the middle acts,

Weidmann leafs through a few picture-book scenes from
Faust's remembered life, presenting him with a lamentable
ensemble: the inevitable outcome makes even his supposed
successes a cause of bitter disappointment. Strip the unimpres-
sive baroque draperies from this sentimental drama and you
find a worn-out, downcast Faust: not even Helen's murder of
Faust's father can save the play. Faust appears as a stubborn
but outdated Everyman who has lost most of his sixteenth-
century vigour. From the Everyman tradition come Conscience, the traitor's despair, the poisoned cup handed to Faust
by the devil, Faust's consciousness of damnation and his dying
cry 'Mercy, mercy!' (though not his incessant grumbling and
self-pity). Following the same tradition, the 'good angel'
Ithuriel (Judas' guardian angel in Klopstock's *Messiah*, here
the devil's adversary) is able to overcome Mephistopheles and
extol the 'unending mercy' of God. 'He receives the penitent in
his fatherly bosom and casts you, oh accursed tempters, into
everlasting hell.' Thus ends the Faust play – or is it the
Everyman play? – of 1775.

In the novel *Faust* by Friedrich Maximilian Klinger
(1791),[38] Faust is the inventor of printing. This means the
propagation of Hell, the genius of a dark truth composed of
satanic visions: visions of a time when madness gripped the
whole of Europe and acts of unspeakable inhumanity were
tolerated.[39] A satanic inspiration, which already counts Judas
among its triumphs, keeps pace with the times; and through
the Book, the propagator of madness, it swallows more than
one Judas – swallows whole continents.[40] 'Soon a fire will break
out in Germany that will engulf the whole of Europe. Already
the germ of insanity is sprouting in ages to come ...'[41] This
devilish onslaught on the world, which transcends the private
sphere and brings Lucifer into politics, is also embodied
through the titanic individualism of Faust ('I overleap the
bounds of humanity'),[42] who is doomed to flee in vain before
Despair. Genius as Faust may be, he is in the unnatural fetters
of those who 'seek through their wiles to increase their wit, so as
to escape from the claws of Despair'.[43] Through his
engagement with the devil he tries to break those bounds by

transcending his own nature, but the attempt is illusory from the start: the devils' council aims from the beginning to drive him to despair. Their charge to Leviathan ends: 'If then despair seizes him, fling him down and return victorious to hell!'[44] At the very outset Faust's family pronounces him 'Lost, alas! Forever lost!',[45] and at the end Faust's dying father says in his misery: 'Forever, alas! forever lies the abyss of damnation between me and thee.'[46] Faust, unable to grasp the nature of God, falls away from him in an echo of Lucifer's fall: treason is indeed the root of despair.[47] Klinger situates his solipsistic Faust, through a series of diachronic interconnections,[48] in a world stripped naked, and thus brings out his single theme: the man who dices with his eternal salvation.

Faust travels with the devil through the world, stopping to behold the sufferings of the righteous and the rewards of wickedness. The despairing, the suicidal and the insane progressively reveal to him the meaninglessness of existence. To Faust, with his emotional self-love, the devil's vengeful revelation of wickedness along their adventurous path seems almost chivalrous, so that he 'almost began to see his alliance with the devil as the brave act of a man who sacrifices his soul for the best of humanity and so surpasses all the heroes of olden times, who risked only their earthly existence'.[49] Faust, last of the knights-errant, Don Quixote without the innocence, 'sat on his horse and rejoiced in excited imaginings of being the Knight of Virtue': a piece of self-deception which 'served to gild for him the prospect of hell'.[50] And Faust, too, has his Sancho Panza.

The devil rode close beside him and let him continue his commentary. But in each of these would-be noble feelings he saw fresh material for future torment and despair ... Already he was savouring the hour when all those shining mirages would fade away, all those bright imaginary pictures be overcast with the colours of hell, and so cleave that rash man's heart as no mortal's heart was cloven before.[51]

And Faust's little train goes by: the Knight, Death, and the Devil.

If, like Faust, you see hell in this world, then hell will seem to you a paradise. More hideous than all the courts of Europe is the papal court at Rome. The devil, Faust's companion, is a 'favourite' of the pope.[52] Dispensations are available even for incest and diabolical pacts! There Faust, now set in hatred of humanity, sees it doomed to destruction in all its 'horrible nakedness', and is moved not to lament that destruction but recklessly to pursue it. Pope Alexander prays to the devil, who sends him to hell. Faust, now a physical and spiritual wreck, is on the point of collapse. An allegorical dream foreshadows it and the devil announces it: 'I'll shred your quivering soul until you stand like a frozen image of despair!'[53] Faust would rush eagerly to hell, but that is not to be: 'I'll slay you with long-drawn despair.'[54] 'Now I'll draw aside the curtain and sling the ghost of despair into your brain.' The devil shows him the outcome of his life and shakes him to the core: 'Madness glowed in his brain, and he cried out in the wild tones of despair.'[55]

Faust's return journey is marked by traces of the heart-rending misery which he left behind him, while the devil fans his memories. Revolutionary rhetoric (Klinger was writing in 1791) is a spent fire – at best it was a 'squint-eyed virtue'. Unhuman masks had hidden humanity from him; in his rage he smote upon the masks, and his blows fell on men. 'Howl and moan, for I'm drawing more horrors from the dark.'[56] 'Now behold all the consequences of your folly, peruse them all . . .'[57] Faust's sick rage had two targets, morality and immorality. It was not private but political.

The misery your hand has woven stretches through the centuries. Generations yet unborn will curse their existence because you soothed your itchings in hours of madness, or set yourself up as judge and avenger of human affairs. See, rash man, the significance of your works, which seems so limited to blind ones like you! Which of you can say, 'Time erases all trace of my existence'?[58]

So the devil makes his reckoning. The victims of the guilty Faust are individuals, peoples, all Europe, his own century, a whole age. Faust freely chose to be master over the ('guiltless') devil, despite the latter's incessant warnings; he used the devil's devices, with consequences which strike him with sheer horror. 'Faust opened his staring eyes and looked to heaven. Devil: "It is deaf to you!"'[59] "See, my eyes are dry and staring: call my indifference despair."[60] Horrified at the irreparable outcome of his guiltiness, Faust falls headlong into despair. In his last moments of freedom this despair hardens into an obdurate[61] clinging *to* despair, as to a jealously guarded possession. Faust's body is torn apart, the punishment of traitors: not by his own hand nor by officers of the law, but the the devil's hand. Under the gallows on which Faust's own son hangs:

It is time to go: you have played your part here, you're beginning another, which will never end. Step out of your circle and bury this unhappy boy; then I'll seize you, rend your quivering, crumbling body from your soul just as a man strips the skin from an eel, chop it in pieces and scatter it abroad, to the revulsion and terror of passers-by.[62]

It is now that Faust shows himself obdurate. 'Then he seized him, with a scornful laugh that hissed over the earth's surface, tore his quivering body apart as a naughty boy tears a fly to bits, scattered the trunk and bleeding limbs horribly and angrily, and made off with his soul to hell.'[63]

In Klinger, Faust's despair is in no way a despair of grace: his presumption provokes the devil, not God. The world is swarming with godless servants of God, the pope goes whoring after the devil. Repentance, prayer, forgiveness and grace have no place, only stark horror, and the devil is in his element. Faust's one glance at heaven is like a vain and ill-directed memory. Faust may feel guilt and foresee the consequences, but this produces not the slightest inclination to repent. His route to hell is one of inexorable logic. The world is flat, with hell beneath, and everything else is mirage. No one's conscience troubles him – except the devil's perhaps. Faust's moral sensitivity is not metaphysical; quickly outraged by others, he is hardened towards himself. Humanity finds transcendence only in the inhuman. In a world without heaven, the only horizon (and admittedly there is one) is hell. Klinger's 'historical' novel announces a new age, or a prophecy of how such an age might be.

Even the next world can know despair: the despair of a Sisyphus. Such is Faust in a fragment by Lenz which places him in the antique hades.[64] The underworld river cannot bear Faust away. Unloved, he cannot sink and drink of annihilation. Lethe refuses him oblivion. When Bacchus comes to fetch him back to the upper world Faust asks him for eternal destruction, and says fearfully:

> Kommst du vielleicht mit zehnfachem Grimme,
> Großes Wesen, meiner Pein
> Neue endlose Stacheln zu leihn?
> Willst du eines Verzweifelten spotten?
> Oder kommst du, wie dein Gesicht,
> Liebenswürdigster! mir verspricht,
> Mich auf ewig auszurotten? –
> Nimm meinen Dank und zögre nicht!
>
> *Bacchus* Keins von beiden. – Dein Herz war groß–
> Faust – – – du bist deines Schicksals los,
> Und, wenn dir die Gesellschaft gefällt,
> Komm' mit mir zur Oberwelt!

Faust sinkt in einer Betäubung hin, die, weil sie der Vernichtung so ähnlich war, eine unaussprechliche Ruhe über sein ganzes Wesen ausbreitet.

Do you perchance come with tenfold cruelty, great one, to add new and endless stings to my torment? Would you mock a man in despair? Or do you come to destroy me forever, as is promised by your looks, O you most worthy of love? Take my thanks and hesitate not! *Bacchus* Neither the one nor the other. You had a great heart, Faust: you are released from your fate, and if you fancy my society, come with me to the world above! (Faust sinks into a daze, which was so like annihilation that it spreads ineffable peace through his whole being.)

There the fragment breaks off. Was annihilation to be Faust's salvation? There would be no annihilation in the upper world. Faust's terror plunges him into apparent annihilation. Will he awake from his 'ineffable peace' into despair? Is that 'Come with me to the world above' the acme of deceit, leading to something worse than hell?[65]

In 1846 Karl Simrock presented a verse puppet-play of Faust, whose ever-changing tonalities, from the weighty to the relaxed, outrank many a more pretentious drama on this theme.[66] Faust's scenes alternate with comic 'Kasperle' scenes in a rapid chiaroschuro, building up to a precarious climax in the last act, which turns a potential drama of salvation into a theological tragedy of classic proportions. In the first scene Faust comes to the parting of the ways of Magic and Theology, and chooses the left-hand path to the cry of 'Woe to thine unhappy soul!' coming from the 'voice on the right'. That is the direction taken by the whole play; in Act II the pact with Hell confirms it. Faust says, 'I abjure God and the Christian faith.' His good angel replies, 'Lost forever is thine unhappy soul.' In Act III, Faust's magic cloak wafts him, along with Mephistopheles, to the refined surroundings of the duke of Parma's court: this represents the first twelve of the twenty-four years bought by Faust through his pact with hell. Exactly halfway through his life of self-indulgence, everything changes. In the brilliantly simple fourth act, Faust looks back and takes stock. Pleasure has lost its savour; he has forfeited eternal bliss for mere appearance; he cannot pray. 'For prayer is the mercy of heaven, and for me there is no mercy. O how I repent! – Repent? Where repentance is, there is also mercy! If only I truly repented, perhaps even I might yet obtain mercy.' In one masterly little scene, Faust's question, 'Can I still come to God?' strikes the devil dumb and he vanishes howling – which means that the devil has broken the pact, for he was bound to speak the truth. Thus the scene declares Faust to be free. He prays: 'I thank you, mother of God! I am redeemed, I am saved! Ah! I can pray again, weep again, the spring of repentance is not sealed.' If the play were following the Everyman pattern it would end there. Faust has three more hours to live.

But the devil's name is treachery. He can lie in silence as well as in words. A play on words robs Faust of grace: 'If you still wish to attain bliss, you could do it only through love.' He offers Helen to Faust, who cries 'Give her me! Give her me!' 'First you must again abjure him to whom you have prayed.' 'I abjure him forever. With this treasure in my arms, I defy both him and you. Give her me!' In a twinkling Faust loses his newly won salvation. He presses Helen to his breast, and the serpent of hell along with her, and is cheated of life, of grace – and of twelve years as well. The pact was to have run for twenty-four years, 'reckoning a year as three hundred and sixty-five days'.

But the devil counts in the nights in which he has also served
Faust, and so gains twelve years. 'At midnight you are mine!'
Two brief scenes suffice to raise Faust to heaven and then
plunge him down to hell. (Lessing's Faust tests the speed of the
devils so as to select the fastest for himself. He was 'quick as the
change from good to evil'.)[67] For what little is left of the puppet
play Faust sits with the knife at his throat. Kasperle, as night
watchman, calls out the hours. Faust can no longer pray: 'God
forsworn, all forlorn.' The 'muffled voice from above' is confined to chilly Latin: 'Fauste! Fauste! praepara te ad mortem
... Fauste! Fauste! accusatus es' (Faust, Faust, prepare thyself
for death ... Faust, Faust, thou art accused.) Faust's recourse
to the Latin liturgy ('Quid sum miser tunc dicturus': Woe is
me! What then shall I say?) is doomed to failure. As Kasperle
calls the hours the voice booms on: 'Fauste! Fauste! judicatus es
... Fauste! Fauste! in aeternum damnatus es' (Faust, Faust,
thou art judged ... Faust, Faust, thou art damned to eternity).
Kasperle would rather have liked to give him a message for his
grandmother:

> Hört, ihr Herrn, ich laß euch wissen,
> Mit dem Teufel seid ihr stets besch—.
> Er hält nicht, was er auch verspricht,
> Bis er euch gar den Hals zerbricht.
> Zwölf ist der Klock, zwölf ist der Klock.

Hear, gentlemen, I'll tell you: you are always b...d by the devil. He
doesn't keep his promises, he just breaks your neck. It is twelve
o'clock, it is twelve o'clock.

   Kasperle and Gretel dance. The puppet play cannot accept
a denouement on the Everyman pattern: it introduces it only to
reject it. If you tangle with the devil there is no escape. Faust
must fall because he did fall. It is not the tempter's fault, it is
Faust's for being tempted. Faust is stumped for words to God
quicker than for discourse with the devil. He breaks the fetter
and it fastens on him once more. Whatever Simrock's sources,
the language of his puppet play reveals a genuine poet.

Faust's way to damnation – of salvation – differs in different
works. In the folk book, in Marlowe and in Klinger the road to

Hell is direct; in the puppet play it turns up towards salvation and then drops steeply down again. In Weidmann the path to the grave is blocked at the last moment by the appeal for grace borrowed from Everyman. In Mountfort Faust goes down via suicide to inevitable destruction; in Lessing he goes up from disquiet into reassurance. In Lenz his desperation in the underworld can have no end; but Goethe's conclusion is that 'He who ever strives, him can we save' ('Wer immer strebend sich bemüht, / Den können wir erlösen').

Examining different treatments of the Faust legend before Goethe, we can see how it was constantly being reworked from different standpoints and towards different ends. The differing historical circumstances known to each author made his version reveal new possibilities of existence in this world under God; the versions are more or less convincing, depending on the way they give new form to received ideas. As regards literary form, Faust can change not only his tone but even his genre, from 'history' to drama (or puppet play) to novel; he can also change his position within the literary examination of human existence in this world, all the way from assured damnation to salvation. We can hardly say that Faust redeemed carries more literary conviction than the genuine, failed Faust: even what is known of Lessing's work cannot change that. This shows how bold was Goethe's decision to put him among the elect. At the end of Part II of Goethe's *Faust*, Gretchen, as one of the penitents (*una poenitentium*) – along with the sinful saints of medieval legend, the *magnae peccatrices* Mary Magdalene, Mary the Egyptian and the Samaritan woman – takes an active part in the salvation of Faust. The path from Judas to Gregorius is retrodden as we go from Dr Faustus to Goethe's Faust.[68]

CHAPTER 8

Bunyan, Günther, and 'Lenore'

In John Bunyan's autobiography, *Grace Abounding to the Chief of Sinners* (1666),[1] we read how for a whole year the Tempter obsessed him with the thought of selling his saviour as Judas had done. In the intense, relentless struggle with the temptation to 'Sell him, sell him, sell him, sell him' he is finally defeated: 'Oh, the diligence of Satan! Oh, the desperateness of man's heart! Now was the battle won, and down I fell, as a Bird that is shot from the top of a Tree, into great guilt and fearful despair.'[2] Through two unrepentant years he expected certain damnation, blasphemously doubting that he could still obtain grace after such a sin; then the words 'Christ's blood forgives all sin' brought him peace. But Christ's words concerning the sin against the holy ghost, for which there is no forgiveness, dragged him back into hopelessness. He would rather have been torn in pieces than fall from grace – than to be let fall by God – and yet such a preference was vain for Bunyan, who stood nearer to Judas than to other fallen sinners like David and Peter, who found forgiveness because they did not commit the one unforgivable sin: 'Whatever I now thought on, it was killing to me.'[3] He sought in vain for a hair's breadth of difference between his sin and the indelible sin of Judas, and could no longer pray 'because despair was swallowing me up. I thought I was as with the Tempest driven away from God, for always when I cried to God for mercy, this would come in, *'Tis too late; I am lost, God hath let me fall, not to my correction, but condemnation: My sin is unpardonable.'*[4] Bunyan repeatedly and inescapably takes to himself the judgement of the Letter to the Hebrews upon Esau, who had sold his birthright just as

Bunyan sold his God: 'For ye know how that afterward, when he would have inherited the blessing, he was rejected: for he found no place of repentance, though he sought it carefully with tears.'[5] Like a man on his way to execution, without help in thinking of all the great sinners who have been saved, looking round him but seeing no God following him to offer mercy, he is conscious only of rejection. Through the window he hears, amidst a rushing wind like a passing angel, this: 'Didst ever refuse to be justified by the Blood of Christ?' His denial breaks the spell and gives three or four days of peace – 'and then I began to mistrust, and to despair again'.[6] The tempter hinders his prayers ... after which the spiritual biography of the sinner settles into a torturing rhythm of repeated and often precipitous alternations between hope (in grace) and despair (of salvation), which lasts for years.

Judas despaired, and went and hanged himself. John Bunyan gives a heartfelt description of years of torment, a baroque chiaroscuro, dark despair illuminated by occasional hope. God spoke in the bible, but now is silent, while Satan and conscience talk incessantly, plunging the sinner into a dramatic and desperate struggle within his own soul: to make sense of the contradictions in what God *did* say. Bunyan's autobiogrpahy repeats and intertwines its leitmotifs like a great organ work, pursuing the heights and depths of a sinner's mind through the different registers, playing with masterly skill on the refined and satanic theology of the Tempter who builds up the sinner's hopes again and again, only to have God dash them down. Even in its moments of deepest emotion the spiritual control is there: this tale of the Elect who forsakes his God is one of the greatest ever treatments of the theme which Judas first gave to the world. Like a foundering ship he is tossed on a sea between hope and despair,[7] heading for wreck on the rocks of a salvation shown by God's work to be impossible: thus he endures the never-ending dialectic of God's contradictory pronouncements. In despair, he cries out against God's inexorable word; like an echo from God comes the reply, 'This sin is not unto death.' And he cries back like one risen from the dead: 'Lord, how canst thou find a word such as this?' God's pledge and

condemnation lie incomprehensibly side by side. Tossed about
all ways, now summoned, now spurned, the sinner goes
through bliss and through despair, and Satan quotes God to
him in contradiction of God. Now up, now down, bereft of
mercy, he reeives rest and peace without comprehension, and
uncomprehendingly sees them slip away once more. The
hideous alternation of vision and daylight, of elevation and fall,
assumes baroque proportions, but its emotion never strays into
histrionics. God's word does not alter. Whatever handhold the
sinner seeks, he cannot stop his swinging between judgement
and mercy. God's next word contradicts his last. In eighteen
scenes of the drama hope dies, blessings fade, promises turn
traitor, when the sinner remembers Esau: 'For ye know how
that afterward, when he would have inherited the blessing, he
was rejected: for he found no place of repentance, though he
sought it carefully with tears' (Hebrews 12:17). What can
break this inexorable rhythm? It is unexpectedly stilled by the
description of Christ 'who of God is made unto us wisdom, and
righteousness, and sanctification, and redemption' (1 Cor-
inthians 1:30). The sinner, in torment because he can forget
not one word of God, can cling to the memory of this one. He
feels his chains fall away. Peace, for which he hardly dared to
hope, is assured him through a vision of Christ. Grace comes as
a mystical surprise. 'Suddenly a voice came to my soul: thy
judgement is in the heavens.'[8] Grace breaks in, calm after
storm, and must show forth:

I never saw those heights and depths in grace, and love, and mercy,
as I saw after this temptation: great sins do draw out great grace; and
where guilt is most terrible and fierce, there the mercy of God in
Christ, when shewed to the Soul, appears most high and mighty.
When Job had passed thorow his captivity, 'he had twice as much as
he had had before', Job 42:10.[9]

Gregorius did penance for seventeen years upon the rock. Was
the long-drawn-out temptation, which Bunyan suffered after
committing in his heart the sin of Judas, in itself a penance?[10]
He speaks of no other. He tells us that of all books, excepting
the Bible, he found Luther's commentary on Galatians the
most full of genuine (as opposed to secondhand) truth about

life, the most full of hope for a wounded conscience. It speaks (he says) of the advent of temptations like blasphemy,[11] despair and so on, and shows how the law of Moses, as well as the devil, death and hell, have a lot to do with them: 'the which at first was very strange to me, but considering and watching, I found it so indeed'.[12]

In 1720 Johann Christian Günther fell from dire need into revolt, cursing the hour he was born, unable to forgive himself the sin of living as an unbeliever, and put into words the complaining sinner's rejection of grace:

> Ihr Lügner, die ihr noch dem Pöbel Nasen dreht,
> Von vieler Vorsicht schwatzt, des Höchsten Gnad erhebet,
> Dem Armen Trost versprecht und, wenn der Sünder fleht,
> Ihm Rettung, Rat und Kraft, ja, mit dem Maule gebet,
> Wo steckt denn nun der Gott, der helfen will und kann?
> Er nimmt ja, wie ihr sprecht, die gröbsten Sünder an:
> Ich will der gröbste sein, ich warte, schrei und leide;
> Wo bleibt denn auch sein Sohn? Wo ist der Geist der Ruh?
> Langt jenes Unschuldskleid und dieses Kraft nicht zu,
> Daß beider Liebe mich vor Gottes Zorn bekleide?
> Ha, blindes Fabelwerk, ich seh dein Larvenspiel.

You liars, still making fools of the common herd, chattering about taking care, extolling the grace of the Almighty, promising comfort to the poor, and giving the supplicant sinner salvation, council and strength – at least with your lips – where is this God hiding, who can and will help? You say he receives the worst of sinners: I will be the worst. I wait, cry out, suffer; so where is his Son now? Where is the Spirit of peace? Will his guiltlessness, the Spirit's strength, not suffice so that the love of Christ and the Spirit may clothe me against God's wrath? Alas, blind work of legend, I see through your mask.

His rejection of God, after an experience of futility which suffocates all patience, calm and effort, extends also to hell, 'about which Christian mouths have been lying for a thousand years' (wovon der Christen Mund / Schon über tausend Jahr den Leuten vorgelogen'). In his indignation, cursing God and man, he desires even to think himself out of existence ('Jetzt läg ich in der Ruh bei denen, die nicht sind', now I would rest among them who are not). But he is no rebellious Lucifer: the desire soon faints and falls. A man cannot escape his own experience if he – or his times – have no language to speak of trust, no words of repentance on their tongue. Lived, historical experience, remembered even beyond death, keeps its own shape, its own tongue, which speaks for those who can speak no more. The force of history, rather than of rhetoric, in the poem drives it towards the redemption of both rejection and curse:

> Verflucht sei Stell und Licht! – Ach, ewige Geduld,
> Was war das für ein Ruck von deinem Liebesschlage!
> Ach fahre weiter fort, damit die große Schuld
> Verzweiflungsvoller Angst mich nicht zu Boden schlage.
> Ach Jesu, sage selbst, weil ich nicht fähig bin,
> Die Beichte meiner Reu; ich weiß nicht mehr wohin
> Und sinke dir allein vor Ohnmacht in die Armen.
> Von außen quälet mich des Unglücks starke Flut,
> Von innen Schröcken, Furcht und aller Sünden Wut;
> Die Rettung ist allein mein Tod und dein Erbarmen.[13]

Cursed be this place, cursed the light! – Ah, eternal patience, how your loving onslaught pulls at me now! Ah, go on, that the great guilt of despairing fear strike me not to the earth. Ah Jesu, speak thou, for I cannot, the confession of my repentance; I no longer know where I should go, and fall fainting into thine arms alone. The strong tide of unhappiness torments me from without; from within, terror, fear and the rage of every sin; in my death and thy mercy alone is there salvation.

Some people believe that in the last extremity God will miraculously intervene, even in cases where his mercy 'would scarcely have come on it by itself'.[14] In the life of Saint Aegidius, heaven spares Charlemagne the necessity of confessing his sins out loud: this is done by proxy, and he is required merely to evince remorse before being forgiven.[15] So in Günther, the protagonist is unconscious and cannot confess his faith, but God does it for him, speaking to the despairing sinner the words which he cannot say for himself. The last word, and the boldest, in these seventy alexandrines is 'mercy': bold because it could not be spoken by this modern sinner's own efforts – but it saves him from the fate of Judas, who looked on his death with different eyes. But why does God receive this sinner who falls, trapped and fainting, into his arms because of a vague and unconvincing memory? 'I no longer know where I should go'! Even Nicolai Lesskow, writing in 1885, expressed himself worried by the uncomfortable question 'how to reconcile this whining of the soul with the precise requirements of Christian doctrine'.[16]

Isidore of Seville, in his 'sinner's lament', had given a model for this struggle to save a beleaguered soul from despair. It is echoed once again in *Lenore*, by Bürger, in which a mother strives to save her despairing daughter. It is not her sins that rob Lenore of all hope, but God taking her lover to Himself. 'God has no mercy', she says. Her mother answers, 'What God does, is well done.' 'Oh mother, mother', exclaims Lenore, 'that is a vain delusion!' Lenore rejects sacrament and salvation, casts aside her mother (who is contemplating, horror-struck, the torments of Hell), and sees only death:

> 'Der Tod ist mein Gewinn!
> O wär ich nie geboren!
> Lisch aus, mein Licht! auf ewig aus!
> Stirb hin! stirb hin! in Nacht und Graus!
> . . .
> So wütete Verzweifelung
> Ihr in Gehirn und Adern.
> Sie fuhr mit Gottes Fürsehung
> Vermessen fort zu hadern,
> Zerschlug den Busen und zerrang
> die Hand bis Sonnenuntergang . . .

'Death is my prize! Would I had never been born! Go out, my light! forever out! Die! Die! in night and horror! . . . So despair raged in her brain and her veins. Presumptuously she continued to struggle against God's providence, smote her breast and wrung her hands till sunset . . .

Her lover is the Grim Reaper. He leads her through night and horror to her bridal bed: 'Cool and narrow! six planks and two little boards! Dead souls, dancing on the graves, howl to her in her despair:

> Geduld! Geduld! Wenn's Herz auch bricht!
> Mit Gottes Allmacht hadre nicht!
> Des Leibes bist du ledig;
> Gott sei der Seele gnädig!

Patience, patience, though thy heart should break! Struggle not against God's almighty power! Thou art free of thy body; God have mercy on my soul!

That wish is but devilish mockery. Lenore is lost. She has lost God in her beloved:

> Ohn' ihn mag ich auf Erden,
> Mag dort nicht selig werden!

Without him I wish neither for happiness on earth nor for bliss elsewhere!

Often, as in Wolfram's *Willehalm*, human love leads to divine love. But a refusal of human love can lead to rejection of God. In despair a man may cling to suffering which turns pleasure in God and the world into a horror of them: his new love, not fully recognised at first, is Death. Victims, however innocent, of a failure of love (*Lenore*) or wrongful enjoyment of it (*Gregorius*) put the blame on God. Lenore is innocent, but she despairs, rebels against God, and damns herself irredeemably. Gregorius takes God's guiltiness, his complaisance, upon himself. He saves his mother from the worst, whereas the theologically inspired apprehension of Lenore's mother –

> Hilf Gott! hilf!
> Geh' nicht ins Gericht
> Mit deinem armen Kinde!
> Sie weiß nicht, was die Zunge spricht;
> Behalt ihr nicht die Sünde!

Help, God, help! Judge not thy poor child! She knows not what her tongue speaks: do not impute this sin to her!

– cannot prevail against her unbridled grief. The ballad genre goes down to destruction; hagiography gives a taste of salvation.

CHAPTER 9

Two novels by Thomas Mann: 'Doktor Faustus' and 'Der Erwählte'

Karl Kerényi, in conversation with Thomas Mann, once called the latter's *Doktor Faustus* a 'Christian novel'. Later Mann wrote to him that this had 'struck me and filled me with the satisfaction one gets from the truth'.[1] For Mann, the despair of Dr Faustus did not have the metaphysical conclusiveness of the fate of Judas – or not to the point that it could bear no kernel of hope. Speaking of 'Dr Faustus' lament', he wrote to Kerényi:

What amazing frivolity, what credulity, is it that makes us go on writing literature? For whom? What future is there in it? And yet a work of literature, even one of despair, must always have optimism, faith in life, as its basic substance – and this is particularly true when dealing with despair: it carries within itself the transcendence of hope.[2]

When in summer 1949 Mann told his friend about his work on his 'Gregorius' novel, Kerényi perceived in this '*manifestly* Christian theme' the 'development of a kernel which was thematically and organically contained within *Dr Faustus*'.[3] Kerényi eagerly anticipated '*the* sequel to *Dr Faustus*, whatever the "*redeemed sinner*" may be called and whatever historical form his "salvation" may take.'[4] Ten years later he retrospectively dubbed *Der Erwählte (The Holy Sinner)* the satyr play after the tragedy:

Der Erwählte restores the humanistic sense of balance, like the satyr play after the tragedy: it was virtually required from the beginning, for objective reasons to do with the innermost form of the narrative.[5]

And indeed the theme of *Der Erwählte* is foreshadowed long before in *Doktor Faustus*. In Adrian's great visionary dialogue with the devil, which seals the pact between them (chapter xxv), Adrian is easily induced to abandon the 'wholly out-dated' theology of repentance and conversion because he has already chosen a theologically new road to salvation based on presumptuous despair. Adrian would invert the old belief in despair as the one unforgivable sin and take it instead as 'the true theological way to salvation', a notion so bold that it alarms even the devil, who with true Christian clarity forbids him to espouse it. In this excerpt, 'I' is Adrian, the Stranger is 'He':

I Meanwhile I should warn you lest you feel all too certain of me. A certain shallowness in your theology might tempt you thereto. You rely on my pride preventing me from the *contritio* necessary to sal-vation, and do not bethink yourself that there is a prideful *contritio*. The remorse of Cain, for instance, who was of the firm persuasion that his sin was greater than could ever be forgiven him. The *contritio* without hope, as complete disbelief in the possibility of mercy and forgiveness, the rocklike firm conviction of the sinner that he has done too grossly for even the Everlasting Goodness to be able to forgive his sin – only that is the true *contritio*. I call your attention to the fact that it is the nighest to redemption, for Goodness the most irresistible of all. You will admit that the everyday sinner can be but very moder-ately interesting to Mercy. In his case the act of grace has but little impetus, it is but a feeble motion. Mediocrity, in fact, has no theo-logical status. A capacity for sin so healless that it makes its man despair from his heart of redemption – that is the true theological way to salvation.

He You are a sly dog! And where will the likes of you get the single-mindedness, the naive recklessness of despair, which would be the premise for this sinful way to salvation? Is it not plain to you that the conscious speculation on the charm which great guilt exercises on Goodness makes the act of mercy to the uttermost impossible to it?

I And yet only through this *non plus ultra* can the high prick of the dramatic-theological existence be arrived at; I mean the most aban-doned guilt and the last and most irresistible challenge to the Everlas-ting Goodness.

He Not bad. Of a truth ingenious. And now I will tell you that precisely heads of your sort comprise the population of hell. It is not so easy to get into hell, we should long have been suffering from lack of space if we let Philip and Cheyney in. But your theologian in grain, your arrant wily-pie who speculates on speculation because he has speculation in his blood already from the father's side – there must be foul work and he did not belong to the devil.[6]

Adrian makes a daring onslaught on the dogma of the sin against the holy ghost, an attempt to root his arrogant expectation of grace in despair: the most presumptuous possible form of *praesumptio*. But the devil uses orthodox Christian theology to refute his arguments – in order to bind Adrian more closely to himself. Such an extravagant speculation on grace will not pay off, says the devil – not for Adrian Leverkühn. In the theological tradition of the West, the two sins of *desperatio* and *praesumptio* have always been at opposite extremes, though since Augustine they have always been considered equally unforgivable. One is the theological despair of grace, the other its opposite, presumptuous expectation of grace: what Mann calls 'true *contritio*' and 'speculation' – a sinful calculation. It was Mann who first had the striking idea of merging them both into a single sin, the worst conceivable sin against the holy ghost, an unbeatable combination! The devil has to bring his 'contrite' victim, if not to his theological senses, at least to a realisation of how pointless it would be to try and *force* God to redeem, instead of repudiating, him. The devil fights on God's side, which is also his own: for the devil would lose the battle if he let God be forced into contradicting himself. The devil stands up for God, lest he himself lose the day.[7]

At the death of the angelic child, Echo, a death for which he admits responsibility, Adrian reaches a higher emotional level than we find in the puppet play of *Gregorius* (see p. 132 below). Echo's prayer for grace for Adrian dies along with him. Adrian bids him farewell in Prospero's words: 'Then to the elements! Be free, and fare thee well!' – recalling those other words of Prospero, 'And my ending is despair'.[8] Adrian Leverkühn's great public confession, in the hour of his death, acknowledges the fate which was sealed by his disputation with the devil. He dies in despair, forsaken of God, a composer of merely diabolical inspiration, knowing that his sands have run out:

My sin is greater than that it can be forgiven me, and I have raised it
to its height, for my head speculated that the contrite unbelief in the
possibility of Grace and pardon might be the most intriguing of all for
the Everlasting Goodness, where yet I see that such impudent calculation makes compassion impossible. Yet basing upon that I went
further in speculation and reckoned that this last depravity might be
the uttermost spur for Goodness to display its everlastingness. And so
then, that I carried on an atrocious competition with the Goodness
above, which were more inexhaustible, it or my speculation – so ye
see that I am damned, and there is no pity for me that I destroy all
and every beforehand by speculation.[9]

Though Adrian Leverkühn is a 'modern' character, in
damning his hero utterly Mann has gone back centuries before
Goethe to the viewpoint of the German folk book and Marlowe's late sixteenth-century *Dr Faustus*. As far as Adrian's art
is concerned, however, the question remains whether his devil-
inspired compositions – 'devil's work, infused by the angel of
death',[10] works springing from a life overshadowed by his pact
with the devil – may find grace even if their author cannot. Are
these works of art, forged by one fully aware of his sinfulness,
damned like the artist himself? In his dying confession Adrian
asks himself: 'with murder and lechery have I brought it to
fullness and perhaps through Grace good can come of what
was created in evil, I know not'.[11]

In this context it is significant that Mann should have chosen
to tell in advance, in the pages of *Dr Faustus*, the story of the
'holy sinner' Gregorius, which was to constitute the theological
counterpoint of Adrian's presumptuous expectation of grace.
It is in fact recounted in some detail,[12] being the 'absolute core'
of Leverkühn's musical adaptation of a series of tales from the
Gesta Romanorum for the puppet theatre. In true post-romantic
style, the work was to be 'art without agony', adapting the
medieval myths with an eye to the comic, the grotesque and
the lively with parody and irony, with 'jaunty intellectual
simplicity', eliciting from the audience a 'mingling of tears and
laughter'.

The intended effect was attained:

The meeting of the Queen with the holy man whom she had borne to
her brother, and whom she had embraced as spouse, charmed tears

from us such as had never filled our eyes, uniquely mingled of laughter and fantastic sensibility.[13]

The 'sensibility' comes from the free grace of a sort of Kleistian marionette, the innocence of a puppet untroubled by conscious thought. The close of Adrian's epoch seem to restore creativity; his parody seems to restore an absolute trust, as if it could indeed be recaptured without any diabolical pact. Through that pact – which he accepts out of despair at his own times and for the sake of his work, not of his own future life – Adrian takes the guilt of an age upon his own head. He hopes to break through to a second eating 'from the tree of knowledge in order to fall back into a state of innocence'.

This extensive treatment of Adrian's *Gregorius* puppet play involves some consideration of differing styles of speech to be adopted in the future: 'such anticipations and overlappings often occur in creative life'.[14] Although the immediate context rather diverges from such associations, it seems clear that Mann is cryptically playing on the fact that in *Dr Faustus* he is already looking creatively ahead to *Der Erwählte*, and that the subject and character of the latter are present embryonically in the former. Once, a puppet play of Faust provided the kernel from which a greater work was to spring. Just the same thing happens here, with the puppet play of Gregorius. *Dr Faustus* already stands in relation to *Der Erwählte* as does the tragedy to the satyr play. Mann called the latter a sequel to *Faustus*,[15] and after finishing it he wrote:

The kernel of the new usually lies in what goes before. So it is in *Faustus*: not only as regards the motif of grace (which is only sketchily treated here, but is exhaustively developed in *Der Erwählte*), but especially in the linguistic relationship. It lies where the baroque and Lutheran perspectives of the German novel reach down through the Swiss speech of the child Echo to the roots of Middle High German.[16]

It is impossible to over-emphasise the change of tone as saint's life gives way to novel, the medieval *Gregorius* to *Der Erwählte*.[17] Mann himself made no attempt to hide it. Hartman's poised, classical style, whose limitations are so seldom perceptible, is matched in *Der Erwählte* by Mann's stylistic experiment (*katexochen*).[18] Hartmann's verse, which gives all speeches the same elevated tone, is replaced by a prose which allows differentiation of character and rank. The change of genre allows Mann to abandon the earnest involvement of the saint's life for a series of formal and theological games, which he describes as if the story itself were of lesser importance. He descibes the tale as

an airy game; it is primarily, I admit, a linguistic entertainment, but not without a heartfelt commitment to the theme of redemption from the depths of sin.[19]

To a certain extent it is a continuation of *Faustus*. ... I am doing it with the same light-heartedness as when I finished *Joseph and his Brethren* and threw aside *The Commandments*. It is above all the comedy I'm after.[20]

What is still to come can only be an epilogue, a pastime, so don't expect too much of this tale of sin and grace, pious and comic all at once, which I'm working on in the mornings without too much urgency.[21]

It's a piece of pious grotesquerie, which makes me laugh a good deal; nevertheless it is all about *Grace*.[22]

I hope I may be excused my theological humorizing, which found itself as early as *Joseph* and has nothing sacrilegious about it. A German critic once wrote that in *Der Erwählte* I was 'teasing' God. Now, I had already been 'teasing' Goethe – why not almighty God as well? I am convinced that He has a sense of humour; otherwise He would never have given life to such a double-sided creature as an author or artist. I even tease Grace a little here and there, although I know and honour her and truly admire 'Thine alchemy'.[23]

Mann kept to this tone for many years when speaking of *Der Erwählte*. It recalls Goethe's description of *Faust Part II* as 'this very serious joke',[24] save for Goethe's sense of shame, which is largely absent from Mann's novel. In it we find no covert meaning, no gold hidden deep beneath the 'theological humour', challenging discovery. Written with a lighter touch than *Joseph* or *Dr Faustus*, *Der Erwählte* skates with fearless ease over the perilous lake of theological problematics.[25] Less solidly anchored in the real world than the great novels, without the ever-shifting religious and historical horizons of the *Joseph* cycle, *Der Erwählte* touches on many matters, but penetrates deeply into none.

In comparison with Hartmann's *Gregorius*, Mann's novel is insistently multifarious, full of charm and enjoyment. His discussion of sin soars high over the ground of theology: it shimmers through the many and various interruptions to the narrative in a 'wilful failure'[26] of the old, grave style. Satan and sin have their part in the deliberately old-fashioned language, which is awkward rather than comic, reminiscent of a historical novel. It is a merging of ancient and modern which is defamiliarised through the motif's apparent transfiguration of the medieval elements. What *Der Erwählte* repeatedly calls 'sin' is the very mark of election: 'Where the spot is, there is true nobility': the literal 'spot' which Gregorius' mother and her brother bear on their brows as a strange sign of their twin birth.[27] Cain bore a mark on his brow, sign of his immunity under the curse of fratricide.[28] So extraordinary is the sin that wonder at it mingles with repulsion. There is no devil, save for the 'boundless indifference' of Nature, who breaks her will on the guileless pair and drives them into their guilty union.[29] But this lack of a devil does nothing to rob the novel of its sting: for human sin is essentially this arrogant wish to rise above the common; this inequitable desire to love what is born equal to oneself; this exclusive striving towards self-transcendence through union with a person stamped with one's own mark of honour, whose hybrid pretentiousness provokes not only the world's favour but also the grace of God.[30]

Grace to the Elect is no free gift of God. The sinner takes the initiative and asks God for grace; God accepts the suggestion as His own and acts upon it. When Baduhenna wants a child, God is assailed with solemn masses, processions, prayers from the Archbishop, until at last He abandons his denials, hesitations and reservations – only to link his concession with a return demand. Baduhenna's child-bed becomes her deathbed. The Archbishop is 'unfavourably affected by the doubtful success which his pressure upon the Almighty had brought about'.[31] By forgiving, one can force God to make the next move. Gregorius goes in search of his parents 'until I find them and tell them that I forgive them. Then will God forgive them, probably He is only waiting for that'.[32] He is driven by the desire to 'pardon them his existence, that God might pardon them all three'.[33] If God does some spontaneous act of mercy, like producing miraculous milk on the rock, then the narrator 'will leave open the question whether a blessed chance obtained in this instance' or whether at this miraculous spring, mercy 'went so far that God himself had caused it to flow anew for Gregorius the sinner'.[34] Realising that he is in receipt of a grace 'which bordered on the arbitrary',[35] Gregorius, now pope, retains 'his bold way of enforcing the divine mercy, in cases where the Deity would scarcely have come on it by himself'.[36] God lets the pope guide His dispensation of grace, though Gregorius reputedly wants to 'pardon unpardonable sins'.[37] He even gets God to release the heathen emperor Trajan from hell, though with a warning:

and the story went that God had let him know, very well, now it had happened and the pagan was installed among the blest, but he would better not dare ask the like a second time.[38]

God's concern is not unfounded, for his Elect is well able to soothe Sibylla's anxiety for her brother's soul:

My father's soul? Woman, have you never heard that we succeeded in praying a pagan Emperor out of hell? Well then, no anxiousness . . .'.[39]

In *Der Erwählte*, the story of Trajan's liberation opens a series of *miracula* such as figure commonly at the conclusion of a saint's life. But Mann gives them an ironising twist in that all the wonders he recounts are not against nature, but against the dogmas defended by the church. It is as if God were being pushed from behind by a compulsion towards grace, which he has to preempt by forcing himself against himself to deeds which are not natural to him. Thus, when the barge bearing the sinful child of sin is set adrift on the sea, its case is almost hopeless, and Clemens has to admit:

I marvel at God's skill how He, when He will, knows how to steer it through dangers which he Himself has heaped up in its path. Verily, it gives occasion for the words to rise to the lips: *Nemo contra Deum nisi Deus ipse.*[40]

Now behold how God brought it to pass, and with the utmost dexterity contrived against Himself that the Lord Grimald's grandson, the child of the bad children, should come happily to shore in the cask.[41]

At the end God must act against himself: the very enormity of the abnormality, when it is weighed against God's grace,[42] tips the balance on grace's side by force of penance and confession:

Great and extreme, woman, is your sin, and to the very bottom you have confessed it to the Pope. This thoroughness to the uttermost is greater penance than when according to your sin-husband's arrangements you washed the feet of beggars.[43]

This extraordinary sinner drives God to equally extraordinary measures: he can calculate, if not with rash *praesumptio* then at least with some boldness, on the depth of his sins provoking a correspondingly and unbelievably high elevation to heaven:

But truly it is wise to divine in the sinner the chosen one, and wise that is too for the sinner himself. For the divining of his chosen state may make him worthy and his sinfulness fruitful so that it bears him up for high flights.[44]

The concluding maxims of the novel are focused on the sinner, not as God, as if requesting God himself to view the high flight of the sinner and acknowledge his own deed of mercy. Whither does he fly? We cannot tell. Mann uses the words 'election' and 'elect' (*Erwählte*), which give the novel its title, to denote Gregorius' elevation to the papacy and his calling by the Romans into the 'new Jerusalem', by which he always means Rome.[45] Only the penitent sees himself otherwise, as one 'whom God has chosen as the lowermost, uttermost sinner'.[46] Hartmann called mother and son 'two of the elect children of God' ('zwei uz erweltiu gotes kint'),[47] meaning that at the Last Judgement they would be elected to the eternal bliss of the redeemed. *Der Erwählte* gives us little more than an expectation of grace which is in part rash, in part (or so it is promised) legitimate: a grace whose 'holy alchemy' leaves it unclear where the 'gates of Paradise' really are.

God does have his little spark of belief in the novel, in the monastery 'Agony-of-God' (*Agonia Dei*)[48] on the island sheltered from travel and changes which

pass over the single man spun round in his own thoughts and are gone, so that, if I may so express my thought, world events do not take him with them, but leave him inexperienced and back in the former stage.[49]

Obviously there is more than meets the eye to the Abbot's pious explanation of the monastery's name, 'God made our sins into his own agony.'[50] God's agony comes from his need to fulfil what man has predetermined. It is not a pre-cast world history which is projected into God, but the human ego, fixated on its own extraordinariness, forcing God himself into the exceptional. That is why God's refuge in an island undisturbed by change, in an ever-changing world, is called *Agonia Dei*. It is refuge also for a sin which forces God, against himself, to grace in cases where he 'would scarcely have come upon it by himself'. Then both God and man must bear the sorrows of God, hear 'what the bell has tolled', if there is to be any thought of progress in God.[51] The name *Agonia Dei* seems to imply a sort of death. Mann said that the story of *Der Erwählte* 'is scarcely likely to be told again after me', and he added:

Since *Buddenbrooks* I seem fated to write 'last' books. And at times the whole of our best literature appears to me like a hasty recapitulation of western mythology, western culture in its last moments, before the curtain falls and all is forgotten.[52]

CHAPTER 10

Sophocles' 'King Oedipus' *and* 'Oedipus at Colonos'

Memory brings modesty and reassurance. It is necessary to culture, to an understanding of permanence in a changing world, to a possible persistence of the past in the present, a past whose influence lives on. The demands of memory are heavy. Rilke, seeing the Belvedere Torso: 'You must change your life.' Times which remember are creative; times which forget fall into excess. All myth is bound together, above all, by that most human of all constants, living with guilt. *Nil humani a me alienum puto.* It would be strange indeed if the damned and the elect did *not* march side by side through history. Adam, the Elect, was damned. The brothers Cain and Abel exhibit both possibilities. One last glance, now, towards Ancient Greece.

The relationship between Oedipus and Gregorius – both exposed as children, both marrying their mothers (and the Judas legend also parallels the patricide) – has often been pointed out, but is of no great significance. The sin of incest is a universal literary motif, and in the Middle Ages the tradition spared neither King Arthur nor Charlemagne. Motifs have no individual spiritual form: they are building blocks which have meaning only in the completed edifice. Incest, innocent or intentional, with mother or sister such as we find in our texts show how sin strikes at our innermost being, how darkness can break into light, how closely the devil observes our devilishness. Sophocles' tragedy and Hartmann's saint-legend are linked, over fifteen hundred years, by more than just a common motif. What counts in art, and in life, is not what happens – happens to a person – but what he makes of it. The world of happenings as such, ranging from the dreadful to the delightful, provides

an easily comprehensible stock of motifs. Every step, every
encounter, everything we read, every hour of history, brings us
experiences which we fail to register, because we cannot live
without a rigorous selection of the things that disturb and affect
us. Otherwise we would be permanently guilty, or sated. A
work of art is superior to life in that it gives us a ready-made
selection from the world of experience, and turns that selection,
along with its consequences, into the form of a human
potentiality which becomes part of the world's heritage. The
incest motif is semiotically neutral: trivial or terrible, gloomy or
lighthearted, crime or encouragement, privilege of the elect or
custom of the gods. What arouses interest is the reception of the
motif as experience, its extraordinary or exemplary power. We
see how the dark wave of fate nears a human shore, looms over
it and breaks on the resistance of moral identity: dashing in
spray against a rock, running over sand and green grass,
changing the lie of the land or bringing a cliff crashing in its
wake. What Oedipus and Gregorius have in common, as
against Judas, is not the incest itself, nor its preliminaries, nor
the inevitable consequences – in which the hero, after an initial
deed of shame like killing his father or sleeping with his sister,
goes on to act if not creditably, then at least with the best of
intentions and under the eyes of an ever-present God or gods –
perhaps even with their assistance. It is in his mastery of the
experience. Judas' story is in fact the closest to Oedipus': both
have an ill-omened oracle, both are exposed, grow up in a
strange land, quarrel with their brothers, kill their fathers and
marry their mothers. But when it comes to the question of
living with guilt, Judas diverges from Oedipus, for Judas'
solution is despair and suicide. It is in their search for self – the
evil exposed to the light of day – that Oedipus and Gregorius,
finding themselves other than they would wish, cast aside
appearances, assume their true identity, and live it. There is no
accusation, no acquittal, but they themselves acknowledge and
stand for what they are.

With one exception, all Karl Reinhardt's comments on the
end of *King Oedipus* apply also to Gregorius:

No judgement is decided here, no expiation: nothing could be more perverse than to see the blinding as an expiation. What we do have is an opposition of truth and seeming, with mankind bound and entangled between them: striving towards the heights of human potential, he is consumed and destroyed, in those fetters still.[1]

While Jocasta (like Judas) hangs herself, Oedipus blinds himself, renouncing light, not life. Oedipus, struck down by horror and his own curse, forsaken of God, goes forth from the horror and shame, from his kingship and from Thebes, to hide the hideousness of it all from himself, and himself from all who know of it. He withdraws into the darkness of years of exile. For years, also, Gregorius flees from the eyes of men, but not into hopeless darkness: on to the rock of his penance, where he will endure seventeen years until the hour of his election. Oedipus' blind wanderings must have lasted about as long: when he returns as an old man, his daughters Ismene and Antigone, children when he left, have grown up. It would be wrong to compare *Gregorius* only with *Oedipus the King*, as if there were no relationship save opposition between the accursed and forsaken pagan hero of antiquity and the medieval Christian who falls, repents and is raised up. By the will of the gods Oedipus, too, becomes one of the elect at his life's end. A full twenty years after *Oedipus the King*, shortly before his death at the age of ninety, Sophocles wrote *Oedipus at Colonos*. This shows us that the sequence of damnation and redemption fulfils an enduring human desire, from Antiquity through the Middle Ages to our own time, to see the hero who has been brought low, but accepted his fate, led back once more into the light. Let us consider the two Oedipus plays as a unity of this kind, and let our last view of our theme be directed at Sophocles' masterpiece in his old age.

Driven forth by his sons, led as a beggar in exile by his daughter's hand, Oedipus, old and frail, comes to Colonos, where at last he accepts his destiny and is comforted. Here, in the holy grove on a rocky hill outside Athens, is the end of his painful road. Here he dwells in peace until at last the mercy of the gods falls on him, and in an ecstatic miracle, releases him from suffering as from life. His daughters by his own mother are his blessing, the foreign grove his home; Theseus renews trust in him;[2] for an instant the light shines through his blindness:

> Sun, daylight, which has been no light
> To me, for years, I saw you once,
> I remember how good you were. And now
> I can still feel you, your life-giving warmth
> On my face, here, for the last time.
> Now I go down with faltering steps
> To the last darkness.[3]

His inner enlightenment shows him the blessing of the gods through the miracle of his death:

> Perhaps
> Some kindly ghost from the dark regions
> Silently opened, and silently took him
> With love, like a child to its bosom.
> One thing is certain. There were no tears,
> No cries of pain, or sound of suffering
> Of any kind. A stranger and more wonderful
> Death than any man has experienced before.
> Some of you won't believe me, I know.
> ...
> If that's what you think, that's your privilege.

The tragedy of *King Oedipus* is followed by *Oedipus at Colonos*, the drama of transfiguration. Oedipus ostracised becomes Oedipus the elect.[4] His departure from the holy place is a sacred mystery. The curse of Thebes, the suffering hero, in dying brings a blessing upon Athens. The protecting spirit of his grave shelters Athens, the place of his refuge and election, against Thebes, the place of catastrophe whence he came. The end of his life, after much suffering, miraculously transcends its beginning, leading out of fate into transfiguration. In the comfort of death lies reconciliation with life.

> *Chorus* The gods blessed his dying. Now he is gone,
> And you must make an end of weeping.
> Pain is the inheritance of every man.

Appendix: Unpublished *Life of Judas* from the Schaffhausen Lectionary

Some illustrations from this Middle High German text, dated 1330 (Schaffhausen, Stadtbibliothek MS Gen. 8, fols, 223^r – 224^v) are reproduced above as figs. 1–4. Here follows the text with accompanying translation. Obvious errors in the MS have been corrected; the MS readings are given in the notes. Abbreviations have been expanded and punctuation normalised. Capitalisation (except at the beginning of sentences) follows the MS. An edition of the MS is planned. On this MS see A. Stange, 'Eine osterreichische Handschrift von 1330 in Schaffhausen', *Jahrbuch der Kunsthistorischen Sammlungen in Wien* NF 6 (1932), pp. 55–76, especially figs. 66 and 67 from the Judas legend; see also p. 70, where O. Mausser pronounces the language to be Bavarian or Lower Austrian. The Krumauer Codex in the National Library of Vienna (cod. 370, painted post 1356), which contains a *Biblia pauperum*, saints' lives and parables and ends with the *Voyage of Brendan*, includes (fols. 102^v, top to 104^r, bottom) a cycle of pictures from the Judas legend, a page of which is illustrated in G. Schmidt, 'Der Codex 270 der Wiener Nationalbibliothek', *Wiener Jahrbuch für Kunstgeschichte* (1956), pp. 14–18, fig. 33.

Von Judas geslæhte vnd von seiner gepvrte vnd seinem leben und wie er gots iunger wart.

Man List, daz ze[1] Jerusalem ein man gesezzen was, der het zwen namen: Rubein vnd Symon. Der was des werden geslæhtes von Juda. Der selb Rubein het ein chonen, di hiez Cyborei. Und do si eines nahtes mit einander wonten nach Adams vnd Even gewonhait, dar nach entslief Cyborei vnd ir traumte gar

ein swærer traum. Des erchom si gar ser vnd sæufte gar pitter-
leich, wand manigem menschen sagt sein hertzze chünftigen
vngemach. Da von sprach si zu ir wirte Symon: Ich han in dem
traum gesehen, daz ich ein vnsæligez chint, einen sun gebern
sol, von dem allez vnser geslæhte, daz Jÿdisch volch, verlorn
wirt. Do sprach Symon zu ir: Du saist ein vnendhaftez mær,
des dv niht sagen soldest, vnd ich wæn, du menst dich wan-
sagen² an. Do sprach Cyborei: Ist, daz ich swanger pin
worden vnd daz ich einen svn gebier, so ist ez an zweifel war
vnd ist dehain wansagen da pei. Dar nach do di zeit irer
gebvrte chom, do gebar si winen svn. Do wurden sich vater vnd
mueter ser fürchtend vnd trahten vaste, waz si tæten, daz si
niht verturben von des chindes wegen. Doch mohten si ir chint
niht getôtten. Vnd doch di vorht, daz ir geslæhte verterben
solde, prahte sue dar zu, daz si daz chint in ein cystel legten
vnd legten die cystel mit dem chinde auf daz mer mit vil
wainen vnd chlagen, wand daz chind gar schon was. Do
chomen des meres ÿnden vnd sluegen di cystel, di was mit
peche wol vermachet, in ein Insel, di haizzet scarioth, vnd
nach der selben Insel haizzet er Judas scarioth. Nu was des
selben landes Chvniginne dvrich chürtzweil zdem mer
gegangen vnd sah daz di cystel auf dem mer hin vnd her
swanchte.³ Do hiez si irs pringen vnd hiez sie zehant aufpre-
chen. Do sah si daz chint in der cystel, daz was vnmazzen
schôn. Nu het si dehain chint vnd sæüfte vnmazzen ser vnd
sprach: Ach herre got, sold ich ein sogetan chint mir ze
fræüden haben, daz vnser Chvnichreich niht erblos wurde.
Vnd da von hiez⁴ di Chvniginne daz chint haimleich ziehen
vnd iah si wær swanger vnd iah dar nach, si hiet einen svn
geborn vnd der levnt wart mit fræüden über al daz Chvnichreich gepraittet. Des freüten sich des landes fvrsten mit der
gemain armer vnd reicher, vnd die Chvniginne hiez daz chint
nach chvnichleicher werdichait mit allem fleizze ziehen. Vnd
dar nach vber lang zeit do wart di Chvniginne swanger von
dem Chvnige vnd do des zeit was, do gebar si einen svn. Di
chinde wuechsen mit einander als zwai geswistrôd vnd spilten
ofte mit einander als chinde tuent. Doch tet Judas dem rehten
svn des Chvniges gar vil laides ze aller stvnt vnd machte in ofte

wainend. Daz was der Chv̆niginne lait, wand si wol weste, daz
Judas ir svn niht was, vnd slueg in ofte vmb sein müeleichait.
Daz half ot niht. Dannoch tet er des Chv̆niges svn vil laides.
Vnd doch zdem lesten do chom ez auf, daz Judas der Chv̆ni-
ginne svn niht was vnd daz er funden was. Do daz Judas
vernam, er schamt sich vnmazzen ser vnd vmb daz selb totte er
vnd mordet des Chv̆niges sun haimleich vnd floh mit ettleichen
levten hintz Jerusalem vnd habt sich in Pylati hof. Der was
zden zeiten Rihter ze Jerusalem, vnd wand ein isleich mensch
seins geleichen sich fræüt, also tet auch Pylatus, wand Judas
seins sinnes vnd poshait vol was, wart er in gar lieb habend,
vnd dar nach machte er in gar gewaltich v̆ber allen seinen hof
vnd swaz er wolde, daz geschah. Der nam Judas wart im von
der Chv̆niginne vor lieb gegeben, wand der nam zden zeiten
der werdist nam was pei den Juden vnder allen namen. Nu
fuegt sich eins tags, daz Pylatus in seinem palas was vnd sah in
einen paumgarten, da waren schôn epfel inne. Der wart in so
ser belangend, daz er nach vertorben was. Vnd der selb pavm-
garte was Rubeins, Judas vaters. Aber weder Judas chant
seinen vater, noch Rubein chande seinen svn. Auch weste
Judas niht, von wanne er chomen wær. So wande auch
Rubein, sein chint wær stunt in dem mer vertorben. Nu sande
Pylatus nah Judas vnd sprach: Mich ist gahens so grozz gyrde
vnd gelust nach den epfeln an chomen, vnd ob ich ir zehant
niht gewinne, so get mir rehte di sel auz. Zehant spranch Judas
pald in den pavmgarten vnd prach der epfel pald ab. In der
zeit do chom Rubein vnd Judas, daz er im sein epfel ab prach,
vnd wurden vaste mit einander chriegend mit red vnd mit
schelten, ainer den andern, vnd zdem lesten begraif Judas
einen stain vnd sluech Rubeinen geleich hinden auf daz hals
pain, daz er zehant tot was. Daz gestuend also vntz auf den
abend. Da wart Rubein toter funden in dem pavmgarten, vnd
man wande, daz er gæhes endes verschaiden wær, wand er ane
wunden was. Do gab Pylatus alles daz guet, daz Rubein
gehabt het, Judasn vnd betwanch di witiben, daz si Judasn ze
einem wirte nemen mueste. Vnd dar nach an einem tage, da
ersæüfte Cyborei gar herticleich. Da vragt sei Judas gar fleizz-
zichleich, waz ir gewurre. Do sprach Cyborei: Laider ich pin di

vnsæligist aller weibe, wand ich mein ainigez chint inz mer
gesancht han vnd han meinen wirt des gæhen endes vertorben
funden. So hat Pylatus mein lait nu gemeret vnd ain lait auf
daz ander gelæt, daz er mich laidigev vnd traurigev zu manne
gegeben hat an meinen danch. Do Judas daz vernam, er
begvnde sei von erste vmb daz chint vragen, vntz daz si imz
allez gæntzleich chvnt getet. Do sagt Judas ir auch allez daz im
widervarn was. Do erfunden si nach ir paider sag, daz Judas
sein mueter ze chonen het genomen vnd daz er seinen vater
ertõttet het. Do praht in Cyborei dar an, daz in sein sünde
rowen, vnd gie zu vnserm herrn Jhesu christo vnt pat in antlaz
aeiner sünde. Do nam in vnser herre an sich vnd machet in der
zwelif poten ainen. Do was er vnserm herren so gehaim vnd so
lieb, daz er im enpfalch in ze nemen, daz man in gab, vnd daz
übrig armen leÿten tailte. Er stal aber ze allen zeiten da von
vnd het verporgens hæüffel mit phenning hin vnd her. Auch
sagent ettleich schrift, daz er ein besunder reht het, swaz man
vnserm herren gab, des was der zehent phenninch sein. Vnd do
sand Marei Magdalen vnsern herren mit der edeln vnd tewern
salben salbte, di wær wol dreier hvndert phenning wert
gewesen, da wærn in dreizzich phenning an gevallen, wær di
salb verchauffet. Vmb den selben geitigen neit verchaufte er
vnsern herren vmb dreizzich phenning, daz er also der dreizzich phenning zue chom.

Nu merchet, wie die selben dreizzich phenning her sein
chomen.[5] Ez sint di dreizzich phenning, da Joseph von seinen
prüedern, herrn Jacobs sünen, vmb verchauft wart in
Egypten lant, vnd sint auch immer mer enther in rehter
erbschaft vil tausent Jar vntz an di Jvden, di vnsern herren
vmb die selben phenning von Jvdasn chauften, vnd sint der
münzz von Ismahel, vnd ie ainer ist als guet als zehen gem-
ainer phenning. Vnd ze gleicher weis als Joseph gewaltich
wart alles landes in Egypten lande, da man wande, daz er
vertorben wær, also wart vnser herre nach seiner marter
gewaltich himels vnd erdreichs, do di Juden wandem, daz er
tot solde sein.

Of Judas' race and his birth and his life and how he became a disciple of God.

Know that in Jerusalem there lived a man who had two names, Reuben and Symon. Reuben was of Judas' lineage. This same Reuben had a wife called Cyborei. And as one night they dwelt together as did Adam and Eve, after that Cyborei fell asleep and dreamed a terrible dream. She was very frightened at it and sighed most bitterly, as when someone's heart speaks to him of future horrors. She spoke of it to her husband Symon: 'I saw in my dream that I must bear an accursed child, a son, through whom all our race, the Jewish folk, shall be lost.' Then said Symon to her: 'You speak of an endless evil, which you should not have spoken of, and I think you are saying a foolish thing.' Then spoke Cyborei: 'If I am with child and bear a son, then surely it will come true and it is you who speak foolishly.' And when her time came, she bore a son. Then the father and mother were very frightened and wondered what they should do, so that they might not be destroyed because of the child. Yet they did not wish to slay their child. And yet the fear that he would destroy their race drove them to lay the child in a chest and lay the chest with the child upon the sea with much weeping and lamenting, for the child was very fair. Then came the sea-waves and drove the chest, which was well sealed with pitch, to an island which was called Scarioth, and after this same island he was called Judas Scarioth. Now the queen of that same land had just come to the sea and saw the chest tossing to and fro on the sea. Then she had it caught and unsealed. There she saw the child in the chest, and it was immeasurably beautiful. She had no child: she sighed immeasurably and said: 'Ah lord God, I should have such a child to my joy, so that our kingdom be not heirless.' And thereupon the queen had the child brought in secretly and gave out that she was with child and after this, that she had borne a son and the news was broadcast over the kingdom with great joy. The nobles of the land rejoiced and so did all, rich and poor, and the queen had the child reared as a king's son with all care. Not long after this the queen was with child by the king and in due time she bore a son. The children grew up together as two brothers and often played with each other as children do. But Judas did much hurt to the king's real son all the time and often made him cry. Then the queen was sorry, for she knew that Judas was not her son, and she often beat him for his naughtiness. But it did no good. He still hurt the king's son very much. And at the last it came out that Judas was not the queen's son and that he was a foundling. When Judas learned this, he was immeasurably ashamed and because of that same thing he slew and murdered the king's son in secret and fled in great haste to Jerusalem and went to Pilate's court. At that time he was ruler of Jerusalem, and because every man is always glad to find another like himself, so was Pilate: because Judas was of like mind with him and full of evil, he took to him greatly, and thereafter made him very powerful over all his court, and whatever he desired, so it came about. The name Judas had been given to him in love by the queen, and at that time this name was honoured among the Jews above every other name. It happened one day that Pilate was in his palace and saw an orchard, in which were beautiful apples. He desired them so greatly that he nearly died of it. And that same orchard belonged to Reuben, Judas' father. But Judas did not know his father, nor did Reuben know his son. Nor did Judas know whence he came. So Reuben also thought that his son was long since drowned in the sea. Now Pilate sent for Judas and said: 'I have so great a desire and lust for these apples that if I do not win them soon, my soul will soon leave my body.' So Judas went soon to the orchard and plucked the apples. At that time Reuben came and found Judas plucking his apples, and they attacked each other with words and with blows, one to the other, and at last Judas seized a stone and smote Reuben right on the back of his neck, so that he fell dead on the spot. That happened in the evening. So Reuben was found dead in the orchard, and people thought that he had come to a sudden end, because he had no wound. Then Pilate gave all the possessions that had been Reuben's to Judas and forced the widow to take Judas as her husband. And after that one day, Cyborei sighed most heartily. Then Judas asked her most courteously what grieved her. Then said Cyborei: 'Alas, I am the unhappiest of women, for I cast away my own son on the sea and have found my husband destroyed by a sudden death. So now Pilate has increased my grief and piled one grief upon another, for he has given me grief and sorrow as my husband, as I think.' When Judas heard this, he began first to ask her about the child, and she told him everything that had happened. Then Judas also told her all that had happened to him. And from what both had said they realised that Judas had taken his mother to wife and killed his father. Then Cyborei brought him to repent of his sins and go to our lord Jesus Christ and ask of him forgiveness for his sins. Then our lord took him and made him one of the twelve apostles. Then he was so close with our lord and so dear to him that he allowed him to receive whatever anyone gave him, and share it out among the other poor folk. But he was always stealing from it and hiding the money, a penny here, a penny there. Some writings also say that he had a special right, that whatever anyone gave to our lord, every tenth penny was his. And then Mary Magdalene anointed our lord with the noble and precious ointment, which would have been worth at least three hundred pence, and out of that thirty pence would have come to him, if the ointment had been sold. By that same greedy treachery he sold our lord for thirty pence, so that he got the thirty pence in any case.

Now mark, how these same thirty pence came about. They were the thirty pence for which Joseph was sold by his brothers, lord Jacob's sons, in the land of Egypt, and thereafter they had been preserved as a true inheritance for many thousand years among the Jews, who bought our lord for those same pence from Judas, and they are the coins of Ishmael, and every one of them is worth ten ordinary pence. And just as Joseph gained power over all the land of Egypt, when people thought that he was dead, so our lord after his passion had power over the kingdoms of earth and heaven, when the Jews believed that he was dead.

Notes

1. JUDAS AND GREGORIUS

1 This study builds on some research published in 1974 under the title 'Desperatio und Praesumptio, Zur theologischen Verzweiflung und Vermessenheit', in *Festgabe für O. Höfler zum 75. Geburtstag*, ed. H. Birkhan, Philologica Germanica 3 (Vienna, 1976), pp. 501–58. This article pursues the theme from patristic texts as far as the early Middle Ages and should be assumed as a prologue to the present study. No further detailed references will be made.

2 H. Kuhn, 'Parzifal. Ein Versuch über Mythos, Glaube und Dichtung im Mittelalter', in *Dichtung und Welt im Mittelalter* (Stuttgart, 1959), pp. 151–80 (p. 172): 'Even in Hartmann's *Gregorius*, which is so deliberately contrasted to the Arthurian poems, no one has yet been able to point to a motivating sin recognized by contemporary or modern theology. There may indeed be some cruel fate at work (*vil stark ze hoerenne*, 'most terrible to hear', line 53), but no sin: Gregorius' heredity, his flight from the monastery, his unintentional incest, his anger against God, are not sins. For in each case the author specifically denies the hero's responsibility. All Chrétien's and Hartmann's works centre on unconscious guilt. It cannot and should not be accounted as a sin. Rather it leads the knight to reject his own not-guiltiness, cease to rely on self-interested deeds and services and, through disinterested service, find beyond himself the lasting *unio* which comes of love.' See also J. Schwietering, 'Parzivals Schuld', in *Philologische Schriften*, ed. F. Ohly and M. Wehrli (Munich, 1969), pp. 362–84 (p. 374): 'Sin is not only a willed action, it is a power which works from generation to generation and creates a state of sin. Parzifal learns of this power of sin, which pervades the whole of life and is an ever-present threat, through his unconscious sin rather than through gross and deliberate errors.'

3 K. Ruh, 'Hartmanns "Armer Heinrich". Erzählmodell und theo-

logische Implikation', in *Mediaevalia litteraria. Festschrift für H. de Boor* (Munich, 1971), pp. 315–29 (p. 328), on acceptance of guilt and suffering as stages in Heinrich's spiritual journey: 'The acceptance of guilt is Hartmann's own addition ... It means an existential consciousness of guilt found in all Hartmann's characters, Erec and Iwein and the "good sinner" Gregorius. What matters is *that* the guilt is accepted, not whether an actual sin has been committed.'

4 'Bemerkungen zu dem Roman *Der Erwählte*', *Gesammelte Werke* XI (1960), p. 688.

5 Thus we are not discussing the question of guilt in *Gregorius* here. For a survey of nearly forty studies of the problem of guilt in *Gregorius* over twenty-two years see Elisabeth Gössmann, 'Typus der Heilsgeschichte oder Opfer morbider Gesellschaftsordnung? Ein Forschungsbericht zum Schuldproblem in Hartmanns *Gregorius*', *Euphorion* 68 (1974), pp. 42–80. A later study is D. K. Goebel, *Untersuchungen zu Aufbau und Schuldproblem in Hartmanns Gregorius*, Philologische Studien und Quellen 78 (Berlin, 1974).

The idea that *Gregorius* is concerned not with incurring guilt but with living with it has been making slow headway in the last ten years. Neither Gregorius nor his mother is aware of any personal sin, 'and yet they both expressly and spontaneously account the sin of incest as a proof of their own deep depravity ... Hartmann sees Gregorius' objective sin as representative of all human sin. His theme is not the psychological explanation of sin, but the polarity of unusual, profound entanglement and the omnipotent, incomprehensible grace of God.' W. Dittman, *Hartmanns Gregorius. Untersuchungen zur Überlieferung, zum Aufbau und Gehalt*, Philologische Studien und Quellen 32 (Berlin, 1966), p. 241. C. Cormeau, *Hartmanns von Aue Arme Heinrich und Gregorius. Studien zur Interpretation mit dem Blick auf die Theologie zur Zeit Hartmann*, Münchener Texte und Untersuchungen 15 (Munich, 1966), p. 143: 'From his youth up, Gregorius fights against the shadows which evil has cast over him. With the best will in the world and without incurring the responsibility for any sin, he falls into a fearful entanglement. He resolves the agonising tension between subjective guiltlessness and objective sin by assuming the unwilled guilt and doing a harsh penance for it. Thereby he rejects any calculation of his own deserts and delivers himself unreservedly to the mercy of God. God's grace and election come in abundant response to this absolute surrender. ... The religious message of the work is that we should cease to rely on our own powers and accept our need of grace: God's election is gracious, always unearned, and immeasurable.' For Arnold, abbot of the Benedictine house in Lübeck, who translated Hartmann's poem into Latin in about 1210, the theme was not the theology of sin, 'not the "how" of sin, but the way that Gregorius behaves as peccator praecipuus': P. F. Ganz, 'Dienstmann und Abt. "Gregorius Peccator" bei Hartmann von Aue und Arnold von Lübeck', in *Kritische Bewahrung. Beiträge zur deutschen Philologie. Festschrift W. Schroder zum Geburtstag* (Berlin, 1974), pp. 250–75 (p. 274).

6 The modern title, 'Gregorius on the stone' (i.e. the stone of penitence) is a striking echo of the older *La vie d'un bon pecheur* (The life of a good sinner: so in A1 and B1, line 2) or *Maere von den guoten sundaere* (Legend of the good sinner), lines 175–6. On the relationship between the Old French and Middle High German texts see H. Schottmann, '*Gregorius* und *Grégoire*', in *Hartmann von Aue*, ed. H. Kuhn and C. Cormeau, Wege der Forschung 359 (Darmstadt, 1973), pp. 73–407. German text in *Gregorius von Hartmann von Aue*, ed. H. Paul, 12th edn revised by L. Wolff, Altdeutsche Textbibliothek 2 (Tübingen, 1973).

7 Gregory the Great, *Moralia* IX.9.12, Patrologia Latina 75, p. 959 col. B, on Job 12:14, 'si incluserit hominem, nullus est qui aperiat' ('he shutteth up a man, and there can be no opening'). 'Quia omnis homo per id quod male agit, quid sibi aliud quam conscientiae suae carcerem facit, ut hunc animi reatus premat, etiamsi nemo exterius accuset?' (For does not every man, through the evil he does, make nothing other than a prison out of his own conscience, so that an awareness of guilt oppresses him even if no one outside accuses him?)

8 Hartmann von Aue warns against sinful trust in youth and putting off penitence until old age:

> du bist doch ein junger man,
> aller dîner missetât
> der wirt noch vil guot rât:
> dû gebüezest si in dem alter wol.

> (lines 12–15)

You are still a young man: your sins can be well taken care of, you can repent of them in your old age.

Cf. Hans Sachs, *Ein comedi von dem reichen sterbenden Menschen, der Hecastus genannt*, ed. A. von Keller, *Werke* vol. 6 (Stuttgart, 1872, reprint Hildesheim, 1964), p. 147. Death's messenger is told:

> Wir aber sind noch frisch und jung.
> Im later ist die buss noch gnung,
> Wenn wir streichen zu dem end.

> Wann ich bin noch ein junger mann.
> Aber wenn ich kom in das alter,
> Wirt ich ein bussfertig hausshalter.
> Des ich über viel jar wol kum.

But we are still fresh and young. Penitence is suited to old age, when we are hastening to our end. Now I am still a young man. But when I grow old, I'll be a respectable penitent. I hope I'll live for many years.

9 Lines 309–52.
10 Lines 150ff.
11 Line 579.
12 Lines 604–5.
13 Line 898.
14 Lines 738–9. There is a fragment of a strophic narrative poem in Latin in which a king of Spain has a son by incest with his daughter and orders him to be killed at birth; in her motherly love, the daughter wraps it in a purple cloth when she lays it in the cask in which it is to be cast adrift. See P. Dronke, *Medieval Latin and the Rise of the European Love-Lyric*, vol. 2 (Oxford, 1966), pp. 520–3, with note on related motifs.
15 Lines 763ff.
16 Line 1285.
17 Lines 1289–90.
18 Line 1403.
19 Lines 1780ff.
20 Line 1820ff. On the search for identity in *Gregorius* see my 'Die Suche in Dichtungen des Mittelalters', *Zeitschrift für deutsches Altertum* 94 (1965), pp. 171–84. M. Wehrli has studied the analogous question of the meaning of true identity, hidden by appearances, in the face of the 'threatening incomprehensibility of human existence', in relation to 'one of the boldest conceptions' of it: Philemon in the mystery play. See his edition and translation of Jacob Bidermann's *Philemon Martyr* (Cologne/Olten, 1960), pp. 327–8.
21 Lines 1935ff.
22 The Abbot predicts Gregorius' sins during his life as a knight: 'plus te peccatum aggrauat, et culpa culpam cumulat' (sin weighs thee down yet more, and heaps misdeed on misdeed, II, 953ff.).
23 Line 2241.
24 Lines 2169–70.
25 Lines 2241ff.
26 Lines 2290–1.
27 Lines 2482–98.

28 Lines 2608ff.

29 Lines 2623ff.

30 Is his *truren* (sorrow, the sin of *tristitia*) when Saul, Jonathan and Absolom, the son who betrayed him, lie slain, the same as Judas' sin of suicide, the sin against the Holy Ghost? Not so F. Neumann: Hartman von Aue. *Gregorius. Der 'gute Sünder'* (edn and commentary), Deutsche Klassiker des Mittelalters NF 2 (Wiesbaden, 3rd edn 1968), p. 227. Arnold of Lübeck does not mention Judas at this point:

> Non credo, quod sic doluit
> dauid cum planctum fecerit
> super saulem et ionathan
> et doluisse forsitan
> multo minus tunc creditur
> quando a casu cognoscitur
> absolonis interitus
> qui vir erat pulcherrimus,
> ut testatur veridica
> regum nobis hystoria
> qui domini iudicio
> interijt suspendio.
> Quid istis quam mors dulcius
> si immineret gladius
> persequentis officio
> *nec erat desperatio*
> *sed cordium contritio.*

(ii, 382–98)

I do not believe that David grieved thus when he made his lament over Saul and Jonathan, and perhaps it is thought that he grieved much less when he heard from Cushi of Absolom's death, who was the fairest of men, as the Book of Kings truly tells us, and who died strangled by the judgement of God. What was sweeter to these two than death, if the sword menaced them through the zeal of their pursuer? Nor was it despair, but contrition of heart.

Here Arnold recalls Absolom, the traitor hanged on a tree, who with Achitophel is the commonest prefiguration of Judas. Cain and Judas, as prototypes of despair, are mentioned (as a warning) only in the epilogue:

> Iam absit desperatio
> cayn nec non confessio
> iude, qui non penituit
> dum laqueo interiit.

Now save us from the despair of Cain and the confession of Judas, who repented not, even when he died in the noose.

The legend of Vergogna, which is closely related to that of Gregorius, also warns against despair, with reference to Mary Magdalena and other holy sinners, once when the daughter is with child by her father, and again when the mother is about to marry the son born of this incest. See A. d'Ancona, *La leggenda di Vergogna, testi del buon secolo in prosa e in verso, e la Leggenda de Giuda, testo italiano antico in prosa e in francese antico in verso* (Bologna, 1869); R. Köhler, in *Jahrbuch für Romanische und Englische Literatur* 11 (1870), pp. 313–24 (314, 316).

31 Lines 2667–80.

32 Line 2685.

33 Lines 3925ff.

34 Lines 3953–4. The elect children of God in the epilogue to the *Rolandslied* are Duke Henry and his wife, who are destined for eternal bliss and were led forth from the world 'unter allen erwelten gotes kinden, / da si di ewigen mandunge uinden' (among all the elect children of God, for they followed his everlasting joys, lines 9029–30).

35 Lines 1526–7.

36 W. Dittmann, *Hartmanns Gregorius. Untersuchungen zur Überlieferung, zum Aufbau und Gehalt*, Philologische Studien und Quellen 32 (Berlin, 1966), p. 181, speaks of 'Hartmann's determined excision of the priest, and hence the confession, from his tale of the good sinner' and so removes the work from any discussion of Hartmann's stance on penitential theology.

37 H. J. Schmitz, *Die Bußbücher*, vol. 1, *Die Bußbücher und die Bußdisziplin der Kirche* (Mainz, 1883), pp. 274, 404, 429, 448, 527, 576, 623, 693, 826; vol. 2, *Die Bußbücher und das kanonische Bußverfahren* (Düsseldorf, 1898), pp. 183, 223, 342, 499, 547, 613, 618, 655, 664, 686.

38 Schmitz, *Die Bußbücher*, 1, pp. 357ff., 657; 11, p. 180.

39 Ibid., 1, p. 787:18: 'Qui peccat cum commatre de Domino Jesu Christo sive de sancto Johanne aut cum sanctimoniali, xvii annos peniteat' (Whoever sins with his godmother in the Lord Jesus Christ or in Saint John or with a nun, he shall do seventeen years' penance'); 19: 'Qui peccat cum propria matre aut cum uxore patris sui, similiter peniteat' (Whoever sins with his own mother or with his father's wife, shall do the same penance); 20: 'Qui peccat cum sorore aut consobrina aut uxore germani sui, xv annos peniteat' (Whoever sins with his sister or cousin or his brother's wife, shall do fifteen years' penance).

40 Augustine, *Enarrationes in Psalmos*, Corpus Christianorum, Series Latina 40 (Turnholt, 1956), p. 2192, on psalm 150, 1, 58–70,

points out the total number of psalms and adds, 'Unde et hac causa non inconuenienter intellegimus istum numerum esse psalmorum. Nam et in illo numero piscium qui capti sunt retibus post resurrectionem missis, ad centum quinquaginta additis tribus, uelut admonitio uidetur facta, in quot partes debeat iste numerus dispertiri, ut ter habeatur quinquagentos. Quamquam ille numerus piscium habeat et aliam rationem multo subtiliorem et iucundiorem, quod decem et septem in trigonum missis, id est, ab uno usque ad decem et septem onnibus computatis, ad eumdem numerum peruenitur. In decem autem lex, in septem uero gratia significatur; quia legem non implet, nisi caritas diffusa in cordibus nostris per Spiritum sanctum, qui septenario numero significatur.' (Whence, for this reason also, we understand that this number of psalms is not unfitting. For in that number of fishes which were caught in the nets cast after the Resurrection, three added to one hundred and fifty, there seems to have been an indication of how many parts that number should be divided into, so that it gives three times fifty. Although that number of fishes also has another much subtler and more cheerful reason, because seventeen set out in a triangle, that is, all the numbers from one to seventeen added together, comes to the same number. In the ten the law is signified, in the seven, grace; for nothing fulfils the law save charity infused into our hearts by the Holy Spirit, which is signified by the number seven.) On the number 153 see H. Meyer, *Die Zahlenallegorese im Mittelalter. Methode und Gebrauch*, Münstersche Mittelalter-Schriften 25 (Munich, 1975), pp. 184ff.

41 E. Auerbach, *Mimesis*, tr. W. R. Trask (Princeton, NJ, 1953), p. 111.

42 *Patrologia Latina*, vol. 172, p. 1075D: 'Septimo decimo ponit beatos parvulos filiae Babylonis tenentes et ad petram allidentes. *Beatus*, inquit, *qui tenebit et allidet parvulos tuos ad petram* (Ps. 136, 9). Parvuli filiae Babylonis sunt suggestiones carnalis delectationis. Hos ad petram allidunt qui ob Christi passionem carnalia respuunt. Hii cum de Babylonia hinc ad Hierusalem remeabunt, ymnum de canticis Syon in aeternum cantabunt.' (He says that seventeen was the number of the happy ones who took the little ones of the daughter of Babylon and dashed them against the stone. 'Happy,' he says, 'shall he be, that taketh and dasheth thy little ones against the stones' [Psalm 137:9]. The little ones of the daughter of Babylon are the urgings of fleshly enjoyment. They who spurn the flesh for Christ's sake will dash them against the stone. They who return from Babylon hither to Jerusalem shall

sing the songs of Sion forever.) Joseph was seventeen when he was sold to Potiphar in Egypt: Genesis 37:2, 37:36.

43 F. Tschirch, '17–34–153. Der heilsgeschichtliche Symbolgrund im *Gregorius* Hartmanns von Aue', in *Formwandel. Festschrift für Paul Böckmann* (Hamburg, 1964), pp. 27–46; on the number 153, pp. 38ff.

44 Ibid., p. 40. In his fifth letter, Abelard says that God's grace fished him and Heliose out of the sea of sin with the net of mercy, and says that this is an exemplary consolation for those who have despaired of God's goodness. In the *Historia calamitatum*, 'the past is understood as sin, thought of as fated; the future is understood as election to God's grace. Thereafter two parallel tracks go through the *Historia calamitatum* itself: one shows the workings of Fortune in external events to be a *tragoedia* for the sinner; the other reveals God's working of salvation as an invisible *consolatio* to the repentant and elect ... The deserved downfall of the *elatus* turns into the loftier victory of the *humiliatus*.' P. von Moos, 'Cornelia und Heloise', *Latomus* 34 (1975), pp. 1024–59 (p. 1052 and note 84).

45 Schmitz, *Die Bußbücher*, I, p. 274: 'Incesti poenam, quae in viro in insulam deportatio est' (The punishment of incest, which for the man is exile to an island).

46 Ibid., I, pp. 274–5 (and cf. p. 527): 'The original meaning of *peregrinus* was exile; only in the sixth century did it come to mean a religious pilgrimage to an unspecified goal, and later, pilgrimage to one of the three most famous destinations ... *peregrinare* was the punishment for certain sexual offences.' Alain de Lille's *Liber Poenitentialis* (*c.* 1200) prescribes, for incest with one's mother, thirty years' penance on bread and water, exile and *peregrinatio* with no more than one night to be spent under the same roof. The penitent must spend the rest of his life in a foreign monastery. Ed. J. Longère, vol. 2, Analecta Medievalia Namurcensia 18 (Louvain/Lille, 1965), chap. II, 129, p. 112. Burkhard of Worms' *Decretum* (*Patrologia Latina* 140, chap. XIX, 5, p. 966) prescribes a lighter penance: 'Fecisti fornicationem cum matre tua? Si fecisti, xv annos per legitimas ferias poeniteas: unum ex his in pane et aqua, et absque spe conjugii permaneas, et numquam sis sine poenitentia. Mater autem tua, si consentiens non fuit, juxta arbitrium sacerdotis poeniteat: et si se continere non vult, nubat in Domino.' (Hast thou committed fornication with thy mother? If thou hast, thou shalt do penance for fifteen years duly reckoned, one of them on bread and water; and thou shalt remain without hope of marriage, and shalt never be without penance. As

for thy mother, if she was not consenting, she shall do penance as the priest shall see fit; and if she will not be continent, she should marry in the Lord.)

47 E. Dorn, *Der sündige Heilige in der Legende des Mittelalters*, Medium Aevum 10 (Munich, 1967), pp. 84ff.

48 Karin Morvay, *Die Albanuslegende. Lateinische und deutsche Texte. Untersuchungen*, Medium Aevum 32 (Munich, 1976): 'Nobis igitur ... Albani vita proponitur prosequenda, cuius exemplis instructa, cuius praesidiis animata, mens nostra nec de viribus praesumere propriis, nec de clementia diffidere audeat Redemptoris' (Thus ... the life of Alban brought before us as an example; our minds, instructed by his example and encouraged by his trials, should not doubt either to presume on their own strength or to distrust the mercy of our Redeemer).

49 Ibid., lines 886ff.

50 Ibid.

51 G. von Buchwald, ed., *Gregorius peccator* (Kiel, 1886), vol. 4, lines 1203–14.

52 The following are the most important items in the abundant critical literature on the apocryphal life of Judas. They contain numerous additional references: W. Creizenach, 'Judas Ischariot in Legende und Sage des Mittelalters', *Beiträge zur Geschichte der deutschen Sprache und Literatur* 2 (1876), pp. 77–207; V. Istrin, 'Die griechische Version der Judaslegende', *Archiv für slavische Philologie* 20 (1898), pp. 605–19; E. K. Rand, 'Medieval Lives of Judas Iscariot', in *Anniversary Papers by Colleagues and Pupils of George Lymen Kittredge* (Boston, 1913), pp. 305–16; P. F. Baum, 'The Medieval Legend of Judas Iscariot', *Publications of the Modern Language Association of America* 31 (1916), pp. 481–632. R. Foulché-Delbosc, 'La legende de Judas-Iscariote', *Revue Hispanique* 36 (1916), pp. 135–49, is an edition of a Spanish life of Judas from the cradle to the grave, dating from 1450–1550, which has some substantial and unique additions. A. Büchner, *Judas Ishcarioth in der deutschen Dichtung* (Freiburg, 1920); P. Lehmann, 'Judas Ischariot, in der lateinischen Legendenüberlieferung des Mittelalters, *Studi Medievali*, new series 3 (1920), pp. 289–346 (also in his *Erforschung des Mittelalters. Ausgewählte Abhandlungen und Aufsätze*, vol. 2 (Stuttgart, 1959), pp. 229–85; quotations from this edition); L. Kretzenbacher, '"Verkauft um dreißig Silberlinge." Apokryphen und Legenden um den Judasverrat', *Schweizerisches Archiv für Volkskunde* 57 (1961), pp. 1–17; K. Lüthi, *Judas Iskarioth in der Geschichte der Auslegung von der Reformation bis zur Gegenwart*, dissertation, Basel 1953 (Zürich, 1955). On Judas

in modern literature see Elisabeth Frenzel, *Stoffe der Weltliteratur. Ein Lexikon dichtungsgeschichtlicher Längsschnitte* (Stuttgart, 1962), pp. 323ff. I have not been able to consult A. Megas, 'Judas in den Volksüberlieferungen', *Jahrbuch des Volkskundlichen Archivs* 3/4 (Athens, 1941–42), pp. 5ff., which according to Marianne Klaar, 'Christos und das verschenkte Brot', *Neugriechische Volkslegenden und Legendenmärchen* (Kassel, 1963), pp. 85–8, 220–1; cf. p. 93, the legend of the 'foul tree' on which Judas hanged himself), reports a version of the Judas legend from Crete (1938), which has survived orally down to our own day.

53 P. Lehmann, 'Judas Ischariot', p. 248. notes 'the persistent linking of the legends of Judas and Pilate. Not only are they often preserved together; they also exhibit many similarities of content and treatment. The Judas story depends on the Pilate story, at least for certain details.' Cf. Creizenach, 'Judas Ischariot', p. 197. On the legends of Pilate and Judas see W. Harms, *Der Kampf mit dem Freund oder Verwandten in der deutschen Literatur bis um 1300*, Medium Aevum 1 (Munich, 1963), pp. 113–19.

Pilate, like Judas, becomes frozen in unbelief and unrepentance and is damned for all eternity. The legend of Pilate the anti-saint developed out of late antique apocryphal stories about him and medieval legendary accretions; eventually, in the high Middle Ages, his childhood and youth were added to constitute a *vita*. In his youth he knowingly murders his half-brother, a king's son (just as Judas kills his foster-brother), and commits another murder in Rome. As the arch-betrayer of Christ he, like Judas, commits suicide and is damned: fearing to be condemned to death by the Roman Emperor, he cuts his throat. He, like Judas, dies guilty of *desperatio*, though Pilate's is not theological. On the origins of the Pilate *vita* see K. Hauck, 'Pontius Pilatus in Forchheim', in *Medium Aevum Vivum. Festschrift W. Bulst* (Heidelberg, 1960), pp. 104–24; Doris Werner, *Pylatus. Untersuchungen zur metrischen lateinischen Pilatuslegende und kritische Textausgabe*, Beiheft zum Mittellateinischen Jahrbuch 8 (Ratingen/Kastellaun/Düsseldorf, 1972), pp. 28, 31: 'Even the final opportunity for inner conversion remains unused: Pilate remains stubbornly far from God, without belief or trust in his mercy and forgiveness of his sins ... To the last he fails to recognise the possibility of salvation, but goes further and further away from God's grace.'

54 The *Alte Passional*, ed. Hahn, 312:68–318:55. The *Vita Judae Scarioth* (ed. P. Lehmann, 'Judas Ischariot') alone reaches an epic length of 912 hexameters, but only by including the passion of Christ and Judas' sufferings in hell.

On the Judas legend in the *Passion* and in the *Thuringian chronicle* of Johannes Rothe (d. 1434), see A. Heinrich, *Johannes Rothes Passion*, Germanistische Abhandlungen, Heft 26 (Breslau, 1906), pp. 92–100. Rothe also introduces the story of the thirty pieces of silver, known since the twelfth century (pp. 97ff., text pp. 112–17); the legend of Pilate (pp. 60–92, text pp. 117–54); and the destruction of Jerusalem (text pp. 154–64). The story of Judas (text pp. 103–12) only goes up to the contrition for incest with his mother which takes Judas to Jesus, whom he betrays – a negative antitype of Moses (lines 258–91). The theme of Rothe's *Passion* is the punishment of the Jews and their associates by the heathen for their part in Christ's passion. In an appendix Heinrich published the *Vita Judae traditoris* from the Wolfenbüttel manuscript, on which see Lehmann, 'Judas Ischariot', pp. 239ff.

55 *Patrologia Latina* 83, pp. 825–68.

56 Isidore's *Synonyma* (pre 612), now awaiting rediscovery, was widely known in the European Middle Ages as a model of both style and piety; from its own century onwards it was also known as *Lamentatio*. The pioneering study, including sources (and preparation for a new edition) is J. Fontaine, 'Isidore de Séville auteur "ascétique": les énigmes des *Synonyma*', *Studi Medievali* 6/1 (1965), pp. 163–95. From the twelfth century the lament of the living sinner was coupled with a lament from a sinner in his grave, the *Planctus animae damnatae*, Analecta Hymnica 46 (Leipzig, 1905; repr. Frankfurt, 1961), pp. 349–50; on the German versions see G. Eis, 'Eine unbekannte deutsche Bearbeitung des *Planctus animae damnatae*', *Neuphilologische Mitteilungen* 65 (1964), pp. 278–85.

57 Book I, 1–21.

58 I, 22–38.

59 I, 39–78.

60 I, 53–4; col. 839C: 'Certissime igitur crede, nullo modo haesites, nullo modo dubites, nullatenus de misericordia Dei desperes. Habeto spem in confessione, habeto fiduciam. Non desperes remedium sanitatis; non desperes salutem, si ad meliora convertaris. Qui enim veniam de peccato desperat, plus se de desperatione quam de commisso scelere damnat. Desperatio auget peccatum, desperatio pejor est onmi peccato. Corrige igitur te, et indulgentiae habeto spem. Depone injustitiam, et spera vitam; depone iniquitatem et spera salutem. Nulla tam gravis culpa est quae non habeat veniam; quamvis enim peccator sis, quamvis criminosus, quamvis sceleratus, quamvis infinitis criminibus nefandis oppressus, non denegatur tibi poenitentiae locus: facile poeniten-

tibus divina clementia subvenit, per poenitentiam indulgentia datur, per poenitentiam delicta omnia absterguntur.'

61 1, 55.

62 G. H. Dreves, ed., *Rhithmus pape Leonis IX*, Analecta Hymnica 50 (Leipzig, 1907, repr. Frankfurt, 1961), pp. 305ff.

63 siglos *J*, ungeblos *K*. Zwierzina reads *vingerblôz*, Neumann *sinne blôz*; I read *tugende blôz*, which is closer to *K* and is supported by *virtutibus spoilant*.

64 J. Szöverffy, *Die Annalen der lateinischen Hymnendichtung* 1 (Berlin, 1964), pp. 381–2. One might also recall earlier works like the poem by Bishop Eugenius of Toledo, (d. 658) which begins

> Criminum mole gravatus
> et reatu saucius
> Carmen insonare nitor
> luctuosis quaestibus,
> Lacrimis ora madescant,
> verberentur pectora.

> (*An. Hymn.* 50, p. 91)

Weighed down with weight of sins and under accusation, I strive to intone a song with grievous lamentations; let my cheeks be wet with tears, let me beat my breast.

Or this ABC poem, *De paenitentia*, by the Patriarch Paulinus of Aquileia (d. 802):

> 1 Ad caeli clara non sum dignus sidera
> Levare meos infelices oculos,
> Gravi depressus peccatorum pondere;
> Parce, redemptor!

> 2 Bonum neglexi facere, quod debui,
> Probrosa gessi sine fine crimina,
> Scelus patravi nullo clausum termino,
> Subveni, Christe!

> 13 Nullum peccatum super terrae faciem
> Potest aut scelus inveniri quodpiam,
> A quorum non sim iniquinatus faecibus
> Infelix ego.

> (Ibid., p. 148)

I am not worthy to lift my unhappy eyes to the bright stars of heaven, weighed down as I am with a heavy weight of sins: spare me, redeemer! I failed to do the good I ought to have done, and endlessly committed shameful sins; I did evil unlimited: help me, oh Christ! ... No sin or wickedness can be found upon the face of the earth by whose filth I am not polluted, unhappy I.

One might also think of the *Versus de ploratu paenitentia* of Gotts-
chalk of Orbais (d. 869) (ibid., pp. 225–6). ~~The *Rhythmus de primo*~~
homine of Herradis von Landsberg (d. 1195) (ibid., pp. 495–6)
deals with Adam's fall, making comparisons not only with the
Good Samaritan (verses 3ff.) but also with the redemption by the
good shepherd (verse 16: 'Deus quaerens venerat / Ovem quem
perdiderat', God had come seeking the sheep he had lost). So also
the *Gregorius*.

Thomas Mann realised that the sins in *Gregorius* could inspire
lamentations. 'Sybil's prayer' in *Der Erwählte*, 'one of my favourite
events in the book', derives from the lament in the *Vorauer Novelle*
and the Arnstein *Marienlied*, but is lighthearted where they are
serious: see the letter to Erich Auerbach in Mann's *Gesammelte
Werke*, vol. 11; letters, 1948–55 and supplement, 1965, pp. 209 (to
Julius Bab) and 246 (to William H. McClain).

65 For older studies see G. Ehrismann, *Geschichte der deutschen Literatur*, II, 2/1 (Munich, 19276), p. 189; later H. Sparnaay, *Hartmann
von Aue. Studien zu einer Biographie* 1 (Halle, 1933), p. 159 (no
knowledge of Rand or Bum): P. Wapnewski, *Hartmann von Aue*
(Stuttgart, 1962), p. 74 (same omission).

66 W. Creizenach, 'Judas Ischariot', p. 119ff.; Lehmann, 'Judas
Ischariot', p. 247; Baum, 'Medieval Legend', pp. 595ff., 600, 608.

67 The illustrations to the German Judas legend in the Schaffhausen
Lectionary (*c.* 1330) use one tree to represent the orchard (*paumgarten*); it recalls the tree of knowledge which caused the Fall. See
figs. 1–4.

68 On *equitatio diabolica* see J. W. Smit, 'The Triumphant Horseman
Christ', in *Mélanges Christine Mohrmann. Nouveau Recueil* (Utrecht/
Antwerp, 1973), pp. 172–90.

69 T. Graesse, ed., *Jacobi a Voragine Legenda aurea* (3rd edn 1890;
repr. Osnabrück, 1965), p. 185.

70 Text in Baum, 'Medieval Legend', p. 491; see Lehmann, 'Judas
Ischariot', pp. 236, 239; F. Ohly, 'Zum Dichtungsschluß "Tu,
autem, domine, miserere nobis"', *Deutsche Vierteljahrsschrift für
Literaturwissenschaft und Geistesgeschichte* 47 (1973), pp. 26–88.
Baum discusses the forty-two MSS of the Latin *vita* of Judas
known to him, but without giving the context in the texts;
unfortunately he gives no comments on the use made of the *vita*.
Hitherto unpublished is the Middle High German Life of Judas in
the Upper German lectionary of 1330 in the town library of
Schaffhausen (MS general 8): the text is given on pp. 143–9 above.

71 S. Rüttgers, ed. and trans., *Der Heiligen Leben und Leiden, anders
genannt Das Passional*, 1: *Winterteil* (Leipzig, 1913), pp. 154–66

(Gregorius), 434–7 (Judas). On the medieval German Gregorius tradition after Hartmann von Aue see N. Heinze, *Hartmann von Aue, Gregorius. Die Überlieferung des Prologs, die Vaticana-Handschrift A und eine Auswahl der übrigen Textzeugen*, Litterae 28 (Göppingen, 1974), pp. 17ff.; on the Old French and Middle English traditions see pp. 14–17.

72 *Sermones ad fratres in eremo* 28: *PL* 40, p. 1285. According to P. Glorieux the sermon derives from a thirteenth-century Belgian original: 'Pour revaloriser Migne. Tables rectificatives', in *Mélanges de science religieuse* 9 (1952), *Cahier Supplémentaire*, p. 31. According to R. Lievens, this particular sermon is not included among the twenty-three Dutch translations of *Sermons ad fratres in eremo: Jordanus van Quedlinburg in de Nederlanden* (Ghent, 1958), pp. 217–18.

73 Hildegard Nobel, 'Schuld und Sühne in Hartmanns Gregorius und in der frühscholastischen Theologie', *Zeitschrift für deutsche Philologie* 76 (1957), pp. 42–79 (pp. 3ff.) was the first to see Judas and Gregorius as type and antitype, but only because of Hartmann's mention of Judas; she shows no knowledge of the Life of Judas, which extends the typological relationship beyond this one point.

On the dating of the Life, which is germane to our purpose: Baum knew forty-two MSS of five different versions of the Latin *vita*; the oldest he discovered in the twelfth-century MS from Saint Victor (Paris, BN lat. 14,489). At least fifteen others are thirteenth-century, leading Baum to conclude that the work must have appeared before the end of the twelfth century (see 'Medieval Legend', pp. 515, 'a period somewhat before the end of the twelfth century'; 516, 'Somewhere in the twelfth century'; 518, 'at least as early as some time in the twelfth century'; and cf. p. 608). Also relevant for the dating is the fact that Baum thought that the Provençal version of the Life, from an MS of about 1350, represented the oldest form of the story, older than any of the Latin versions (pp. 557–8, 608, 618, 620). He would put back the origin of the Life to the eleventh century: 'The probable date of its appearance is late in the eleventh century, when incest was a familiar theme; but the earliest manuscript evidence we have is for some time in the second half of the twelfth century' (p. 629). Lehmann ('Judas Ischariot', p. 285) was able to indicate another twelfth-century MS of the Life (Oxford, Bodleian Laud. Misc. 663), which was written in a known hand of *c.* 1185. Baum gives good reasons for considering this text, belonging to the *R* group and giving an extended version of the Life, as earlier than the

Provençal, Greek and Latin *A* texts, which are themselves earlier stages in the development of the *vita*. Lehmann was able to assign the Munich MS lat. 23,390 saec. XII–XIII, which was already known to Steinmeyer, to the *R* group. He goes so far as to claim that the 'longest and most stylistically polished' *vita*, version *H* (thirteenth and fourteenth-century MSS) is 'of twelfth-century French origin'. He thinks it safe to assume (p. 239) that 'from the first half of the twelfth century' there existed a shorter form containing only the pre-biblical part of Judas' life. 'All in all we would not be far wrong in believing that soon after 1100 ... an oriental, maybe Syrian tale of Judas became known and was translated into Latin; then this (probably very sketchy) original underwent multiple elaborations ... The oldest Latin versions of Judas' story known to us, however, seem to be of French origin and to date from the twelfth century, or not much earlier' (pp. 247–8). Thus we may legitimately conclude that the Life of Judas most probably appeared around the middle of the twelfth century, so that there is no chronological reason why it should not pre-date the Old French *Vie du pape Grégoire*.

74 On medieval knowledge of Oedipus and the relationship between the Oedipus story and the early lives of Judas see Baum, 'Medieval Legend', pp. 609–18.

75 F. Ohly, 'Halbbiblische und außerbiblische Typologie', in *Schriften zur mittelalterlichen Bedeutungsforschung* (Darmstadt, 1977), pp. 361–400.

76 Version *H*, text in Baum, 'Medieval Legend', pp. 501–8; see also pp. 518ff.

77 Hartmann von Aue's loaded *war umbe* (why?, line 355 – i.e. why does God admit some possibilities and not others?) corresponds here to the *cur* in the question to *crudelis fortuna* addressed to Judas as victim: 'Miser Iuda et infelicissime, quo tuo vel tuorum parentum crimine contigit tibi tot tantisque malis natum esse? Cur misera illa mater tua cum te concepit non statim abortivit? Cur autem natus? Cur exceptus genibus? Cur lactatus uberibus? Cur natus non statim es paternis et maternis manibus necatus? Esset certe modo tibi melius; parricidale autem crimen fuisset tuis miseris parentibus tuo crimine venalius. Cur autem vel in mare proiectus non statim es emersus et a tanto abysso suffocatus? Esset tibi vel mare vel aliquis beluinus venter sepulchrum nec postea celo terreque perosus tam infelici morte perisses inter utrumque. Sed cum mori poteras adhuc sine crimine, pepercit tibi inter fluctus nescio quis deus, quamvis ether, venti et pelagus ut perires totis pugnabant viribus. Incertum est, inquam, quis deus hoc

discrimine te eripuit; et elementa dum te laborant obruere, visa sunt pocius obsequium tibi prestitisse' (pp. 503–4: O miserable and most unhappy Judas, through what sin of yours or your parents were you born to so many and such great ills? Why did your unhappy mother not abort as soon as she conceived you? Why were you ever born? Why taken on her lap? Why suckled at her breasts? Why did your mother and father not kill you with their own hands as soon as you were born? It would certainly have been better for you; and the sin of parricide would have been more venial for your unhappy parents than yours was. And why, when thrown into the sea, did you not sink at once, to be drowned in that great abyss? The sea, or the belly of some whale, would have been your sepulchre, and you would not have died such a miserable death later, between heaven and earth and hated of both. But when you could have died still without sin, some god or other spared you amidst the waves, though the air, the winds and the sea strove with such might for your death. It is uncertain, I say, what god snatched you out of that danger; and while the elements strove to overwhelm you, they seemed rather to do you service.) Later Judas goes to his mother and tries 'ab ea scrutari et querere textum huius tragedie' (to question her and find the text of this tragedy, p. 507); he goes with his mother to Jesus 'ut ei suarum miserarum tragedias narrent' (to tell him the tragedy of their miseries, p. 508).

78 Baum, 'Medieval Legend', p. 520; cf. pp. 546, 595ff.
79 Line 2685.
80 See pp. 76–7.
81 Oedipus' lament, ed. W. Wattenbach, *Zeitschrift für deutsches Altertum* 19 (1876), pp. 89–92.
82 Verse 18.

2 THE DESPAIR OF JUDAS

1 *De civitate Dei* I, 17.
2 *Moralia* XI, 9, *PL* 75, p. 959B; Pseudo-Bernard, *Meditatio in passionem et resurrectionem Domini*, ch. 7, *PL* 184, p. 752 D: 'Poenitentia enim ductus peccatum suum valde ponderavit' (for, guided by penitence, he had truly weighed up his sin).
3 K. A. Hahn, ed., *Das Alte Passional* (Frankfurt, 1845), p. 318.
4 G. Morel, ed., *Offenbarungen der Schwester Mechthild von Magdeburg oder das fließende Licht der Gottheit* (Regensburg, 1869; repr. Darmstadt, 1963), III, 21, p. 82.
5 Ed. F. Khull (Tübingen, 1882).

6 E. Wolter, *Das St. Galler Spiel vom Leben Jesu. Untersuchungen und Text*, Germanistische Abhandlungen 41 (Berlin, 1912), compares Nicholas of Lyra, *Postilla* (Antwerp, 1634), on Matthew 27:2: 'In hoc plus peccavit quam in tradendo Christum: cuius ratio est quia in traditione Christi peccavit contra eius humanitatem directe: sed in desperatione illa peccavit directe contra eius divinitatem, quia contra infinitatem divinae misericordiae.' (In this he sinned more than in betraying Christ: the reason being that in the betrayal of Christ he sinned directly against his humanity, but in that despair he sinned directly against his divinity, that is, against the infinity of the divine mercy.)

7 Jerome, *Tractatus siue homiliae in psalmos*, on Psalm 108:7, *CCL* 78, 212, 101ff.: 'Paenitentia Iudae peius peccatum factum est. Quomodo peius peccatum factum est paenitentia Iudae? Ivit, et suspendio periit; et qui proditor Domini factus est, hic et interemptor sui extitit. Pro clementia Domini hoc dico, quod magis ex hoc offendit Dominum, quia se suspendit, quam quod Dominum prodidit. Oportebat orationem ipsius esse in paenitentiam, et uersa est in peccatum.' (Judas' penitence became his worst sin. How did Judas' penitence become his worst sin? He went and hanged himself; and he who had become the betrayer of Our Lord, also thereby became his own murderer. I say this concerning the mercy of God, that he offended Our Lord more in this, that he hanged himself, than because he betrayed Our Lord. His prayer should have turned into penitence, but it turned into a sin.)

8 Doultreman (cited by Spanner, see note 8 below) thinks of Judas as hanging himself like a spider: 'vitae taedio, conscientiae angore, proditi et damnati Magistri dolore, demum admissi sceleri horrore' (tired of life, tormented by his conscience, grieving for the betrayal and condemnation of his Master, and horrified by his acknowledged crime).

9 A. Spanner, *Polyanthea sacra*, 1 (Venice, 1741), p. 433, citing Doultreman, book 1, ch. 5, sect. 3 (Christ speaking): 'Vale usque ad sonitum tubae horribilis, quo aures tuae, ad inspirationes meas modo surdae, ambae tinnient' (Farewell until the sound of the last trump, to which your ears shall ring that once were deaf to my voice).

10 *Die Gedichte Heinrichs des Teichners*, ed. H. Niewohner, 3 vols., (Berlin, 1953–6).

11 These lines also appear in Poem 689, lines 58–65; cf. also Poem 91, lines 43–56.

12 Poem 78; cf. 53 and 435, lines 207–8.

13 Poem 464, lines 1753ff. Teichner opines (423, line 82) that the disciples, who had fled from the Cross, only lost their 'faintheartedness' at Pentecost. After Pentecost Judas would not have abandoned them: 'si hieten all zweifel gallen / vor dez heiligen gaistes chunft' (they all harboured shameful doubts before the coming of the Holy Ghost, 423, lines 88–9). Judas was worse than Peter, who repented and did penance after his denial of Christ (569, lines 108–21). However, if Judas had not betrayed Christ, we should be roasting in Hell for ever: 'er was uns ein nutzer man / er hat sich selb nicht recht getan' (he was useful to us, he did not deal justly with himself, 462, lines 159–60). For further examples of despair in Middle High German literature see L. Kretzenbacher, 'Zur *desperatio* im Mittelhochdeutschen', in H. Fromm, W. Harms and U. Ruberg, ed., *Verbum et signum*, II: *Beiträge zur mediävistischen Bedeutungsforschung. Studien zu Semantik und Sinntradition im Mittelalter* (Munich, 1975), pp. 299–310.

14 Matthew 26:69–27:5.

15 On the relationship of the *Erlösung* to the German passion plays see R. Bergmann, *Studien zur Entstehung und Geschichte der deutschen Passionsspiele des 13. und 14. Jahrhunderts*, Münstersche Mittelalter-Schriften 14 (Munich, 1972), pp. 127–68.

16 Rupert von Deutz, *In Mattheum* book 11, *PL* 168, p. 1564B–D. Judas desired not only the death of Christ, but also to obliterate his name, his teaching and all memory of him (p. 1566c–D); he hanged himself in disappointment at his failure to achieve this. Rupert greatly develops the typology of Achipotel (and Absalom) and Judas; on this cf. *PL* 167, 1136B–C. Further references to Peter and Judas in *PL* 219, p. 260D.

17 *Die Passion des Herrn (Passauer Passionale). Gepredigt im Passauer Dom im Jahre 1460 von Dr. Paul Wann (d. 14 9)*, edited (from the Munich MS Clm 2818), translated and with introduction by F. X. Zacher (Augsburg, 1928), pp. 58–61 (on Peter's denial); pp. 84–5 (on Judas' contrition and death in comparison with Peter's).

18 This quotation is not to be found at the reference given by Wann (Augustine, *Tractatus in Joh.* 124, *CCL* 36, pp. 680–8); nor is it in Tractate 113, which deals with Peter's denial.

19 Page 60. Wann stresses the gravity of Peter's sins: 'Let us consider how gravely Peter sinned and how low he fell! First he simply lies; then he repeats the lie, swears oaths, even perjures himself. ... For what reason did he fall so low? ... As soon as he went among impious folk, he became an apostate and a perjurer'

(p. 59). He is alluding to people who 'like David and Peter, fell into sin and evildoing' (p. 61).

20 Wann expounds regarding both Peter and Judas: 'Except eternal damnation there could be no harsher punishment from God than if he refused to warn people against sin or call on the fallen to repent and so aid them. But Peter shows us that God's goodness desires both: to keep us from sin and to save us out of sin.'

21 After the silver pieces had rolled clinking before the High Priest's feet, to the savage curses of Judas, 'there came only a cold laugh from their side as they exulted in his anguish. Then the anger in Judas turned to darkest despair, he no longer saw or heard anything around him, he felt nothing any more save the urge to flee from his hideous deed and know no more of his own life. In this state of mind he stormed out of the city, down into the vale of Hinnom, where twisted olive trees stood around evil-smelling rubbish-heaps, and hanged himself. It must have been a fearful death. Perhaps at the last moment Judas still wanted to escape from the noose. He dangled and struggled on the rope. It broke in two and the corpse, heavy as lead, fell down, down and – horror of horrors! – burst asunder, so that the entrails gushed out' (p. 84). This depiction of Judas' death has the same baroque detail of his sufferings as we find in the late medieval passion stories. Whether Judas tried to free himself in fear of death or because, too late, he repented, Wann does not say.

22 Page 85. For a stylistic comparison between the scenes of Judas's betrayal and repentance in the Latin and German passion plays see A. Brinkmann, *Liturgische und volkstümliche Formen im geistlichen Spiel des deutschen Mittelalters*, Forschungen zur deutschen Sprache und Dichtung 3 (Münster, 1932), pp. 30–7, 80–5.

3 THE PENANCE ON THE ROCK

1 It is not our intention here to give a complete account of the sources of the Gregorius story, but to deal with some material which has not hitherto been fully considered, and to show how and why it was adopted. A reconsideration of the material as a whole would involve some stress on the dating of the texts we have compared above, in order to give the study a more solid historical basis. The most recent study of the sources is A. van der Lee, 'De mirabili dispensatione et ortu beati Gregorii Papae. Einige Bemerkungen zur Gregorssage', *Neophilologus* 53 (1969), pp. 30–45, 120–73, 251–6. E. Dorn, *Der sündige Heilige in der Legende des Mittelalters*, Medium Aevum 10 (Munich, 1967) was

the first to relate the legend of Saint Metro to Gregorius (pp. 80–3). Other points relevant to this chapter emerged from my seminar on the saints' lives, which gave rise to Dorn's book: see his page 9, note 2.

2 Secondary material in Dorn, *Sündige Heilige*, pp. 22–3; F. Dingermann, *Adambuch, Lexikon für Theologie und Kirche*, I (second edn 1957), p. 133; F. Stegmüller, *Repertorium biblicum medii aevi*, I (Madrid, 1940), pp. 26–35; H. Charles, *The Apocrypha and Pseudepigraphica of the Old Testament*, II (Oxford, 1963), pp. 123ff. (survey). Extensive bibliography in the most recent study: B. Murdoch, 'An Early Irish Adam and Eve: *Saltair na Rann* and the Traditions of the Fall', *Mediaeval Studies* 35 (1973), pp. 146–77, esp. pp. 146–52 and, on the penance of Adam and Eve, pp. 167–71. I did not have access to B. O. Murdoch, 'Das deutsche Adambuch und die Adamlegende des späten Mittelalters', in W. Harms and L. P. Johnson (ed.), *Deutsche Literatur des späten Mittelalters*, Hamburger Colloquium 1973 (Berlin, 1975), pp. 209–24. I am grateful to my colleague K. H. Rengstorf of Münster for directing my attention to the *vitae* of Adam.

3 W. Meyer, ed., *Vita Adae et Evae*, Abhandlungen der Bayerischen Akademie der Wissenschaften, philos.-philol. Klasse 14/3 (Munich, 1878), pp. 221–4; in German in E. Kautzsch, ed., *Die Apokryphen und Pseudepigraphen des Alten Testaments*, II (Tübingen, 1900; repr. Hildesheim, 1962), pp. 12–28.

4 Kautzsch, *Apokryphen*, p. 512.

5 Ed. G. Eis, *Beiträge zur mittelhochdeutschen Legende und Mystik. Untersuchungen und Texte* (Berlin, 1935), pp. 241–55.

6 K. Hoffmann and W. Meyer, ed., *Lutwins Adam und Eva*, Bibliothek des Literarischen Vereins 153 (Tübingen, 1881): 'Adam und Evas Buße auf dem Stein', lines 988–1056.

7 Since edited by H. Fischer, 'Die Buße Adams und Evas', *Germania* 22 (1877), pp. 316–41.

8 H. Vollmer, *Ein deutsches Adambuch. Nach einer ungedruckten Handschrift der Hamburger Stadtbibliothek aus dem 15. Jahrhundert*, Programmschrift des Johanneums (Hamburg, 1908). For other texts from the fourteenth to the sixteenth century see J. van Dam, 'Adam und Eva (Adams Klage)', in W. Stammler, ed., *Die deutsche Literatur des Mittelalters. Verfasserlexikon*, I (Berlin/Leipzig, 1933), cols. 4–8; Dorn, *Sündige Heilige*, pp. 27–8.

9 Fischer, 'Die Buße', pp. 317–18.

10 After Murdoch, 'Early Irish Adam', p. 168.

11 Ibid., p. 170.

12 Dorn, *Sündige Heilige*, p. 25 and references.

13 Evidence for the Slav apocryphal literature on Adam in L. Kretzenbacher, 'Jordantaufe auf dem Satansstein. Zur Deutung südosteuropäischer Fresken und Ikonen aus den Apokryphen und Volkslegenden', in *Bilder und Legenden. Erwandertes und erlebtes Bilder-Denken und Bild-Erzählen zwischen Byzanz und dem Abendlande*, Aus Forschung und Kunst 13 (Klagenfurt, 1971), pp. 49–74 (pp. 57–66). L. Kretzenbacher, 'Hunger treibt Urvater Adam zum Pakt mit dem Teufel', in *Teufelsbündler und Faustgestalten im Abendlande*, Buchreihe des Landesmuseums Kärnten 23 (Klagenfurt, 1968), pp. 42–53.

14 E. Preuschen, *Die apokryphen gnostischen Adamsschriften* (Gießen, 1900), pp. 32–3.

15 For the evidence see Kretzenbacher, 'Jordantaufe', colour plates II–V, plates XIV–XVII.

16 C. Selmer, ed., *Navigatio sancti Brendani abbatis, from Early Latin Manuscripts, Edited with Introduction and Notes*, Publications in Mediaeval Studies 16 (Notre Dame, 1959).

17 Selmer, *Navigatio*, ch. 25, pp. 65–70 and notes (pp. 90–1). On the fuller Lisbon version of the fourteenth century see C. Selmer, 'The Lisbon *Vita Sancti Brendani Abbatis*', *Traditio* 13 (1957), pp. 313ff. On the Judas chapter in the *Navigatio* see also L. Kretzenbacher, 'Sankt Brandan, Judas und die Ewigkeit', in *Bilder und Legenden*, pp. 150–76 (pp. 153–6); L. Kretzenbacher, 'Wie "ewig" ist die Ewigkeit?', *Adeva-Mitteilungen* 18 (March 1969), pp. 7–17. On the idea of the Sunday *refrigerium* accorded to damned souls, already current in early Christian times, see A. Graf, 'A proposito della *Visio Pauli*', *Giornale storico della letteratura italiana* 11 (1888), pp. 344–62. Further bibliography in Selmer, *Navigatio*, pp. 90–1. A full account of research on this topic, overlooked by Selmer, is P. F. Baum, 'Judas' Sunday Rest', *The Modern Language Review* 18 (1923), pp. 168–82. Baum (pp. 169–70) thinks that Judas' *refrigerium* on the rock features in a fuller *Navigatio* from as early as *c.* 900. It did not appear in the (Anglo-Norman) vernacular until *c.* 1125. Baum also mentions (pp. 170–8) many later versions of the scene – some as recent as the nineteenth century – both inside and outside the Brendan context (early examples of the latter in *Baudoin de Sebourc* and *Esclarmonde*, a continuation of *Huon de Bordeaux*); there are also complete poems. On the history of the Sunday rest granted to souls in Hell see pp. 178ff.

18 On this preferential treatment of Judas see Baum, 'Judas' Sunday Rest', pp. 181–2. Graf ('*Visio Pauli*') had already distinguished between the theology of sympathy (*sentimento*) and of doctrine (*dottrina*).

19 C. Schröder, ed., *Sanct Brandan. Ein lateinischer und drei deutsche Texte* (Erlangen, 1871), pp. 49–123; the Judas scene occupies lines 936–1091. Cf. the more recent German versions on pp. 143ff., 178ff. In the twelfth-century *Life of Tundalus*, which is of Irish origin, King Cormac has to endure the fires of hell in the dark for three hours every day for unexpiated adultery and the murder of a noble, which he failed to repent in life. The rest of the time, however, he dwells in a beautiful house of jewels, full of light, in the antechambers of heaven, because he showed mercy to the poor. A. Wagner, *Visio Tnugdali. Lateinisch und Altdeutsch* (Erlangen, 1882): Latin prose version pp. 44–5, Middle High German version by Alber, lines 1653–716, pp. 170ff. Cormac is released from his torment at the prayer of all and sundry: see Schröder, *Sanct Brandan*, p. 47.

20 W. Haug, 'Vom Imram zur Aventiure-Fahrt. Zur Frage nach der Vorgeschichte der hoch-höfischen Epenstruktur', in W. Schröder, ed., *Wolfram-Studien* (Berlin, 1970), pp. 264–98, proposes (p. 284) a 'proto-*Navigatio*' 'as the basis of both the *Navigatio* and the "Voyage"'.

21 Schröder, *Sanct Brandan*, pp. 58ff., lines 356–426; cf. the more recent German versions pp. 133–4, lines 284–344; pp. 188–9.

22 Nancy Iseley, ed., *De passione Judae*, Studies in the Romance Language and Literatures 2 (Chapel Hill, University of Carolina, 1941), pp. 29–40, lines 16–28.

23 *Invectiva de translatione sancti Metronis*, PL 136, pp. 451–72; the following draws heavily on Dorn, *Sündige Heilige*, pp. 80–3.

24 Bishop Augustinus Valerius of Verona (1565–1616), referring to an 'ancient lectionary' in the cathedral there: *Acta Sanctorum*, May, II (1738), p. 303.

25 *Invectiva*, p. 303F: 'Ostenduntur adhuc in ipsa ecclesia S. Vitalis catena et lapis cui alligatus fuit s. Metro, dum poenitentiam ageret.' (In that church they still exhibit the chain of St Vitalis and the stone to which St Metro was tied during his penance.)

26 Rather is trying to make himself clear even to those who do not know the place.

27 *Invectiva*, pp. 458C–459C.

28 W. Pabst, 'Die Selbsbestrafung auf dem Stein. Zur Verwandschaft von Amadis, Gregorius und Ödipus', in *Der Vergleich. Festgabe für H. Petriconi* (Hamburg, 1955), pp. 33–49. The following is based on Pabst.

On the survival of Gregorius in religious exampla and saints' lives from the fifteenth century see O. Schwenke, 'Gregorius de grote sünder. Eine erbaulich-paränetische Prosaversion der

Gregorius-Legende im zweiten Lübecker Mohnkopf-Plenarium', *Niederdeutsches Jahrbuch* 90 (1967), pp. 63–88 (with references to other texts of the same kind). The 'folk book' of Gregorius survives only in an edition of 1810–13; it probably had a seventeenth-century source close to the *Gesta Romanorum*. J. Elema and R. Fan der Wal, 'Zum Volksbuch *Eine schöne merkwürdige Historie des heiligen Bischofs Gregorii auf dem Stein genannt'*, *Euphorion* 57 (1963), pp. 292–320; see also Elema, 'Imäginares Zentrum', in *Studien zur deutschen Literatur* (Assen, 1968), pp. 91–123.

29 It is questionable whether Pabst's idea of a 'profane antithesis', Amadis as a 'secularised Gregorius' (p. 39) is sufficient. Pabst denies that the 'romance's secularising of the saint into a knight' is no more than 'sleight of hand on the romance author's part – strictly speaking, a mere trick' (p. 41). 'The "mere trick" in fact marks the birth of the Spanish courtly romance and so the beginning of a new literary epoch. This sleight of hand is most truly epoch-making' (ibid.). I would prefer to see the 'birth' of the modern novel as a gradual osmosis of the saint's life and the romance; cf. J. Scheietering, 'Zur Autorschaft von Seuses Vita', in *Mystik und höfische Dichtung im Hochmittelalter* (Tübingen, 1962), pp. 107–22; also in F. Ohly and M. Wehrli, ed., *Philologische Schriften* (Munich, 1969). pp. 409–19; M. Wehrli, 'Roman und Legende im Hochmittelalter', in *Worte und Werte. Bruno Markwardt zum 60. Geburtstag* (Berlin, 1961), pp. 428–43; also in M. Wehrli, *Formen mittelalterlicher Erzählung* (Zurich/Freiburg, 1969), pp. 155–76.

30 Pabst, 'Selbstbestrafung', points out that 'the self-punishment of the falsely accused lover on the stone (or mountain), and his suicidal despair' (p. 43) became a 'governing, central theme' as far as Cervantes. The Judas *vita* casts doubt on his assumption that suicide prompted by despair was unknown in the Middle Ages, and could only have got into the fifteenth-century romance from classical antiquity.

4 THE *MATHEMATICUS*: PUTTING THE BLAME ON FATE

1 Pseudo-Quintilian, *Declamatio* 4.4.23, in G. Lehnert, ed., *Quintiliani quae feruntur declamationes XIX majores* (Leipzig, 1915), pp. 71ff.

2 *PL* 171, pp. 1365–80; also ed. (together with the *Passio s. Agnetis* of Petrus Riga) by B. Hauréau (Paris, 1895). W. Cloetta sees the *Mathematicus* as the best of the medieval 'epic tragedies': *Komödie*

und Tragodie im Mittelalter, Beiträge zur Literaturgeschichte des Mittelalters und der Renaissance 1 (Halle, 1890), pp. 113–19, with references to older studies. See also W. von den Steinen, 'Les sujets d'inspiration chez les poètes latins du XIIe siècle: Bernard Silvestris et le problème du destin', *Cahiers de Civilisation Médiévale* 9 (1966), pp. 373–83; W. Wetherbee, *Platonism and Poetry in the Twelfth Century* (Princeton, 1972), pp. 153–8; on authorship, A. B. Scott, 'The Poems of Hildebert of Le Mans: a New Examination of the Canon', *Medieval and Renaissance Studies* 6 (1968), pp. 42–83 (p. 81): 'Hauréau's arguments for Bernard as author are not perhaps completely convincing, but there can be no doubt that Hildebert is not the author.'

3 W. Freytag, *Das Oxymoron bei Wolfram, Gottfried und anderen Dichtern des Mittelalters*, Medium Aevum 24 (Munich, 1972), makes no mention of the *Mathematicus*.

4 On the ending see von den Steinen, 'Bernard Silvestris', p. 378. I am convinced that Patricida must go off to kill himself, as are Hauréau (edition, pp. 7–8) and Wetherbee (*Platonism*, p. 157) but not Cloetta (*Komödie*, pp. 117–18).

5 Wetherbee, *Platonism*, pp. 152–3. 156–7.

6 *PL* 171, p. 1376B.

7 Cantus VII: ibid., pp. 1371ff.

8 In king Patricida's farewell speech to the Romans he says (p. 1380B–C):

> Agrestis tam voce fuit, quam veste Camillus,
>   Gratus apud superos rusticitate sua.
> Non pictis nugis rigidi placuere Catones;
>   Sermo patens illis et sine veste fuit.
> Agresti Latio monstravit Graecia blandum,
>   Graecia perplexum, Graecia grande loqui.
> O gravis illa dies, qua simplex et rude verum
>   Sorduit, et picti plus placuere soni!
> Aequor inaccessas utinam fecisset Athenas,
>   Non foret eloquii Roma nitore nocens.

Camillus was a countryman in both voice and clothing, but his rustic simplicity was acceptable to the gods. The severe Catos did not please by gaudy trifles: their speech was straightforward and unadorned. Greece showed rustic Latium how to speak in a mild, complex or grandiloquent way. A sad day, that, when what was simple and plain lost favour, and gaudy words were more pleasing! If only the sea had made Athens inaccessible, Rome would not have become harmful by the glitter of false eloquence.

9 Von den Steinen, 'Bernard Silvestris', p. 381 says: 'The unfortunate Gregorius feels guilty, and according to the author he *is*

guilty before God. He is guilty although he has not willed, or will-ingly done, any evil. Thus Hartmann makes no distinction between fate and guilt: *fatum* is simply dubbed *peccatum* ... How a man becomes guilty is not understood, he just is so; and here lies the resemblance to Patricida.' Speaking of Gottfried von Stras-burg: 'For Tristan and Isolde, perfection lies not in victory over fate, but in complete surrender to the fate of "love" ... What Gottfried is at pains to point out is that Tristan and Isolde do not try to shake off their *fatum* as if it were *peccatum*.'

10 K. Reinhardt, *Sophokles* (3rd edn, Frankfurt, 1947), p. 108: 'Before the Stoa and the victory of astrology there is no pre-determined fate.'

5 THE *VORAUER NOVELLE*: 'ONE SHALL BE TAKEN AND THE OTHER LEFT'

1 A. E. Schönbach, *Studien zur Erzählungsliteratur des Mittelalters*, I: *Die Reuner Relationen*, II, *Die Vorauer Novelle*, Sitzungsberichte der Akademie der Wissenschaften in Wien, phil.-hist. Klasse 139–40 (Vienna, 1898–9): Latin text in vol. I, pp. 43–56.

2 Chap. 2, p. 44: 'Sed terribilis in consiliis super filios hominum novit Dominus, qui sunt eius, et de consimili massa perditionis facit aliud quidem vas in honerem, aliud vero in contumeliam, dum cui velt miseretur et quem vult indurat.' (But the lord, dreadful in his judgements over the sons of men, knows his own, and out of a mass of indistinguishable sinners he makes one a vessel to his honour, another a vessel of reprobation, for he pities and condemns whom he will.)

3 Chap. 5, p. 46: 'Cum jam completa essent peccata illorum quasi amor reorum, advenerat tempus, quod meruerant: et alteri mox redditum est, prout gessit, sive bonum sive malum; alter dilatus est, ut in eo estenderet Deus pietatis et bonitatis sue divicias.' (When their sins were fulfilled, such as love between guilty men, the time came which they had deserved: and to one was soon given according to his deeds, whether good or evil; the other was spared for a time, that in him God might show the riches of his compass-ion and goodness.)

4 Chap. 6, 'De desperatione eius' (On his despair), p. 48.

5 Chap. 7, p. 50: 'Quem Deus a tempore, hunc etiam a fructu peni-tentie non exclusit, sed reconciliatum et bone spe factum dimittit.'

6 Chap. 9, p. 53.

7 The motif of the traitor torn to pieces, which reappears in the Faust legend (see below), I hope to discuss in a separate study.

8 Chap. 9, p. 54.

9 For the so-called *Vorauer Novelle* see Schönbach, *Studien*, II; Middle High German text pp. 42–68. Studies: H. de Boor, *Die deutsche Literatur im späten Mittelalter. Zerfall und Neubeginn*, I, *Geschichte der deutschen Literatur* 3/1 (Munich, 1962), pp. 562–3; L. Kretzenbacher, 'Die Vorauer Novelle von der Hohen Schule der "Nigromancie"', in *Teufelsbündner und Faustgestalten im Abendland*, pp. 54–64; idem, 'Zur desperatio im Mittelhochdeutschen', in Fromm *et al.*, *Verbum und Signum*, II, pp. 266–310 (pp. 305–8).

10 Among whom is Wolfram. The master of the Black Arts welcomes the truants from the cloister in very fair French: 'ben seeiz venu, bea sir, / minen kinden und ouch mir' (welcome, fair sirs, to my children and to me, lines 147–8). In *Parzifal* the envoy of Amphlises, queen of France, greets Gahmuret with 'Bien sei venuz, beas sir / miner vrouwen unde mir' (welcome, fair sir, on my Lady's part and mine: 7611–12, cf. translation by A. T. Hatto, Harmondsworth, 1980, p. 49).

11 Meaning God's curse (*vluoch*), lines, 164, 248, 299, 484; meaning revenge, to avenge, lines 388, 481.

12 Cf. *Gregorius*, lines 3927–9: 'swie groz und wie swære / miner sunden last waere, / des hat nu got vergezzen' (however gross and heavy my burden of sin may have been, God has now forgotten it). In Roland's dying prayer he counts on God forgetting his sins: 'Ultra quam dici fas est me reum et peccatorem esse confiteor, sed tu ... peccatoris facinora in quacumque die ad te conversus fuerit et ingemuerit, oblivione in perpetuum tradis' (I confess I am more guilty and sinful than is fit to be spoken, but thou ... on whatever day the sinner has turned to thee and repented, dost consign his sins to oblivion forever, *Pseudo-Turpin* XXIII, 1291ff.). God's forgetfulness of sins is well documented in Christel Meier, 'Vergessen, Erinnern, Gedächtnis im Gott-Mensch-Bezug. Zu einem Grenzbereich der Allegorese bei Hildegard von Bingen und anderen Autoren des Mittelalters', in Fromm *et al.*, *Verbum et Signum*, I, pp. 143–94.

13 Numerous instances of *verzagen* (to despair) in Kretzenbacher, 'Zur *desperatio*'.

6 JUDAS AND EVERYMAN

1 E. Roy, *Le mystère de la passion en France du XIVe au XVIe siècle. Etude sur les sources et le classement des mystères de la passion. Accompagnée de textes inédits: La passion d'Autun. La passion bourguignonne de Semur. La passion d'Auvergne. La passion Secundum legem debet mori, Revue*

Bourguignonne 13 (Dijon/Paris, 1903), pp. 281, 284–5, 343. In 1841 G. P. Philomneste, a theologian of cheerful disposition, published his *Praedicatoriana ou Révélations singulières et amusantes sur les prédicateurs, entremêlées d'extraits piquants des sermons bizarres, burlesques et facétieux, prêchés tant en France qu'à l'étranger* (Dijon, 1841). On the title page the editor calls himself 'Auteur des amusements philologiques'. This is an anthology of more or less amusing extracts from sermons from the twelfth to the nineteenth century, products of exaggerated rhetoric and overblown allegory gathered together in a series of amusing stories (which is also one purpose of allegory) – which claims to be a 'collection intended to bring momentary distraction and relief to those of the faithful who are somewhat disposed to spleen or melancholia' (p. 318). In an appendix (pp. 375–98), Philomneste prints as 'legende inédite' (p. 316), a life of Judas from the Old French: *Vie de Judas Scariota, lequel fut sénéchal de N. S. Jésuchrist et le vendit* (Life of Judas Iscariot, who was seneschal to our lord Jesus Christ and sold him). Though it is different from his sermon extracts, he finds it 'just as amusing by its form, as a relic of the ancient tongue' (p. 318). He calls it an extract from a 'Life of Christ' of which he gives no other details, and thinks it was invented to increase the fear which Judas, the arch-traitor, had inspired in people through all the ages. Rival etymologies of the name 'Iscariotes' lead him (pp. 375ff.) to legends of the traitor's origins in Jerusalem (as in the *Vita*), Corfu (where he has worthy successors to this day), Saint-Jean-d'Acre (where the thirty pieces of silver were minted) or various parts of 'our own fair France', e.g. Sablé in the Sarthe: 'Perfidus ille Judas Sabloniensis erat'. In the competition to remove Judas' cradle to some unfavoured spots it was the Normans who drew the short straw (p. 378):

> Judas était Normand,
> Tout le monde le dit;
> Entre Caen et Rouen ce malheureux naquit.
> Il vendit son Seigneur pour trente marcs comptant;
> Au diable soient tous les Normands!

Judas was a Norman, everybody says so; the cursed fellow was born between Caen and Rouen. He sold his Lord for thirty marks down. To the devil with all Normans!

Follows the text of the *Vita* (pp. 379–95), with an account of its survival into Jean Michel's *Mystère de la Passion* (here dated to 1402) in the 1507 edition (pp. 395–8).

2 Paris, Bibliothèque Nationale Res. H. 506; Life of Judas fols

62r–66r. Summary of contents: Reuben sleeps with Cyborea, who dreams of crimes committed by her unborn child: he will kill a queen's son and then Reuben, marry his mother and betray the Saviour to the Jews for thirty silver pieces. Reuben thinks the dream is a temptation by the devil. The mother suckles the child for a month, then, in fear of him, casts him adrift in a barrel; the sea casts it up on the island of Scarioth. Its queen, longing for a child, finds Judas and is pleased by his beauty. She hides him, gives out that she is pregnant and passes him off as her child. When she gives birth to her own child, he has to endure beatings from Judas, who is bigger. His howls anger the queen, who informs Judas of his origins and threatens to exile him if he hits her son again. Judas, alone with the victim in the queen's house, kills him with his knife. Judas flees to Jerusalem and enters Pilate's service, Pilate being impressed by his beauty. Always zealous in Pilate's service, he brings him the apples from Reuben's beautiful apple tree, which Reuben would willingly have given him. But by hewing down the branches with his sword and so damaging the tree, he quarrels with Reuben, his father. Judas kills him with the sword. Cyborea complains to Pilate, who advises Judas to take the rich widow to wife; he does so. One day, thinking tearfully of the son she cast away twenty-seven years earlier, she tells Judas about her dream and what she did. He realises his accursed fate and repents. On his knees he begs his mother's forgiveness, and obtains it. He goes to Jesus, who forgives his sins, accepts him as one of the disciples and makes him an apostle and his treasurer. The story is linked by flashback and anticipation with the Passion narrative, supposed to have been composed jointly by Nicodemus, Gamaliel and Joseph of Arimathea. After Jesus' arrest Judas disappears from the story. The end of the Life of Jesus tells of Mary's death and the miracles worked by John the Evangelist in Asia Minor.

3 G. A. Runnalls, ed., *Le Mystère de la Passion ,Nostre Seigneur du manuscrit 1131 de la Bibliothèque Sainte-Geneviève* (Geneva/Paris, 1974).

4 A. Hartmann, ed., *Das Oberammergauer Passionsspiel in seiner ältesten Gestalt* (Leipzig, 1880; repr. Wiesbaden, 1968), p. 40). In the epilogue to Sebastian Wild's sixteenth-century passion play the herald mentions Judas' end: 'Zu letzt henckt er sich selbst zu lohn; / Der Teuffel furt die Sell faruon' (In the end he hanged himself and so was requited; the devil bore away his soul, lines 2114–15, p. 182).

5 In the Donaueschingen Passion play there is a deliberate contrast between Peter's lament for his denial and Judas' lament. E. Hartl,

ed., *Das Drama des Mittelalters* iv (Leipzig, 1941), lines 2400–21 (Peter) and 2438–70 (Judas). E. Benz, *Die Monologue des Judas Ischariot* (Munich, 1951) invents another final monologue by Judas before his suicide (pp. 42ff.).

6 G. Milchsack, ed., *Das Egerer Fronleichnamsspiel*, Bibliothek des literarischen Vereins in Stuttgart (Stuttgart, 1881), pp. 186ff. On the 'year-fire' as a burning of Judas see M. Zender, 'Volksbrauch und Politik. Lichterumzüge und Jahresfeuer von 1900 bis 1943', *Rheinische Vierteljahrsblätter* 38 (1984), pp. 355–85 (p. 380, note 61).

7 J. E. Wackernell, ed., *Altdeutsche Passionsspiele aus Tirol* (Graz, 1897): the Judas scene pp. 103ff. The Halle Passion calls Judas 'the despairing' (p. 322). The Brixen Passion borrows the scene from the Sterzing play (p. 397).

8 The Greek folktale has this to say of the 'stinking tree' from which Judas hanged himself: 'And why is it an evil-smelling plant? When Judas discovered what was afoot – his master was to be crucified through his treason – then he realized his guilt and resolved to hang himself. He went to one tree to fix the noose, but the tree would not allow it; he went to the next, and the same thing happened. None of the trees wanted to be polluted by hanging the traitor. He went also to the stinking tree – and it agreed. Judas cast the noose around it and hanged himself. From then on the plant has been accursed, and smells so vile that nobody can go near it – but before it smelt as sweet as musk, and hence was once called the saints' bush.' Marianne Klaar, ed., *Christos und das verschenkte Brot. Neugriechische Volkslegenden und Legendenmärchen* (Kassel, 1963), p. 93. The *Itinerary* of Antonius of Placentia (*c.* 570; ed. Geyer, CSEL 39, p. 170, 19) reports that pilgrims used to view the tree from which Judas hanged himself. Cf. Ilona Opelt, 'Das Grab des Riesen Goliath', *Jahrbuch für Antike und Christentum* 3 (1960), p. 17.

9 R. Froning, ed., *Das Drama des Mittelalters* (Stuttgart, 1891–2; repr. Darmstadt, 1964): Judas' death, pp. 470ff.

10 There is a shorter version in the St Gallen passion play: E. Hartl, ed., *Das Benediktbeurer Passionsspiel. Das St. Galler Passionsspiel*, Altdeutsche Textbibliothek 41 (Halle, 1952), pp. 104–5:

> Bi Juda si vch kunt gedan,
> wie ir sollent ruwen han:
> kein sunder dar an verzwiueln sal,
> got ist grozen gnaden vol.
> Hete er sich nit irhangen,
> godes gnade hede in inphangen.

(lines 1029–34)

By Judas you should learn how you should repent: no sinner should despair of it, for God is full of great mercy. If he had not hanged himself, God's grace would have received him.

A contrast to the laments of Judas and, later, Faust is to be found in the 'Play of Frau Jutta' (1480; ed. E. Schröder, Bonn, 1911). Jutta, a sinful female Pope, responds to a warning of imminent death with a prayerful lament referring to the salvation of various sinners: Adam, Peter, Thomas, Paul, Matthew, Theophilus, Mary Magdalene, Zaccheus, Longinus and the Penitent Thief:

> Das sint alles gewesen sündige Man,
> Die doch nu die seligkeit von dir han.
> Vergib mir auch die sünde mein,
> Barmhertiger Gott durch die bitter marter dein,
> Vnd lass mich herr nicht verderben,
> Vnd in meinen sünden so kleglich sterben.

(lines 1039–44)

They were all sinful men, but now they have bliss from you. Forgive me also my sins, merciful God, through thy bitter agony; and let me, Lord, not be destroyed, and die so miserably in my sins.

11 Froning, *Drama des Mittelalters*, p. 702. 'Poor' or 'unhappy' Judas is always 'lost', as he says himself (p. 700):

> Ach mich viel armen mann,
> das ich das leben ye gewan!
> ach das ich ye wart geborn!
> ich muss ummmer und ewiglichen syn verlorn!

(lines 3606–9)

Alas for me, man most unhappy! Alas that I ever had life! Alas that I ever was born! I must be lost eternally and forever!

On Judas' death in medieval drama see W. Buhl, 'Der Selbstmord im deutschen Drama vom Mittelalter bis zur Klassik', unpublished dissertation (Erlangen, 1950), fols. 13–18.

At the Harrowing of Hell, the saviour first sings to the elect 'Venite benedicti patris mei' (Come, those blessed of my father), and then says to the damned the words which seal their fate:

> Blibet, ir vorfluchten, in der ewigen pin!
> Do solt er ewiglichen in sin.
> Du armer sunder, nu ganck von mer!
> Trost und gnade vorsagen ich dir.

(lines 7255–8)

O ye damned ones, remain in everlasting pain! There you must forever be. Thou poor sinner, now go away from me! I deny thee consolation and mercy.

As early as the Benediktbeuren passion play (pre 1250) it is the devil who leads Judas to his hanging. See *Carmina Burana. Die Gedichte des Codex Buranus lateinisch end deutsch*, critical edition by A. Hilka and O. Schumann, completed by B. Bischoff (Zurich and Munich, 1974), p. 792.

12 P. Wackernagel, *Das deutsche Kirchenlied von der ältesten Zeit bis zu Angang des 17. Jahrhunderts*, 3 vols. (Leipzig, 1864–70; repr. Hildesheim, 1964), I, p. 210, no. 347:

> O tu miser Iuda, quid fecisti,
> quod tu nostrum dominum tradidisti?
> Ideo in inferno cruciaberis,
> Lucifero cum sociis sociaberis,
> Kyrie eleison.

O thou unhappy Judas, what hast thou done, that thou hast betrayed our lord? Therefore thou wilt be tormented in hell, and wilt be with Lucifer and his companions. *Kyrie eleison.*

In Wolfram's *Parzifal* King Clamide speaks with striking boldness about Judas. In order to win Kondwiramurs, whom he desires as his wife and whom he has besieged unsuccessfully in Pelrepaire, he would be quite ready to incur the damnation of Pilate and 'that wretched Judas', 'who joined the traitors with a kiss when Jesus was betrayed' ('arme Judas ... der bî eime kusse was / an der triwenlôsen vart / dâ Jesûs verrâten wart'). For one embrace from Kondwiramurs he would bear God's punishment on both Judas and Pilate, 'whatever punishment their Maker has in store ... I would accept their torment' ('swie daz ir schephær ræche / die nôt ich niht verspræche'). If he won his beloved, then 'come what might thereafter! ('swiez mir dar nâch ergienge'). *Parzifal*, p. 219, 24–220, 4; Hatto, p. 118. Nothing could show more starkly the immoderacy of Clamide's desire than this hyperbolic readiness to sell his salvation to gain his beloved. In the *Rolandslied* the traitor Genelun is seen as a follower of Judas: 'Genelun geriet michel not, / den armen Iudas er gebildot' (Genelum counselled great torment; he imitated unhappy Judas, lines 1924–5).

13 Wackernagel, *Deutsche Kirchenlied*, II, pp. 486–7. nos. 615–18. W. Bäumker, *Das katholische deutsche Kirchenlied*, I (Freiburg, 1893; repr. Hildesheim, 1962), pp. 205, 462ff. On the fourteenth-century 'song of Judas', its appearance, survival and influence on fifteenth and sixteenth-century satire, and on folk poetry, see A. Taylor, '"O du armer Judas"', *Journal of English and Germanic Philology* 19 (1920), pp. 318–39.

14 In 1541 Luther wrote a parody of 'Ach du armer Judas, was hastu

getan . . . ': an antipapal political song, mocking and pugnacious, beginning 'Ach du arger Heintze, was hastu getan'. It has twenty-four verses and casts Luther's opponents in the role of Judas. Wackernagel, *Deutsche Kirchenlied* 3, pp. 1270ff.

15 Roy, *Mystère de la Passion*, pp. 134–5.

16 Chaucer highlights the problem of the theodicy of the betrayer in the *Nun's Priest's Tale* (*Works*, ed. F. N. Robinson, 2nd edn, Oxford, 1957). This retelling of the story of the fox, the hen and the cock is full of literary and historical allusions, and reflections of world literature, which make it into much more than a fable. The fox's betrayal of the cock is set against a series of examples from Homer, the Bible and the song of Roland, and the narrator considers the problem of predestination versus free will with reference to Augustine, Boethius and Bishop Bradwardine:

> Wheither that Goddes worthy fortwityng
> Streyneth me nedely for to doon a thing,
> – 'Nedely' clepe I symple necessitee;
> Or elles, if free choys be graunted me
> To do that same thyng, or do it noght,
> Though God forwoot it, er that it was wrought;
> Or if his wityng streyneth nevere a deel
> But by necessitee condicioneel.
>
> (lines 3243–50)

The narrator laments:

> O false mordrour, lurkynge in thy den!
> O newe Scariot, newe Genylon!
> False dissymulour, O Greek Synon,
> That broghtest Troye al outrely to sorwe!
> O Chauntecleer, acursed be that morwe,
> That thou into that yerd flought fro the bemes!
>
> (lines 3226–31)

17 G. Paris and G. Raynaud (ed.), *Le Mystère de la Passion d'Arnould Greban* (Paris, 1878), lines 11017–77. The monologue falls between the calling of the Apostle Matthew and that of James son of Alpheus; in Greban the calling of James is followed by that of Judas. K. Kruse, 'Jehan Michel: *Das Mystère de la Passion Jesu Christ jouée à Paris et Angiers* und sein Verhältnis zu der Passion des Arnould Greban und zu den beiden Valencienner Passionen', unpublished diss. (Greifswald, 1907), fol. 12, note 3; fol. 15, note 1. On Judas in Michel in comparison with Greban's *Passion* see also pp. 33, 35–8, 42–3. Reproduction of the Judas scenes from Michel's *Passion*, fols. 75–6 (monologue on his first entrance), 79–87 (Judas' farewell dialogue with Cyborea). On other

French versions of the Life of Judas see E. Roy, *Le Mystère de la Passion en France du XIVe au XVIe siècle* (Dijon, 1904), pp. 284–5.

18 J. Kirkup, *The True Mystery of Passion. Adopted and translated from the French Medieval Mystery Cycle of Arnoul and Simon Greban* (London, 1962), Part 4, Scene 3, pp. 86–90. In 1937 Gustav Cohen put together a Judas play out of the passion plays by Greban and Michel, having previously (1936) drawn a play of Mary Magdalene out of Michel's work. Favourable review of the Paris performance of the Judas play by G. d'Houville in *Revue des Deux Mondes* 107 (1937), pp. 669–72.

19 O. Jodogne (ed.), *Jean Michel. Le Mystère de la Passion (Angers 1486)* (Gembloux, 1959).

20 A. Spanner, *Polyanthea sacra*, 1 (Venice, 1741), p. 432 s.v. 'Judas', cites suggestions that the germ of Judas' treason was Christ's acceptance of Mary Magdalene.

21 Such as this excerpt from Judas' speech:

> Raige restrainte redoubtable,
> rendant redoubtee renforce,
> raige enragee tant ragable
> dont raige ragant me rent force,
> fault il qu'en efforçant m'efforce
> et que de force renforcee
> je forçonne et que me proforce
> a forcer ma fin forcenee?
> Ma despite ame aforcenee
> me tient en gref deul tant suspens
> de mon malfaict ne me repens,
> puis que desespoir tant me larde.
> Mourray je ainsi, las,
> estranglé d'un las
> sans quelque espoir de solas?
> Ha, Desesperance, las,
>   la fin as
> ou la mort me veult actraire!
> Dueil de tous estas
> me quierent a tas!
> Couvoitise, grand port as
>   quand notas
>   et portas
> l'offre qui m'est tant contraire!

(lines 23, 785–810)

[Approximate translation.] O fearful confined rage, bringing fearful reinforcement, enraged rage most enrageable for which raging rage restores my strength, must I gain strength by struggling, and strive with re-strengthened strength and force myself to force my insane end? My vile maddened soul holds me so suspended in terrible suffering that I cannot repent my crime, since despair so harrasses me. Alas, shall I die so, strangled in a noose, with no hope of consolation? Alas, Despair, you have the end to which death wishes to draw me! Torments of all kinds seek me in hordes! Covetousness, you did a great thing when you observed and brought the offer which has brought me so much harm!

22 H. Giese, 'La Passion de Jésus-Christ jouée à Valenciennes l'an 1547', diss. (Greifswald, 1905), pp. 23–6 (the childhood of Christ in parallel to that of Judas); 30–1 (after murdering the young prince at a game of chess on the island, Judas becomes Pilate's seneschal; he kills his father and marries his mother); 33–4 (Cyborea realises Judas is her son; lamentations by both; Judas becomes a disciple of Jesus); 48–56 (the betrayal, the arrest, Judas' repentance and suicide attended by Desesperance).

23 G. England and A. W. Pollard (ed.), *The Towneley Plays*, Early English Texts Society E.S. 71 (London, 1897), pp. 393–6.

24 C. W. Dunn and E. T. Byrnes (ed.), *Middle English Literature* (New York, 1973), pp. 153ff. On the English Judas ballad see E. Seemann, 'Die europäische Volksballade', in R. W. Brednich, L. Röhrig and W. Suppan (ed.), *Handbuch des Volksliedes* I (Munich, 1973), p. 54; M. Lüthi, 'Familienballade', ibid., pp. 95–6. Lüthi thinks the fact that Judas' sister inveigles him into betraying Christ is an argument for classifying the poem as a ballad, since 'the ballad tends to put everything into a family context' (p. 96).

25 *Anticlaudianus*, PL 210, pp. 481–574; new edn by Bossuat, *Alain de Lille, Anticlaudianus. Texte critique avec une introduction et des tables* (Paris, 1955). English translation and commentary by J. J. Sheridan, *Anticlaudianus or the good and perfect man* (Toronto, 1973).

26 Ed. K. Strecker, MGH Poetae latini aevi carolini IV/2 (Berlin, 1896; repr. 1964), no. 53, pp. 582ff.

27 Hans Folz, *Die Reimpaarsprüche*, ed. H. Fischer (Munich, 1961), pp. 164–73; on the dating, H. Fischer, 'Hans Folz. Altes und Neues zur Geschichte seines Lebens und seiner Schriften', *Zeitschrift für deutsches Altertum* 95 (1966), pp. 12–36.

28 Lines 17ff.

29 Lines 21–2.

30 Lines 29ff; cf. *verzagnus* (desperation), line 127.

31 Line 97.

32 Line 212.

33 Line 224: 'gross neüe irrung und ler' (great new error and teaching).

34 Lines 259ff.

35 Thomas Naogeorgus, *Judas Iscariotes. Tragoedia nova et sacra, lectu et actu festiva et iucunda*, n.p., n.d. (1552); Nuremburg, Stadtbibliothek Sign. Phil. 2835, 8°. See also P. H. Diehl, *Die Dramen des Thomas Naogeorgus in ihrem Verhältnis zur Bibel und zu Luther*, diss. (Munich, 1915), pp. 70–81; H.-G. Roloff, 'Thomas Naogeorgs *Judas* – ein Drama der Reformationszeit', *Archiv für das Studium der neueren Sprachen und Literaturen* 123 (1971), pp. 81–107.

36 The workings of conscience in Judas are emphasised by an earlier author, Maximus of Turin, in a sermon on the end of Judas and that of heretics (58.2–3, *CCL* 23, 233–4: 'Sua ergo sententia Iudas condemnatur. Mirum forte sit uobis, quod non eum populus iudicaverit, non praeses addixerit. Hoc sacrilegi solet esse iudicium, ut inpietatem suam ipse dum recordatur et puniat, et scelus suum dum recognoscit et iudicet. Omnium enim supergreditur sententias, quia sua conscientia sua sententia condemnatur ... Tali ergo haereticus quali et Iudas poena damnatur, ut idem sui et reus sit sceleris et iudex sit ultionis. Tali, inquam, haereticus quali et Iudas poena damnatur.' (Thus Judas was condemned by his own judgement. You may wonder why the people did not judge him, nor a judge condemn him. This is the usual punishment for a sacrilegious man: in that he acknowledges his own impiety, he punishes it; in that he admits to his own crime, he avenges it. He was condemned by his own conscience, his own judgement, and so went beyond the judgements of all others. ... Therefore every heretic is condemned to the same punishment as Judas, to accuse himself of his own crime and be judge of his own punishment. The heretic, I repeat, is condemned to the same punishment as Judas.)

37 'Peccatum zeucht unter sich ad desperationem oder uber sich ad praesumptionem. Das heist alles beydes peccatum impoenitibile, quia peccatum aut nimium cognoscitur aut plane non cognoscitur.' *Tischreden*, in the Weimar edition of Luther's works, vol. 1 (Weimar, 1912), p. 115, no. 73; referred to in Roloff, 'Thomas Naogeorgus', p. 96, note 17. Roloff thinks that *Judas Ischariotes* is so closely bound up with its time as to make any 'interpretation' of it inappropriate: it seems to give 'no reason to interpret the events in terms of universal human conduct' (p. 89). But this is contradicted not only by the tone of the ending, but also the link with the plays of Sophocles. Roloff fails to take proper account of the meaning of despair prompted by conscience and sees Naogeorgus in the light of fashionable ideology, comparing the *Judas* with Brecht's didactic plays and so insisting that 'The figure of Judas

can and should not arouse pity and terror. Terror of what? The devil? Christ was the stronger, and the sin could have been repaired by belief in the grace of redemption.' But for Judas, in true Lutheran terms, the sin was not reparable. Judas' words as he put on the noose constituted the unforgivable sin against the holy ghost: 'non est receptus uspiam. Maiora sunt peccata mea quam quae queant remitti.' (There is no refuge anywhere. My sins are so great that they cannot be forgiven.) If *Judas Ischariotes* did indeed 'affect society by means of literature, even in the sixteenth century' (p. 16), then that effect cannot have been as superficial as Roloff suggests: the play must have lent itself to the 'interpretation of the events in terms of universal human conduct' which Roloff professes not to find in it – especially, in this case, for the benefit of Christians.

38 In the twelfth century Werner of St Blaisien assured his readers that real contrition of the heart brought certain forgiveness and protection against damnation, even if confession, penance and priestly absolution were not available at the last moment, because God would accept the will in lieu of the deed: 'confidenter pronuntio, quod in eo summus sacerdos complet, quod mortalis non potuit et apud Deum jam factum constat quod homo quidem vere voluit' (I confidently assert that in this the great High Priest fulfils what the mortal one could not, and God considers what a man really and truly desires to have been done indeed: *Deflorationes Patrum, PL* 157, p. 1184.) For references to the effectiveness of contrition in the hour of death without benefit of penance (as in the case of the Penitent Thief), from the early Middle Ages and the *Artes Moriendi*; see Susan Brooke Snyder, 'The Paradox of Despair: Studies of the Despair Theme in Medieval and Renaissance Literature', unpublished diss. (Columbia University, 1963), University Microfilms, Ann Arbor, nr. 64/9173, p. 33. On the dangers of deathbed despair see pp. 34–5, and idem, 'The Left Hand of God: Despair in Medieval and Renaissance Traditions', *Studies in the Renaissance* 12 (1965), pp. 42–3.

39 *Everyman*, ed. A. C. Cawley (Manchester UP, 1961). God sees himself betrayed by Man, his elect:

> And thereto I had them all electe;
> But now I se, lyke traytours dejecte,
> They thanke me not for the pleasure that I to them ment,
> Nor yet for theyr beynge that I them have lent.

> (lines 54–7)

Everyman sees himself betrayed by all about him:

O false Good, cursed thou be,
Thou traytor to God, that hast deceyved me
And caught me in thy snare.

(lines 451–3)

At his graveside Everyman is betrayed by Fellowship, Kindred, Beauty, Strength, Discretion and finally Knowledge:

Take example, all ye that this do here or se,
How they, that I loued best do forsake me.

(lines 867–8)

Repentance after death is impossible, and so

For than mercy and pyte doth hym forsake.

(line 913)

Only Good Deeds stands by Everyman. – In the *Hecastus* of Macropedius (1539), only Fides and Virtus help the hero to a blessed death. Ed. J. Bolte in *Drei Schauspiele vom sterbenden Menschen*, Bibliothek des Literarischen Vereins in Stuttgart 269–70 (Leipzig, 1927), pp. 63–150:

FIDES   Non deseram vel hinc euntem vel patris Summi tribunal iudicis
        cum accesseris.
VIRTUS Nec ego Fide suffulta modo te deseram.

(lines 1676–8)

Faith I will not leave you as you depart hence, nor when you come before the judgement seat of the father, the supreme judge. *Virtue* Nor will I ever leave you, if I am upheld by Faith.

In *Everyman* Strength, Discretion and Knowledge promise to stay with Everyman:

we will not fro you go . . .
wyll by as sure by the
As ever I dyde by Judas Machabee

– but immediately break that promise at the graveside.

40 The Munich play of the Dying Man (1510), ed. Bolte (*Drei Schauspiele*, pp. 1–62), warns us:

Darumb merckt auff! lernet wol sterben!
dardurch mügt ir die ewigen freüd erwerben.
Das ist die größt kunsst, (glaubt sicherlich)
Die wir mügen lernen hye auf erdtreich.

(lines 263–6)

And so beware! Learn to die well! Thus you may earn eternal joy. That, believe me, is the greatest art that we can learn here upon earth.

Cf. lines 791, 803, 1193, 1377. The Preface to Christopher Ischyrius' *Homulus*, a Latin translation of the Flemish drama of *Elckerlyc*

(1537; ed. A. Roersch, Ghent/Antwerp 1903, p. 2) introduces the play's theme of the nuptials of the Soul after death with Christ the Bridegroom: 'Estque in ea augustissima Christianae vitae institutio atque bene moriendi ars felicissima.' (And in it [the nuptials] there is the noblest Christian institution, and the art of dying well is the most blest of all.)

41 Hans Sachs, *Hecastus*, ed. A. von Keller, in Works, vol. 6 (Stuttgart, 1872, repr. Hildesheim, 1964, p. 168, lines 6ff., and cf. p. 172, line 12) calls the rich man 'the man who despaired'. He is translating Macropedius:

> Quid restat itaque mihi miserrimo nisi
> Vitae et salutis una desperatio?
>
> (lines 1024–5)

> Miserrimum
> Me praedicas. Quanto magis enim haec replicas,
> Tanto magis mihi dolorem exageras
> Barathroque desperationis admoves.
>
> (lines 1299–302)

What remains to me in my great misery but to despair both of life and of salvation? . . . You say I am most unhappy. And the more you assert this, the more you heap anguish upon me and thrust me towards the pit of despair.

42 Page 175, lines 5–13; following Macropedius:

> Obstat mihi scelerum meorum enormitas,
> Quae iram tremendi iudicis mihi provocat.
>
> (lines 1331–2)

The greatness of my wickednesses stands against me and provokes the wrath of the fearful judge.

43 Page 175, lines 26–7; following Macropedius, lines 1390ff.

44 Page 177, line 31. In the Munich play of 1510 the devil challenges the faith of the dying men:

> ob er sy möcht fieren auss der pan
> Und sy möcht pringen auff zweiffels pfat.
>
> (lines 600–1)

Whether he could lead them astray and bring them on to the path to doubt.

The devil 'rayczt in zů verzweyfflung' (tempts him to despair, line 1016), and the Augustinian warns:

> O mensch, verzweifel nit an der barm gots und seiner gnad!
>
> (line 1029)

Ob du gethan hetest aller menschen sünd auf erdtrich
Unnd die nye gepeycht oder gepiest hetest gentzlich,
Dennoch solt du verzweyflen nicht

(lines 1041–3)

O man, despair not of God's grace and his mercy! ... Even if you had committed the sins of all men on earth, and never confessed or done penance for them at all, still you should not despair.

From the examples of the Good Thief, Mary Magdalen, the woman taken in adultery, Peter and Paul, who were all great sinners ('die all groß sünder und sünderin gewesen sind', line 1053) we learn:

Ey wer wolt dann in seinen sünden verzagen?
O mensch, betracht die unaussprechlich barmherczikait!

(lines 1056–7)

Who would then despair in his sins? O man, see this ineffable mercy!

And still the dying man falls into despair because of his sins ('in verzaghnuß von wegen seiner sünd', line 1064), and so cannot repent. The devil drives him deeper into despair and advises suicide (lines 1070–96):

Der sterbend verzagt an gots barmherczigkait wie Chaym und schreyt mit graussamlicher ungedultikait allso:

... mein sünd sein größer dann gotes barmherczikait.
Darum er mir dye nit vergeben mag.
auwe, auwe des enngstlichen tag!   (lines 1097–1106)

The dying man, like Cain, despairs of God's mercy, and cries out with hideous impatience, thus: 'My sins are greater than God's mercy, so that he cannot forgive me them. Alas, alas, the dreadful day!'

The devil denounces the soul to God, saying that it never had any proper repentance or regret, and so it despaired of God's mercy ('nye gehabt rechte rew unnd laid, / dazß hat sy verszweyfelt an deiner barmherczikait', lines 1111–12); and God delivers it to eternal damnation. Only with the third dying man does the devil fail in his attempt to drive him to despair (line 1322), because the warnings against despair (lines 1258, 1309, 1349) win the struggle over the soul, and it goes to heaven, setting an example for the dying Merchant. The Munich play, like the later *Mercator* of Naogeorgus (1540; see pp. 95–100), opposes examples of death in despair and death in faith, souls bound for hell and for heaven, for eternal damnation and eternal bliss.

45 Page 180, line 20.
46 *Homulus*, lines 212ff. The hero calls himself 'omnium infelicium infelicissimus' (the most unhappy of all unhappy men) and,

wishing to anticipate death, lays the sword to his own throat. According to the stage directions, the last words of Act II are to be spoken 'cum summa animi desperatione' (with supreme despair of the mind). They are 'Numquam magis solus fui, quam hodie, infelix ego disperij' (Never was I more alone than today. Unhappy I, I am lost, line 517.)

47 L. Goldscheider, *Michelangelo. Gemälde, Skulpturen, Architekturen. Gesamtausgabe* (Cologne, 1964), Plate 230.

48 *Homulus*, line 756: 'Caput inter vtrasque collocabo manus' (I shall put my head between my two hands). The stage direction gives a description of Homulus in his despair: 'Reclinabit sedens Homulus inter manus caput instar meditabundi cogitabundique paulisper in propatulo, vt videatur ab omnibus' (Homulus should sit back with his head in his hands, in plain view, for a while like one meditating or thinking deeply, so that all can see him). His speech begins 'Actum est. Terras percurri omnes. Nemo est cui ego fidam.' (It is all over. I have travelled all lands. There is no one I can trust.)

49 Thomas Naogeorgus, *Mercator*, ed. Bolte in *Drei Schauspiele*, pp. 161–319. The German verse translation by Jacob Rulich (1591) is edited by H. Wiemken, *Vom Sterben des reichen Mannes. Die Dramen von Everyman, Homulus, Hecastus und dem Kaufmann. Nach Drucken des 16. Jahrhunderts übersetzt, hg. und eingeleitet* (Bremen, 1965), pp. 219–417.

50 Rulich's Prologue (p. 221), following Naogeorgus' Prologue, lines 14ff. In his dedicatory epistle Naogeorgus rejects the doctrine of salvation through works, which conscience cannot accept: 'Luctabatur simul et operum tumida fiducia peccatorumque immensa gravitate, donec peccata (quod fit) effecere, ut iam iam oblita illa fiducia vitam et salutem plane esset desperaturus, ni e supernis iussus esset sperare.' (There was a struggle between overweening confidence in works and the immense weight of sin, until (as often happens) the sins quickly made him forget that confidence, so that he would have despaired wholly of life and salvation, if heaven had not commanded him to hope, p. 164.)

51 Rulich, p. 273; cf. Naogeorgus: 'Non est, quod speres gratiam ... modo desperatio claudat vitam' (you have no reason to hope for grace ... soon may despair close his life, lines 919, 932). His catalogue of sins (Rulich, pp. 265ff., 282–3) cannot be outweighed by the catalogue of good works. Conscience suggests Judas to him as a patron (p. 285).

52 Rulich, p. 322, after Naogeorgus, lines 1638ff.

53 Naogeorgus' epistle dedicatory, p. 164.

54 Rulich, p. 325.
55 Naogeorgus, lines 1689–70.
56 Ibid., line 1765.
57 Rulich, p. 330.
58 Ibid., p. 334.
59 Naogeorgus, line 1843: it would be 'immensa caecitas, / Nec caecitas solum, sed et superbia' (that would be colossal blindness; and not only blindness, but also pride, lines 1844–5).
60 Rulich, p. 355; cf. Naogeorgus, lines 1857ff.
61 Rulich, p. 335; cf. Naogeorgus, lines 1862ff.
62 Naogeorgus, lines 1761–1987; Rulich, pp. 330–42.
63 Rulich, p. 343.
64 Rulich, p. 344; Naogeorgus, lines 2005ff.
65 Naogeorgus, lines 2152, 2161–2; Rulich, p. 353: 'zur Verzweiflung gar / er uns gern brächt durch seine Wort ... da wir ... zweiffleten an der Seligkeit' (to despair he would gladly bring us by his words ... so that we ... despaired of bliss).
66 Satan in Naogeorgus: 'Cur tam sero venitis, electi mei?' (Why do you come so late, o my chosen?). Rulich, p. 373: 'Glück zu, ihr Auserwählten mein' (Greetings, O my chosen).
67 L. Kretzenbacher, *Die Seelenwaage. Zur religiösen idee vom Jenseitsgericht auf der Schicksalswaage in Hochreligion, Bildkunst und Volksglaube* (Klagenfurt, 1958).
68 Rulich omits all speeches by Peter and Christ in Act v and begins the act with the scene in which Satan and St Michael make a mockery of the duke's, bishop's and Franciscan's assurance of salvation. In Naogeorgus this scene is preceded by speeches in which Peter and Christ attack the pope and his church (lines 2053–2553).
69 In Hans Sachs' *Hecastus* the messenger of Death applies the scales metaphor to the rich man, and the doctor metaphor to the priest. Ed. von Keller, p. 154, lines 14ff.; p. 175, line 33.
70 Numerous illustrations in Kretzenbacher, *Die Seelenwaage*. On scene setting in the baroque *Ordensdrama* and in the folk plays see pp. 188, 208–22.
71 Naogeorgus, line 3138; Rulich, p. 412.
72 G. Müller, *Deutsche Dichtung von der Renaissance bis zum Ausgang des Barock* (Potsdam, 1927, repr. Darmstadt, 1957), p. 74.
73 Rulich, p. 366, following Naogeorgus:

> Ingentem prorsus, qua me presit ad inferos.
> Sperare nec ullo potui pacto gratiam
> Et iam iam Satanae ultro me volui addicere;
> Sed ecce caelesti sum afflatus numine.

(lines 2321–4)

Indeed a great [sin], by which he crushed me down into hell. Nor could I in any way hope for grace, and I was on the point of surrendering myself willingly to Satan, but behold! a celestial spirit breathes upon me.

74 Pages 80–161.
75 Ibid., p. 81.
76 Ibid., p. 98.
77 Ibid., p. 102; Death counters (p. 109), 'Narren sinds, die ihre Penitentie sparen / so lang, bis sie von hinn müssen fahren' (they are fools who put off their penitence right up to the time when they must go from hence).
78 Ibid., pp. 125–6.
79 Ibid., p. 129.
80 Ibid., p. 126, 130.
81 Ibid., p. 140. 'Confession' uses the Middle High German synonym for 'doubt' (*zwivel*), which is *missetrôst*: 'Homule, vor allem bewahr dich vor Mißtrost' (Homulus, above all beware of misdoubt, p. 134). The devil 'wollt ihn gern mißtröstig machen' (would gladly make him misdoubtful, p. 158).
82 Ibid., p. 158.
83 Ibid., p. 142.

7 FAUST: SAVED OR DAMNED?

1 R. Petsch, ed., *Das Volksbuch vom Doctor Faust (Nach der ersten Ausgabe, 1587)* (Halle, 1911). On versions of the Faust story see C. Dédéyan, *Le thème de Faust dans la littérature européenne*, 4 vols. (Paris, 1954–67).
2 An epigram on the verso of the title page of the 1589 edition and some distichs at the end both play on Faust's name by calling him the *infaustissimus* of all *infausti*, most unfortunate of the unfortunate. Texts in Petsch, *Volksbuch*, pp. li–lii.
3 Petsch, *Volksbuch*, p. 10, 'Vorred an den christlichen Leser' (Foreword to the Christian reader).
4 Faust misuses the 'glorious gift' of understanding to deny both God and man, 'darvmb du niemandt die Schuldt zu geben hast, als deinem stoltzen vnd frechen Mutwillen' (and you cannot blame anyone for that, save your own proud and insolent mischief; p. 41, cf. p. 101).
5 'Vorred', p. 7.
6 Pages 17–18.
7 'Despair' here means the spirit of revolt, not a hopeless situation; the signing of the pact is described thus: 'and this fall is nothing other than his proud rebelliousness, despair, rashness and pre-

sumption, just as it was with the giants of whom the poets say that they piled one mountain on another and sought to make war on god; or like the evil angel, who set himself up against God, wherefore because of his pride and arrogance he was cast down by God' (p. 20). Here, 'despair' (*Verzweiflung*) is the rebellious and intransigent element in his nature.

8 Pages 18, 23, 118: it is his 'stiffnecked and godless will' which spurs Faust to sign the pact with the devil.

9 Pages 20, 28, 30–1, 48: Lucifer is 'Dr Faustus' rightful lord, to whom he bound himself'.

10 Page 31.

11 Page 34; on the 'despair' cf. pp. 36, 38. Harsdörfer's story 'The despairing repentance' begins by contrasting the penitence of Judas and of Peter: Judas flung the money into the temple and 'despairing of God's grace, hanged himself and burst asunder. In contrast, Peter's penitence broke out in tears of contrition, and did not let him let go of God's grace. The penitence of the damned is that of Judas: they are tormented day and night, without hope and trust in the divine mercy.' *Heraclitus und Demokritus: Das ist: C. Fröhliche und Traurige Geschichte* ... (Nuremberg, 1661), ch. 83, pp. 469–73.

12 Mephistopheles is not one of those devils or damned souls who have no more hope of grace (because God has forgotten them), but one of the spirits who can 'hope and wait hour by hour'. Like Cain, however, he has no hope for himself: 'But my sins are greater than can be forgiven me, wherefore I must endure this hellish and well-deserved punishment and torment and must be forever damned, and cannot ask or hope for any grace or favour from God' (p. 39). The spirits hover in the air, lower than heaven (p. 43).

13 Pages 100ff.

14 On God's forgetfulness of the damned see Meier, *Vergessen*, pp. 143–94.

15 Pages 113–14.

16 Page 115.

17 Page 119.

18 Page 111.

19 Pages 54, 102, 112. In his will he bequeaths Wagner land, a golden chain, some silver vessels, a few household goods and his books (pp. 110–11).

20 Page 119.

21 Ibid.

22 Page 120.

23 Page 121.
24 Page 122.
25 Ibid.
26 Some time before Marlowe's *Faustus* the Calvinist Nathaniel
   Woodes wrote a *Conflict of Conscience*, whose hero, Philologus,
   renounces the Protestant faith and follows Judas' path of despair
   leading to suicide. There is a revised version in which the hero
   overcomes his despair and so escapes damnation, but Philologus
   became a stock warning against despair in England. See A. Sachs,
   'The Religious Despair of Doctor Faustus', *Journal of English and
   Germanic Philology* 63 (1964), pp. 625–47 (pp. 629ff.). The idea
   that intercession for the despairing could win them God's mercy,
   which is alien both to the Faust literature and to theology,
   inspires the last words of Prospero's epilogue to *The Tempest*:

   > Now I want
   > Spirits to enforce, art to enchant;
   > And my ending is despair
   > Unless I be reliev'd by prayer,
   > Which pierces so that it assaults
   > Mercy itself, and frees all faults.
   > As you from crimes would pardon'd be,
   > Let your indulgence set me free.

27 *The Tragical History of the Life and Death of Doctor Faustus*, ed. J. D.
   Jump (London, 1962); see also Sachs, 'Religious Despair',
   pp. 625–47.
28 In Milton's *Paradise Lost* (IV, 73–8), the despairing Satan sees
   himself as Hell:

   > Which way shall I fly
   > Infinite Wrath, and infinite despaire?
   > Which way I fly is Hell; my self am Hell;
   > And in the lowest deep a lower deep
   > Still threatning to devour me opens wide
   > To which the Hell I suffer seems a Heaven.

   See A. Sachs, 'Religious Despair in Richard the Third', in *Roman-
   ica et Occidentalia. Études dédiées à la mémoire de Hiram Peri (Platum)*
   (Jerusalem, 1963), pp. 234–45 (p. 238).
29 As far back as the folk book Faust is carried forty-seven miles up
   into heaven by a flying dragon, so that 'he could see the whole
   world, Asia, Africa and Europe, all together'. On his way down
   Faust sees the world like an egg-yolk, less than a handspan long
   (p. 58), whereas a planet seemed as big as the whole world
   (pp. 58, 73).
30 William Mountfort, *The Life and Death of Doctor Faustus* (London,

1697), introd. A. Kaufmann, The Augustan Reprint Society Publication no. 157 (University of California, Los Angeles, 1973), p. 23.

31 Ibid., p. 26.

32 On these stories, dating from the fifth and seventh century, which are closely related to Faust's, see E. Dorn, *Sündige Heilige*, pp. 44–9. On the legends of Proterius' slave and Theophilus' pact with the devil, see Kretzenbacher, *Teufelsbündner*, pp. 28–41.

33 *El mágico prodigioso*, ed. and trans. B. W. Wardopper as *The Prodigious Magician*, Studia Humanitatis (Madrid, 1982).

34 On this story see Kretzenbacher, '... ein Comedi gehalten von Ciperiano und Justina', in *Teufelsbündner*, pp. 17–27.

35 In *Die Faustdichtung vor, neben und nach Goethe*, III (Darmstadt, 1969), pp. 7–26.

36 Page 20.

37 P. Wiedmann, 'Johann Faust. Ein allegorisches Drama', in *Die Faustdichtung* III, pp. 29–118.

38 'Fausts Leben, Taten und Höllenfahrt. Ein Roman in fünf Büchern', in *Die Faustdichtung* II (Darmstadt, 1969). Afterword by C. Siegrist in the Frankfurt edition of 1964. Quotations are from the first edition.

39 As early as 1597, Augustin Lercheimer was complaining that printers were allowed to sell such 'devil's filth' as the Faust book 'without fear or shame'. Petsch, *Volksbuch*, p. 246.

40 Page 295. Satan is delighted that Faust 'has turned the little poisoned spring of human intelligence into a mighty flood'.

41 Page 46; p. 30: 'horrors will lay waste Europe and outmatch all the madness that men have raved in from the beginning.'

42 Page 62.

43 Page 21.

44 Page 44.

45 Page 23.

46 Page 264.

47 '*Devil* Fool!' To be avenged on you I wish to describe what you have lost in the glowing colours of heaven, and then abandon you to despair' (p. 55). '... hell will mock your wrath. For every tear, despair will wring a drop of your blood from your crazed brow' (p. 57).

48 Philosophers have 'long anticipated the devil' (p. 58).

49 Page 150.

50 Page 151; p. 187: Faust as 'the second Hercules' who 'cleanses Europe's proud thrones of these monsters'.

51 Page 151.

52 Page 231.
53 Page 270.
54 Page 272.
55 Page 217.
56 Page 280.
57 Page 281.
58 Pages 274–5; cf. p. 287: 'Can Man wrest from the midst of the huge crowd the seed of evil which he deliberately planted there?'
59 Page 282.
60 Page 286.
61 Faust's last words are, 'What you see in my eyes are tears of obstinacy, tears of awful indignation: it is not you, devil, but my heart which vanquishes me. (p. 290).
62 Page 289.
63 Page 290. Satan greets him in hell, (p. 292): 'Hm! Quite a fellow, and seems to have shrugged off his humanity altogether. Despair, presumption, hate, wrath, pain and madness have cloven deep furrows in his soul.' Satan shows him his place in hell (pp. 296–7): 'Lock him the in the horridest corner of hell; there let him languish in gloomy solitude and brood upon his deeds and upon the moment which can never be amended. Let no shade go near him! Go and hover alone and lost in the land where dwell no hope, no consolation, no sleep. Let the doubts which tormented you in life nag at your soul forever, and let none ever reveal to you the answer to that riddle the search for which has brought you to this place.'
64 *Fragment aus einer Farce, die Hollenrichter gennannt, einer Nachahmung der Batrachoi des Aristophanes* (Fragment of a farce called Hell's Judges, after the *Frogs* of Aristophanes), by Jakob Michael Reinhold Lenz, in *Die Faustdichtung*, III, pp. 147–8.
65 I take the scenes as in the text of the fragment, without going into the possibility that it is a literary satire. In Aristophanes' *Frogs* Dionysos goes down to Hades to bring Euripides back to the upper world for the benefit of the State. But Aeschylus shows himself worthier to return to the light of day, so that Euripides has to stay in the underworld. Faust, like Euripides, could hope for no good from the upper world, and it for none from him.
66 *Puppenspiel von Doktor Johannes Faust. In der Bearbeitung von Karl Simrock*, in *Die Faustdichtung*, I, pp. 271–341.
67 G. E. Lessing, *D. Faust*, ibid., III, p. 16.
68 Since the Enlightenment a new theological judgement on Judas has been developing, one never conferred on him in the Middle Ages: instead of being one of the damned he is found, uniquely

and astonishingly, among the elect. The process of canonisation is already under way: perhaps in the end we may be able to talk of 'Judas, saved or damned'. For the time being see W. Jens, *Der Fall Judas* (Stuttgart, 1975).

8 BUNYAN, GÜNTHER, AND *LENORE*

1 John Bunyan, *Grace Abounding to the Chief of Sinners*, ed R. Sharrock (Oxford, 1962); G. Misch, *Geschichte der Autobiographie*, IV/2 (Frankfurt, 1969), pp. 795–802. On the Puritan tradition of 'spiritual autobiography' in seventeenth-century England see Sharrock's introduction, pp. xviiff.

2 Page 43, lines 20ff.

3 Page 48, line 5.

4 Page 49, lines 21ff.

5 Hebrews 12:17. Bunyan repeatedly applies this verse to himself: 43/28; 44/28; 45/20; 46/29; 49/25; 52/21; 52/27; 55/9; 60/18; 62/7; 65/4; 65/32; 66/3; 66/33; 67/5; 68/5; 71/5; 71/17.

6 Page 54, line 1.

7 Page 58, lines 6ff. This tossing to and fro on the sea, betwixt hope and despair, occurs earlier in Hugh of Saint Victor and in Gottfried von Strasbourg's *Tristan*: see Ohly, 'Desperatio und Praesumptio'.

8 Page 72, line 17. The sentence is not biblical.

9 Page 78, lines 19–24.

10 His description of this inner theological torment occupies 38 pages (41–78), over a third of the work.

11 I.e. the sin against the holy ghost.

12 Page 41, line 9. I could not use the following work by Bunyan: *The Jerusalem Sinner Saved; or, Good News for the vilest of Men: being a help for despairing souls. Showing, that Jesus Christ would have mercy in the first place offered to the biggest sinners. To which is added an answer to those grand objections that lie in the way of them that would believe, for the comfort of those that fear they have sinned against the Holy Ghost*, in H. Stebbing, ed., *The Complete Works of John Bunyan* (Hildesheim/New York, 1970), vol. II, pp. 454–88.

13 Johann Christian Günther, *Sämtliche Werke*, ed. W. Krämer, II, p. 123.

14 Thomas Mann, *Der Erwählte*, tr. H. T. Lowe-Porter as *The Holy Sinner* (Harmondsworth, 1961), p. 209.

15 F. Ohly, 'Die Legende von Karl und Roland', in P. Johnson, H. H. Steinhoff and R. Wisbey, ed., *Studien zur frühmittelhochdeutschen Literatur. Cambridger Colloquium 1971* (Berlin, 1974),

pp. 292–343 (pp. 332–3). Considers the Life of Saint Aegidius as one of the 'problematic saints' lives which, in their own literary and narratological way, try to answer some theologically disturbing, and perhaps dogmatically uncertain, question which lies on the fringes of what is dogmatically allowable – or sometimes clearly beyond them'.

16 Nikolai Lesskow's story 'Anziehende Männer' (Attractive Men, 1885) gives a striking example of the 'breath from heaven' which inspires witnesses to a suicide to weep and pray for the victim's salvation, stunned and shaken, in a noble attempt to spare the feelings of a woman: 'Mehr wert als eine niedre Wahrheit / Ist ein erhabener Betrug' (a noble deception is worth more than a vile truth). Over his coffin is intoned the poetic lament of John of Damascus, which ends, 'O Herr! Wenn die Posaune schallt, / Am letzten Tag und Weltenende – / Laß Deinen Diener ein alsbald / In Deine seligen Gelände' (O Lord! At the last trump, at the end of the world, let thy servant at once enter thy blessed country). 'And, ladies and gentlemen, I can truly tell you no more than that at this we ... so besieged God with prayers! ... and also with tears, and with such sobbing! ... How great was sweet Sasha's sin according to the church's teachings, they who mourned him knew not at all; but they prayed so tirelessly that he should be received "into the fields of the blessed" that I really do not know how this lamentation of souls could be reconciled with a punctilious observance of religious teaching ... For my part I would not be able to make sense of it ... But Thou, who canst do all things, who gavest light to the eye and withheldest it again, and lettest "beauty" fade away as a thing of no account, "forgive" and "pardon" him and "remember not his sins"'. Nikolai Lesskow, *Gesammelte Werke*, ed. J. von Guenther (Munich, 1964), III, pp. 124–5.

9 TWO NOVELS BY THOMAS MANN: *DOKTOR FAUSTUS* AND *DER ERWÄHLTE*

1 *Mythology and Humanism: the Correspondence of Thomas Mann and Karl Kerényi*, tr. T. A. Gelley (Ithaca/London, 175), p. 22.
2 Page 151.
3 Page 175.
4 Page 176.
5 Page 23.
6 *Doktor Faustus*, English translation by H. T. Lowe-Porter (Penguin, 1968), p. 240. All quotations are from this translation

(slightly adapted). On the subject of Mann's attitude to Christianity, which is not discussed here, see K. Aland, *Martin Luther in der modernen Literatur* (Witten/Berlin, 1973), pp. 184–294.

7 The devil would have been really enraged by the 'Good News for Judas Iscariot' ('Gute Botschaft für Judas Ischariot') offered by the theologian H. Gollwitzer in *Krummes Holz – aufrechter Gang. Zur Frage nach dem Sinn des Lebens* (Munich, 1970), pp. 271–96. Gollwitzer adjures God to mend his ways and become more inoffensive and less cunning: 'Judas, who betrayed him, should be in no worse a position here than Peter, who denied him, Paul the persecutor, and all the disciples, who deserted him. Neither his treason nor his suicide is enough to put him beyond the pale of forgiving, life-giving love ... The only real, divine forgiveness is limitless forgiveness. The New Testament as a book shows concern for the murderers of Jesus, who destroyed the meaning of Israel which came to them through Jesus, and so destroyed themselves as well. Judas is their extremest representative, for whom not even the evangelists dare put in a word. But because any setting of bounds to forgiveness would imperil the whole, it can be said that ... the New Testament shows concern for Judas Iscariot and brings him good news' (pp. 282–3). 'Judas is dead long before he hangs from the tree. Whether he hears the voice saying "Thou shalt live" before or after his suicide is immaterial. For the voice is for all, and it does not yield to death, because it comes out of a death which happened "for all"' (p. 296).

8 Cf. p. 193, note 26.

9 Page 482.

10 Page 477.

11 Page 482.

12 Pages 306–8. See H. J. Weigand, 'Thomas Mann's *Gregorius: Der Erwählte*', *The Germanic Review* 27 (1952), pp. 10–30, 83–95, also in H. J. Weigand, *Surveys and Soundings in European Literature* (Princeton, 1966), pp. 243–89 (243–7). In *Die Entstehung des Doktor Faustus. Roman eines Romans* (Amsterdam, 1949), Mann writes about his work on *Faustus* in the late autumn of 1945: 'I was on chapter 31, which brings in the end of the war, the "serving women" and Adrian's turning to his puppet-opera, and "I was reading a lot in the *Gesta Romanorum* in the evenings. The most beautiful and astonishing story is the one about the birth of Pope Gregorius. His election, earned through his birth from brother–sister incest and his own incest with his mother – which in fact is all forgiven through seventeen years of unbelievably ascetic

penance on the lonely rock. Extreme sinfulness, extreme penance: only this chain of consequences can create saintliness." I knew nothing about the numerous versions of the legend; in particular, I had scarcely heard of Hartmann von Aue's Middle High German poem. But I liked it so much that I immediately began to contemplate taking the material away from my hero and making a little archaic novel out of it myself' (p. 130). He also mentions reading the *Gesta Romanorum* in early 1943 (p. 22). He says that despair is the 'fundamental motif' of his book: 'The approach of sterility, inbuilt despair which predisposes one to make a pact with the devil' (p. 60). The devil appears as the 'background hero of the book' (p. 66). Mann confessed that he loved no creature of his imagination (except perhaps Hanno Buddenbrook) as much as Adrian Leverkühn: he was 'led astray in his "coldness", his isolation from life, his lack of "soul", this urge to link and reconcile spirit and desire, in his "inhumanity" and "despairing heart", his conviction of damnation' (p. 82). When Mann would have let the conclusion of the work, in which 'after all the gloom, there is an approach of hope, of grace', slip into excessive optimism, he followed Adorno's advice to re-write it. Now he gave the very last pages 'the cautious form which they now have: only then did I find expression for the "transcendancy of despair", the "miracle which surpasses belief" and the oft-cited poetic closing cadence with the final reversal from mourning to "a light in the night"' (p. 195). In the Thomas Mann Archive in Zurich is the notebook in which Mann, as a student, conscientiously took notes on Willhelm Hertz's lecture on Hartmann's courtly romance of Gregorius. On this see H. Wysling, 'Die Technik der Montage. Zu Thomas Manns *Erwähltem*', *Euphorion* 57 (1963), pp. 156–99 (pp. 180–1).

13 Page 309.
14 Pages 308–9.
15 Letter to A. E. Meyer, 28 April 1948.
16 To H. J. Weigand, 5 November 1951. Mann based Echo's evening prayers on sayings in Freidank's *Bescheidenheit* ('Modesty'), which he found in vol. 2 of S. Singer's *Sprichwörter des Mittelalters* (Bern, 1946). See J. F. White, 'Echo's Prayers in *Doctor Faustus*', *Monatshefte* 42 (1950), pp. 385–94. The last of Echo's five prayers goes:

> Merkt, swer für den andern bitt',
> Sich selber löset er damit.
> Echo bitt für die ganz Welt,
> daß Gott auch ihn in Armen hält. Amen.

(Mark, whoso for other pray
Himself he saves that way.
Echo prays for all gainst harms,
may God hold him too in His arms! Amen.)

(p. 452)

The saying in Freidank (39, lines 18–19) runs: 'Merkt, swer für den andern bit, / sich selben lœset er dâ mit', and comes from Hartmann's *Gregorius*, which Mann did not know at the time. In Hartmann Gregorius has been manacled to the rock as a penance, and is unwilling to take on the office of Pope offered him by the messengers from Rome. But he hopes that the meeting with these messengers will help him to salvation, since they could intercede for him:

> nû lât mir daz hiute
> ze einem heile sîn geschehen
> daz ir mich hie habet gesehen
> und geruochet iuch erbarmen
> über mich vil armen
> und gedenket mîn ze gote.
> wir haben von sînem gebote,
> swer umbe den sündære bite,
> dâ lœse er sich selben mite.

(lines 3564–72)

Now may this work to my salvation this day, that you have seen me here and taken pity on my most unhappy state, and had a kindly thought for me. God's messenger told us that he who prays for sinners saves himself along with them.

Hartmann quotes himself in *Der Arme Heinrich*:

> man giht, er sî sîn selbes bote
> und erlœse sich da mîte,
> swer vür des andern schulde bit.

(lines 26–8)

They say that he who prays for others is his own messenger and saves himself therewith.

See further in Neumann's edition of *Gregorius*, p. 232 (on lines 3570ff.) and 194 (on the same lines). Additional ref. in the *Mittelhochdeutsches Wörterbuch*, i, p. 170.

A second prayer by the child Echo, who is innocent as one elect from birth, affects Adrian more deeply than does the *Gregorius* puppet play. It takes up the saying from Romans (5:20), 'Where sin abounded, grace did much more abound', which is the fundamental meaning of the Gregorius story:

Swie gross si jemands Missetat,
Got dennoch mehr Genaden hat.
Mein Sünd nicht viel gesagen will,
Gott lächelt in seiner Gnadenfüll. Amen.

(A man's misdeed, however great,
On God's mercy he may wait,
My sin to Him a little thing is,
God doth but smile and pardon brings. Amen.)

(p. 452)

The youth Echo, who prays 'for us all' (as Adrian says) and dies before Adrian's end, can no longer reach the latter with his prayers: he is lost. Nevertheless they are a strong pointer forward to *Der Erwählte*, in which the reverence for 'what is beneath us' which Goethe described in *Wilhelm Meister* lives on. Goethe's explanation of that 'reverence' seems to be evoked by Mann through one small point of style, a tiny quotation, in his analysis of the Gregorius material: 'And all the shocking circumstances accompanying the hero's life *not only are no hindrance* to his final elevation to be the Vice-Regent of Christ on earth, but make him, by God's peculiar favour, called and destined to that seat' (p. 306). Goethe, considering 'Christian' reverence for what is beneath us, says, 'and part of it was ... to see even sin and wrongdoing *not as hindrances*, but encouragements to esteem and honour what is holy' (Complete Works, Hamburg edition, vol. 8, p. 157). The same thought evokes the same expression. Mann was fond of this kind of well-hidden, but deeply revealing quotation.

17 Quotations from Lowe-Porter's translation.
18 To H. J. Weigand, 5 November 1941: 'This gave rise to an idea about language, or the idea for an experiment on language; the Gregorius story ... supplied the subject.' He had 'in all probability greatly exaggerated' his 'Christian, supranational or pre-national Middle Ages: in the first place, I admit, it was a linguistic entertainment.' While working on the text he wrote to S. Singer: 'What I am trying is really a pure experiment, a vaguely medieval setting which hovers in a sort of linguistic internationalism' (13 April 1948).
19 To H. J. Weigand, 5 November 1951.
20 To A. E. Meyer, 28 April 1948.
21 To A. E. Meyer, 17 March 1948. To Karl Kerényi, 17 July 1948: 'I have, since completing this synthesis and recapitulation of my small world, done some other things and broached new paths. But whatever I accomplish henceforth can only be an epilogue and pastime' (p. 167). Golo Mann, with a turn of phrase similar to his

father's, repeats the point, calling *Der Erwählte* his favourite among his father's minor works: 'I'm amazed to think that this delightful jest could follow directly after the heartrending *Faustus*: this meaningful folk tale, this poetry which makes you laugh and cry, this supreme accomplishment of the promise to "spread some higher cheerfulness through the world"' (*Frankfurter Allgemeine Zeitung*, 31 May 1975).

22 To A. E. Meyer, 17 February 1948.

23 To H. J. Weigand, 5 November 1951. After the election Gregorius speaks these lines:

> Shall I find my life's black story
> Turn to lustre in thy glory?
> With what wonder do I see,
> Lord, Thy heavenly alchemy
> Clear the flesh's shame and pain
> Back to purity again,
> To the spouse and son of sinning
> Highly from the Highest winning
> Leave for earthly need where'er
> To open Paradise's door!

> (p. 204)

24 To Wilhelm von Humboldt, 17 March 1832. Even Goethe's remark to K. E. Schubarth (3 November 1920) lacks the blasphemous tone which is intentionally present several times in *Der Erwählte*: 'You have the right feeling about the denouement. Mephistopheles must only half win his bet, and if half the guilt lights on Faust, then the old lord's right to forgive steps in straight away, to make the happiest possible ending for the whole.'

25 In both the incests, suicide from despair is evoked as it were *en passant*. Sibylla's brother Eisengrein concludes that 'we [should] fling ourselves all three straight down from the highest louver of our donjon into hell' (p. 31). Gregorius says, 'If I do not like Judas, who hanged himself out of remorse and disgust at his own act, I shall have time to think it over' (p. 155). Here and repeatedly, it is assumed that Gregorius, the child of incest, is 'very very sinful' (p. 44) from birth.

26 H. Wysling, 'Thomas Manns Verhältnis zu den Quellen. Beobachtungen am *Erwählten*', in P. Scherrer and H. Wysling, ed., *Quellenkritische Studien zum Werk Thomas Manns*, Thomas Mann-Studien 1 (Bern/Munich, 1967), p. 259.

27 After a childhood illness 'a mark remained in the forehead of each, a scar and a flat hollow, in exactly the same place and the same shape, namely like a sickle' (p. 12). In the morning when

both rise from their beds, Wiligis is 'nude like a pagan god, his sickle mark in his tumbled hair' (p. 14); his sister has 'the sign on her forehead quite plain since her hair had been drawn back for the night' (p. 14). For the first time she feels bound to her race: 'for of us two no one is worthy, neither of you nor of me, worthy is one of the other, since we are wholly exceptional children high of birth ... and born together out of death, each of us with our graven sign on our brow, they come of course only from chicken-pox ... but the origin of the sign does not signify, *tout de même* it is the pale little hollow that is important' (p. 19). 'They were, with the sickle-sign on their brows and one carrying the child of the other, not equal to the parting' (p. 38). After the brother dies his 'forehead with the sign in the black hair' (p. 48) is never again to be seen. Even at the age of sixty Sibylla's extraordinary beauty shows, 'this charm marked with the pale sickle underneath the bands' (p. 215).

28 Genesis 4:11–15.
29 Page 139.
30 Self-love in *Der Erwählte* can be seen as a theme long adumbrated in Mann, the possibility of uniting nature and spirit: P. Szondi, 'Thomas Manns Gnadenmär von Narziss', in *Satz und Gegensatz. Sechs Essays* (Frankfurt, 1964), pp. 71–8.
31 Page 10.
32 Page 97. Gregorius is to do penance on his sinful parents' behalf and so bring them to God: 'and by a godly life atone for the misdeeds of his parents' (p. 44). On the rock he 'through harshest penance ... had redeemed his parents and himself from sin', in the happy belief that God 'had something of a blessing in mind for him' (p. 168). The monk Clemens takes a more conservative approach, telling the story as evidence of 'God's immeasurable and incalcul-able loving-kindness' (p. 36), and being ready at the end to praise God, 'overwhelmed by the voice of divine mercy' (p. 99).
33 Page 142.
34 Page 168. In the chapter entitled 'The Revelation', it is again left unclear whether what is seen is a dream or a revelation, a true vision or the deformed progeny of an afternoon nap. The uncertainty is maintained through the multiple viewpoints of the visionaries and the observers.
35 Page 209.
36 Ibid. M. Wehrli, 'Roman und Legende', pp. 169–70, thinks that even in Hartmann's *Gregorius* the miracle is 'not a free gift of grace from God: it is stipulated by the hero'. He 'takes on God's power as he would take on an adventure'.

37 Page 211.
38 Page 209. On the story of Trajan's deliverance from hell by Pope Gregory the Great see F. Ohly, *Sage und Legende in der Kaiserchronik*, 2nd edn (Darmstadt, 1968), pp. 119–28; Ohly, 'Karl und Roland', p. 332, on the story of Gregory and Trajan as example of a theological problem narrative. Mann got this story from F. Gregorovius, *Geschichte der Stadt Rom im Mittelalter* (1859–72), II, p. 87, which uses the same phrase 'he should never even think of it again' ('er solle sich nie mehr beikommen lassen'). See Weigand, 'Thomas Mann's *Gregorius*', p. 254. Mann knew the story's true place in history: 'it was really Gregory the Great who did it, and I always liked it – when it was Trajan who declared Christianity a *religio illicita* and let a state persecution loose on it' (to Anna Jacobson, 11 October 1950). (After Wysling, 'Technik der Montage', p. 160.) On the story of Trajan and Gregorius see also L. Kretzenbacher, *Versohnung im Jenseits. Zur Wiederspiegelung des Apokatastasisdenkens in Glaube, Hochdichtung und Legende*, Bayerische Akademie der Wissenschaften, phil.-hist. Klasse, Sitzungsbericht 1971/7 (Munich, 1972), pp. 30–40.
39 Page 226.
40 Page 53.
41 Page 65.
42 Page 217. Cf. Sibylla on p. 216: 'There has probably never come before him such superfluity of sinfulness and it is fitting he should hear of it. He alone can weigh this extravagant excess with the fulness of God's grace and measure whether the latter will be exceeded or whether God's grace, even in excess, in turn is equal to it and balances my sin. One cannot tell.'
43 Page 223.
44 Page 227.
45 The title of the novel is also from Gregorovius, who usually calls the Pope the 'chosen' or 'elect', a word which Mann underlined. Wysling, 'Technik der Montage', p. 162.
46 Page 197.
47 Hartmann, *Gregorius*, line 3954. At the Last Judgement the angels 'congregabunt electos eius a quattuor ventis' (Matthew 24:31: 'They shall gather together his elect from the four winds'). In the *Rolandslied* Duke Heinrich and his wife belong among 'allen erwelten gotes kinden' (all the elect children of God) who find their way to eternal joy (lines 9029–30).
48 Pages 54, 57, 72, 75, etc. The name 'Notgottes' (Agony of God) still lives on, attached to a monastery in the Rheingau above Rüdesheim; Mann got it from a study of Germanic literature and

legend, published in America. See E. A. Philippson, 'Uber zwei "Erfindungen" in Thomas Manns Roman Der Erwählte', in H. Kuhn and K. Schier (ed.), *Märchen, Mythos, Dichtung. Festschrift für F. von der Leyen* (Munich, 1963), pp. 487–9.

49 Page 57.

50 Page 69.

51 Apparently the 'agony of God' here surpassed the 'anxiety of God' (*Gottessorge*) in the *Joseph* cycle. In his lecture on *Joseph and his Brethren* (1942) Mann spoke of it as part of his current notions of the philosophy of religious history and of his own religious consciousness. However, *Der Erwählte*, which like *Joseph* is a 'late-born soul', lacks the symbolic human representativeness of the Joseph novels and *Faustus'* character as a vicariously German (or more widely relevant) story.

52 To H. J. Weigand, 5 November 1951. 'A little work like this belongs to the late cultural period prior to barbarism, which the times look on with an almost alien eye.' Mann, *Altes und Neues* (Frankfurt, 1953), p. 247.

10 SOPHOCLES' *KING OEDIPUS* AND *OEDIPUS AT COLONOS*

1 K. Reinhardt, *Sophokles* (third edn, Frankfurt, 1947), p. 144.

2 Ibid., p. 216: 'A man, conscious of his human qualities, rises superior to another's predicament and saves him suffering; that other appreciates and thanks him for his gift: a scene like this, made up of such knowing and such liberation, such giving and taking, with no pomp and circumstance, had never before been seen on the Athenian stage, for all its rich inheritance. It may be that Theseus seems a somewhat shadowy character beside Oedipus, but there is no doubt that Theseus was to Sophocles the highest manifestation of humanity he ever attempted to create: *his* Theseus, lord of *his* Athens, that great certainty, repose and warmth as against the hesitations and passions of the plaything of the fates.'

3 Quotations are from the free English translation by Don Taylor, in *The Theban Plays* (London, 1986).

4 K. Stackmann, 'Der Erwählte. Thomas Manns Mittelalter-Parodie', *Euphorion* 53 (1959), pp. 61–74 (p. 73): 'The decisive development of the Oedipus myth, from catastrophe of revelation to the obtaining of grace through penitence, is the contribution of the medieval Christian West.' This remark holds true as regards medieval attitudes to Oedipus but needs to be modified in rela-

tion to *Oedipus at Colonos*, which however is independent of any concept of penance and grace.

NOTES TO APPENDIX

1 caret MS
2 MS *warsagen*
3 MS *swannte*
4 caret MS
5 On the story of the thirty pieces of silver see L. Kretzenbacher, 'Verkauft um dreißig Silberlinge. Apokryphen und Legenden um den Judasverrat', *Schweizerisches Archiv für Volkskunde* 57 (1961), pp. 1–17.

Index

207